T0311976

CAMBRIDGE SOUTH ASIAN STUDIES

PUBLIC EXPENDITURE
AND INDIAN DEVELOPMENT POLICY
1960–1970

CAMBRIDGE SOUTH ASIAN STUDIES

These monographs are published by the Syndics of Cambridge University Press in association with the Cambridge University Centre for South Asian Studies. The following books have been published in this series:

1 S. Gopal: *British Policy in India, 1858–1905*
2 J. A. B. Palmer: *The Mutiny Outbreak at Meerut in 1857*
3 A. Das Gupta: *Malabar in Asian Trade, 1740–1800*
4 G. Obeyesekere: *Land Tenure in Village Ceylon*
5 H. L. Erdman: *The Swatantra Party and Indian Conservatism*
6 S. N. Mukherjee: *Sir William Jones: A Study in Eighteenth-Century British Attitudes to India*
7 Abdul Majed Khan: *The Transition in Bengal, 1756–1775: A Study of Sayid Muhammad Reza Khan*
8 Radhe Shyam Rungta: *The Rise of Business Corporations in India, 1851–1900*
9 Pamela Nightingale: *Trade and Empire in Western India, 1784–1806*
10 Amiya Kumar Bagchi: *Private Investment in India, 1900–1939*
11 Judith M. Brown: *Gandhi's Rise to Power: Indian Politics, 1915–1922*
12 Mary C. Carras: *The Dynamics of Indian Political Factions*
13 P. Hardy: *The Muslims of British India*
14 Gordon Johnson: *Provincial Politics and Indian Nationalism*
15 Marguerite S. Robinson: *Political Structure in a Changing Sinhalese Village*
16 Francis Robinson: *Separatism among Indian Muslims: The Politics of the United Provinces' Muslims, 1860–1923*
17 Christopher John Baker: *The Politics of South India, 1920–1936*
18 David Washbrook: *The Emergence of Provincial Politics: The Madras Presidency, 1870–1920*
19 Deepak Nayyar: *India's Exports and Export Policies in the 1960s*
20 Mark Holmström: *South Indian Factory Workers: Their Life and Their World*
21 S. Ambirajan: *Classical Political Economy and British Policy in India*
22 M. M. Islam: *Bengal Agriculture 1920–1946: A Quantitative Study*
23 Eric Stokes: *The Peasant and the Raj: Studies in Agrarian Society and Peasant Rebellion in Colonial India*
24 Michael Roberts: *Caste Conflict and Elite Formation: The Rise of a Karava Elite in Sri Lanka, 1500–1931*
25 John Toye: *Public Expenditure and Indian Development Policy 1960–1970*

PUBLIC EXPENDITURE
AND INDIAN
DEVELOPMENT POLICY
1960–1970

JOHN TOYE

Fellow of Wolfson College
and an Assistant Director of Development Studies
University of Cambridge

CAMBRIDGE UNIVERSITY PRESS

CAMBRIDGE

LONDON   NEW YORK   NEW ROCHELLE

MELBOURNE   SYDNEY

CAMBRIDGE UNIVERSITY PRESS
Cambridge, New York, Melbourne, Madrid, Cape Town, Singapore, São Paulo

Cambridge University Press
The Edinburgh Building, Cambridge CB2 8RU, UK

Published in the United States of America by Cambridge University Press, New York

www.cambridge.org
Information on this title: www.cambridge.org/9780521230810

© Cambridge University Press 1981

This publication is in copyright. Subject to statutory exception
and to the provisions of relevant collective licensing agreements,
no reproduction of any part may take place without the written
permission of Cambridge University Press.

First published 1981
This digitally printed version 2008

A catalogue record for this publication is available from the British Library

ISBN 978-0-521-23081-0 hardback
ISBN 978-0-521-05002-9 paperback

CONTENTS

LIST OF TABLES

PREFACE

Most of the data collation and writing of this work was done in 1972–74, while I was a Graduate Assistant at the Centre of South Asian Studies, University of Cambridge. I am deeply obliged to Mr B. H. Farmer, Director of the Centre, for his unfailing support and encouragement both at the time, and since, in bringing this work to completion. I should also like to thank the staff of the Centre for assisting my research in innumerable ways.

Dr P. P. Howell, Secretary of Cambridge University's Overseas Studies Committee, was instrumental in making possible my second research visit to India in early 1976 and kindly spared me from other duties while writing up was finished.

I began my work on Indian public expenditure as a Research Fellow of the School of Oriental and African Studies of the University of London. I am grateful to the School for help in arranging study leave in India in 1971–72. The help of many officers of the Government of India's Central Statistical Organization and of the state governments' Statistical Bureaux during my visit was freely given, and is gratefully acknowledged.

Over the years I have enjoyed and benefited from conversation with colleagues and friends on the topics covered in this work. It would be impossible not to mention Terry Byres (who criticized the first draft with great acuteness), Valpy FitzGerald, David Lehmann, Suzy Paine, Prabhat and Utsa Patnaik and the late Bill Warren. Ashwani Saith furnished me with some useful Indian statistics and Tom Tomlinson was good enough to comment in detail on an earlier version of Chapter 2.

The original text was further improved by the wise comments of Pramit Chaudhuri, who saw it as examiner of my doctoral dissertation, and of Shri L. K. Jha and an anonymous scholar who refereed it for publication in the Cambridge South Asian Studies series. I have tried to incorporate their views, as fully as possible, into the revised text. Nevertheless, I should make it clear that the errors and misjudgements which undoubtedly remain are my responsibility alone.

I wish to thank the Trustees of the Houblon-Norman Fund of the Bank of England for a grant of £150 towards the cost of having this manuscript typed.

My greatest debt is to my wife, Janet, without whose encouragement, support and intellectual guidance the work would not have been started, let alone completed. I dedicate this book to her.

Cambridge   JOHN TOYE
September 1979.

LIST OF ABBREVIATIONS

A.R.C. The *Administrative Reforms Commission*, a body charged by the Government of India with recommending changes in the machinery of government and administration, active between 1966 and 1970.

C.S.O. The *Central Statistical Organisation* of the Government of India, an organization responsible for central government statistics and national statistical policy.

D.A. *Dearness allowance*, an additional payment made to government and certain other public sector workers to compensate them wholly or in part for rises in the cost of living.

D.M.K. The *Dravida Munnetra Kazhagam*, or Dravidian Progressive Federation, a pro-Dravidian political party operating in Madras (now Tamil Nadu) since 1949.

G.F.C.F. *Gross fixed capital formation*, the addition to the stock of immoveable productive assets, without deductions in respect of replacement investment.

G.N.P. *Gross national product*, the aggregated production of the citizens of a country, without deductions in respect of capital depreciation.

I.A.S. The *Indian Administrative Service*, an all-India cadre of top-level administrators, established in 1947 as a successor body to the old Indian Civil Service.

N.C.A.E.R. The *National Council for Applied Economic Research*, a non-profitmaking research institute.

N.D.C. The *National Development Council*, set up in 1954 as a forum for discussion between members of the Indian Planning Commission and the chief ministers of state governments.

N.D.P. *Net domestic product*, the aggregate production originating within a country's borders, with a deduction in respect of capital depreciation.

N.N.P. *Net national product*, the aggregated production of the

	citizens of a country, with a deduction in respect of capital depreciation.
N.P.C.	The *National Planning Committee of the Indian Congress*, active between 1938 and 1949.
P.L.480	United States *Public Law Number 480* (the U.S. Agricultural Trade Development and Assistance Act) passed in 1954, which regulated the forms in which United States Government foodstuffs and financial credits were given to India.
R.B.I.	The *Reserve Bank of India*, established in 1929 and subsequently coming to perform the functions of a central bank for India.
S.D.P.	*State domestic product*, the aggregate production originating within the borders of a state government in India.
S.N.A.	The *System of National Accounts* recommended by the United Nations as a model for international practice at various different times.
S.P.E.	*State public expenditure*, the total public expenditure of a state government.
S.S.B.	*State Statistical Bureau*, the organisation of each state government responsible for the compilation of state-level statistics.
U.T.	*Union Territory*, a small or remote area of India whose second-tier government is less elaborate and more closely controlled by the central government than areas under a state government.

Introduction

This work has three major aims. The first aim is of a technical kind, and the second and third aims are broader, historical ones.

The technical objective was to place the analysis of Indian public expenditure on a sounder and more informative statistical base than that on which it has hitherto rested. For a number of reasons which are explained in some detail in Chapter 3 the national accounts classification of public expenditure is, when its advantages and disadvantages are balanced out, more useful for macroeconomic analysis than any existing scheme for ordering public expenditure data. At the time when this task was begun, in the early 1960s, the analysis of Indian public expenditure was caught in a pincer attack, between those who seemed quite ignorant of the national accounts method of expenditure analysis, and those who, following Professor Myrdal, were convinced that national accounts categories could have no meaning in the economic circumstances of contemporary India.

The original plan for this work was that it should document as fully as possible all public expenditure data in India that had been reclassified on a national accounts basis, in order to build up continuous and fully reconciled time-series data for the central and state governments and, if possible, for local authorities. This was to have been done with a critical commentary on the nature and limitations of this kind of data. The original plan had to be drastically modified, however. The economic classification of central government spending came easily enough to hand. Twenty-eight economic classifications of state government budgets (as detailed in Appendix A) were also collected. Although

I had succeeded in gathering together more economic classification of government expenditure than anyone seemed to
know, or care, existed, it nevertheless quickly became clear
that these data were still much too fragmentary to be worth
collating and reconciling. The limited fruit of my earlier
statistical explorations is to be found in Chapter 3 which is
a comparative guide to, and assessment of, Indian statistics
on public expenditure.

Fortunately for me, one day when I was discussing national
income statistics with Central Statistical Organization (C.S.O.)
officials at Sardar Patel Bhavan, I stumbled on the information that the Central Statistical Organization had been engaged
on the task of reclassifying all governments budgets since
1960/61, for the purpose of building up certain components
of the statistics required to conform with the United Nations
1968 System of National Accounts. The Director of the C.S.O.
was kind enough to make available to me the worksheets on
which this task had been done. Inspection and some random
checks showed that the work had been done to a very compet-
ent standard. In the absence of copying facilities, it was then
necessary to spend a whole month making a facsimile of these
worksheets by hand. Once this was done, I had a data set which
was in most, but not all, respects more comprehensive than
the other, fragmentary set which I had collected so laboriously.

Once in possession of a copy of the C.S.O. worksheets, it
was possible to make progress with my second aim, namely
to trace the relationship between changes in public expenditure and the implementation of macroeconomic planning in
India. The data set restricted the period for which this could
be done to 1960/61 to 1969/70. Experience as a junior
Treasury official in the 1960s suggested that the integration
of public expenditure control with the extensive economic
dirigisme required to make a macroplan successful is an
extremely difficult administrative and political task in a
smallish developed country with a relatively centralized government. One was naturally curious to discover how it was per-
formed in a vast, developing country with a quasi-federal
structure of government, but where the commitment to planning appears *prima facie* much more strongly entrenched than
in the U.K., with its single, abortive National Plan of 1965.

The matching up of Indian public expenditure statistics with comparable data on the main macroeconomic aggregates quickly indicated that the relationship between actual public expenditure trends and the macroeconomic objectives of the Indian plans was, in the 1960s, initially not very strong and becoming progressively weaker. Part Two of this work is a detailed exploration of this relationship. The picture of the finances of the public sector at the all-India level is given in Chapter 4. Chapter 5 considers how far the public authorities were responsible for causing the industrial recession in the late 1960s by their own expenditure programming. Changes in the degree of centralization of public expenditure are examined in Chapter 6. Chapter 7 presents a measure of the inter-state differences in public expenditure growth, and tries to account for them. Chapter 8 looks at changes in the centralization of government capital formation and saving, and tries to account for differences between states in their capital formation growth rates. These empirical analyses, taken together, show a growing disjunction between the reality of government spending and the planning objective of rapid capital accumulation on public account.

At this point one could have continued, in a vein familiar in the literature on public finance in developing countries, with recommendations for improving the integration of public expenditure control with planning. To do so, however, seemed rather otiose. The disjunction between expenditure control and planning does not appear to result from some kind of intellectual mistake on the Indian side, and, if it did, foreign 'experts' with the requisite advice are not in short supply. The failure of understanding seemed to be more on the part of foreign observers who repeatedly have failed to take the full measure of Indian-style planning. The third, and most ambitious, aim of this work is to sketch the broad historical trajectory of Indian planning, in a way that accounts for its early history, its zenith between 1955 and 1963/64, and its subsequent decline.

This sketch is centred on a phenomenon which has here been called 'mimetic nationalism', for want of a better phrase. Chapter 2 begins with an attempt to define the concept of 'mimetic nationalism' and goes on to interpret the early history of the state accumulation policy in India with the aid of this concept. Chapter 9 attempts to draw together the threads of the different arguments that have occupied the previous chapters. It shows the way in which mimetic nationalism shaped the concrete features of the Indian state accumulation policy, the concrete ways in which Indian public expenditure control (or, rather, lack of it) undermined the Indian state accumulation policy, and the concrete inhibitions which a federal government places on Indian public expenditure control.

The story is left, perhaps rather abruptly, with the year 1970. Too much has happened since then to be easily incorporated into the present text. The author hopes that, in due course, he, or some other person with a taste for this kind of enquiry, may write a companion volume covering developments in the 1970s.

Part one
General

1

Public expenditure and state accumulation in theory

Economists have used a number of different basic ideas to provide their perspective on the phenomenon of public expenditure. For a variety of reasons, some of which will be mentioned shortly, most of these intellectual approaches very quickly run into the sands of irrelevance or absurdity. But some critical comment on them is required to explain why they have not been delved into and explored at greater length in the bulk of the work which follows. By the same token, some justification is needed for the particular theoretical thread which has been picked up in this work, namely the relationship between public expenditure and state accumulation.

I COMMENTS ON ECONOMIC APPROACHES TO PUBLIC SPENDING

The theory of public expenditure best known to the general economist is that of Adolph Wagner, a German thinker of the so-called Historical School, whose influence flourished in the fourth quarter of the last century. Wagner's famous 'law' of expanding state activity has, at least at a superficial level, some relevance for present day students of economic development. Wagner predicted that as the process of economic development took place 'government expenditure must increase at a faster rate than output'.[1] Because of the mistiness of his prose style, the precise formulation of his prediction is controversial, but he is usually understood to mean that government expenditure divided by gross national product (G.N.P.) is a positive function of G.N.P. divided by

[1] Peacock and Wiseman (1967), p. 17.

3

population.[2] The causes alleged to account for this relationship were three influences that would increasingly augment the demand for state activity. They were (a) for the protective and administrative services of the state, as society became more complex; (b) for cultural and welfare services (including income redistribution through transfer payments); and (c) for the takeover by the state of those industries which private entrepreneurship was unable to operate on the scale or with the technology that were (in some undefined sense) required.

Wagner's prediction has been tested with data from a number of developed and underdeveloped countries. Most of the data examined seem to be consistent with the overall relationship postulated by Wagner.[3] But, although it might be plausibly claimed that Wagner correctly identified a nearly ubiquitous feature of modern economic growth, he did not succeed in explaining why this feature is so generally found. He did not conceptualize rising income per head as an independent variable which directly caused an increase in the dependent variables, the state's share in output. Further, he did not always clearly seperate what he thought would happen from what he hoped would happen. Wagner was filling out a scenario for social progress, which comprehended the quantitative and qualitative improvement – simultaneous, interdependent and inevitable – of income per head, technical skills, urban life and, last but not least, public morality. As a philosopher of history, he concerned himself little with the details of subordinate causes. He also gave no consideration to what would happen to government spending in times of social retrogression, such as wars or depressions.

Despite wide influence based on superficial plausibility, Wagner's law is not very useful in helping one to understand the public expenditure trends in today's underdeveloped countries. These countries tend not to have reliable time-series data for more than about twenty or thirty years. Before that time, estimates of national output, and sometimes even of public spending, tend to rest on very shaky foundations. In

2 Gandhi (1971), pp. 44–6
3 Bird (1971), p. 8 and (1970), pp. 72–5; Goffman and Mahar (1971), p. 63; Reddy (1970), p. 90.

any case, they relate to a period in which the forces of social retrogression – two international wars and a desperate depression – were dominant. Since Wagner's law is a generalization about development in the very long run, there is not much point in trying to test it with time-series data for a medium-term period such as the ten years 1960–70 covered by the present study of Indian public expenditure.

Professors Peacock and Wiseman, in their pioneering study of public expenditure growth in the U.K. give war and social upheaval a central place in their theory. They postulate that increased government spending is a primal urge of politicians and bureaucrats which is held in check only by taxpayers' democratically enforceable view of the 'correct' level of taxes.[4] The taxpayers' view of the correct level of taxes is revised drastically upwards in times of war or social upheaval. Consequently, graphs of public spending show a ratchet, or 'upward displacement' effect.

A recent study of Indian public expenditure has taken over the Peacock and Wiseman approach lock, stock and barrel and tried to apply it to Indian data. It is claimed therein that in the Indian data 'the displacement effect is found clearly'.[5] This is a somewhat misleading statement of the author's own conclusions, which show the relative size of India's public sector declining between 1911 and 1921, and a 'displacement effect' during the Second World War which 'disappeared immediately thereafter'. The only statistically evident displacement occurs in the period 1947–66. To save the Peacock and Wiseman thesis, this period is then described as a 'period of social disturbance' despite the fact that, at any rate after 1951, social change has been neither rapid nor violent and wars have been short, localized and non-cataclysmic. We shall see in Chapter 5 that the attempt to make Indian data conform to Peacock and Wiseman's U.K. results on the question of expenditure centralization result in equally absurd statistical and logical contortions. Reddy's work is, unfortunately, eloquent testimony of the inapplicability of Peacock and Wiseman's theory to India.

4 Peacock and Wiseman (1967), p. xxxiii.
5 Reddy (1970), pp. 90–5; and (1972), p. 46.

Apart from long-run historical studies of public expenditure trends, recent economists have theorized about public expenditure from two perspectives, one derived from microeconomics, and the other from macroeconomics. The microeconomic perspective derives from a revival of the concept of a 'public good', which had been developed outside the Anglo-Saxon public finance literature by Italian, German and Swedish economists. This revival, led by Professor Samuelson, can be seen as an attempt to cast the mantle of neo-classical legitimacy over at least some public expenditure, once a large and permanent public sector had become an element of every advanced capitalist economy.[6] Theorizing about 'public goods' is essentially a discussion of a certain type of market failure, and of how social welfare can be optimized when this type of market failure exists. As such, this perspective is purely normative. In one of the classic texts of this style of theory, Professor Musgrave notes that he will omit entirely what he calls 'the sociology of fiscal politics'.[7] It clearly has nothing to say about why public spending totals and patterns are the way they are.[8]

Nevertheless, certain neo-classical economists have not understood the nature and limits of the public goods literature and have introduced propositions from it as if they were descriptive statements about the real world.[9] That governments would actually maximize social welfare if they knew how to will seem sufficiently improbable to some. But to this improbability must be added the prior impossibility, as argued by Professor Arrow, of constructing a social welfare function while remaining both rational and democratic. Despite various ingenious attempts, a recent review of the 'Arrow problem' concluded that 'no clear-cut solution has been found to Arrow's paradox'.[10] If this is so, economists who persist in suggesting that governments actually do maximize social welfare are plainly latter-day Panglossians.

A variant of this microeconomic perspective on public expenditure is the attempt to construct a theory of political

6 Samuelson (1954), pp. 387–9.   7 Musgrave (1961), p. 4.
8 Cf. Bird (1970), pp. 4–6.
9 E.g. Hirsch (1970), p. 1; Grubel (1969), p. 105.
10 Pattanaik (1971), p. 161; cf. Winch (1969), p. 169 and Tullock (1967), p. 263.

behaviour by applying the logic of utility maximization to political phenomena. If one assumes that voters are rationally maximizing their own utility, and politicians in a representative government are maximizing their votes at elections, one can derive a number of predictions about, *inter alia*, how public finance issues will be resolved. On closer examination it turns out that the number of public finance predictions that can be validly derived is very few. In addition, the assumptions on which these theories proceed can be shown to be very dubious.[11]

The economist's macroeconomic perspective on public expenditure is provided by post-Keynesian macroeconomic models. Oddly enough, in Keynes' own writing a government sector was never treated as a specific and separate entity. With the refinement of Keynesian-style models it is now so treated, and government revenues and expenditures are somewhat disaggregated by economic impact. But these models are policy models. They are built so that policy makers can be advised on the macroeconomic consequences of alternative fiscal policy changes. They do not incorporate any assumptions about the way in which the government itself behaves. Thus budgetary changes are exogenous to the model, which, as has been candidly admitted, 'is in effect an admission of ignorance' about the causes of government behaviour.[12]

A good recent example of a macroeconomic policy model is that of Leuthold and Due.[13] Here the authors postulate a government objective, or set of objectives, such as stabilization and growth, and then determine the type of fiscal policy that is most conducive to that objective or set of objectives. But, despite the relative competence with which this model is built, it is difficult not to remark how remote it remains from the economic reality of an underdeveloped economy such as India's. The basic Keynesian conceptual framework is retained, with its built-in trade-off between unemployment and inflation, despite its inappropriateness when, as in India, particular structural supply rigidities persist and non-integrated markets remain. Output materializes, in the model,

11 Toye (1976), pp. 433–47.
12 Peacock and Shaw (1971), pp. 64–5.
13 Leuthold and Due (1970), pp. 517–33.

from a Cobb–Douglas production function, a decision which gains it mathematical tractability at the expense of realism. Capital aggregation problems are ignored, land is excluded as an input to production and the income shares of the factors of production which are included are constrained to take certain values. Balance of payments disequilibria are assumed away, and foreign trade flows are controlled solely by variation of customs duty. As for the government itself, its expenditure excludes transfer payments by assumption and its consumption expenditure is assumed to be a constant proportion of national output during growth – despite empirical evidence which is consistent with Wagner's 'law'. Despite the formal advantages of reasoning with the aid of a fully articulated macroeconomic model, one is inclined to forgo them on the grounds that they imprison reasoning in a cage of unrealism.

As a reaction of impatience with these main strands of public expenditure theory, a large number of economists (particularly in the U.S.A. in the 1960s) tried to proceed with an almost purely empirical method. Starting with a large volume of statistical information, they searched it systematically for regularities that could form the basis of inductive generalizations. Because of the absence of sufficient reliable time series data, these studies, whether they were international comparisons[14] or inter-state comparisons within the U.S.A.,[15] relied heavily on cross-section data. Quite apart from the problem of ensuring parity of purchasing power when making such comparisons, no necessary logical connection exists between the determinants of international or inter-state differences at one time and the determinants of changes in a single nation or state over a period of time.[16] The absence of a clear *a priori* theory encouraged the practice in these studies of selecting as determinants variables that appeared to 'explain' the highest proportion of total variance. Not only is this dubious from the point of view of statistical theory. It has the added disadvantage that it leads to a plethora of arbitrary and irrecon-

14 E.g. Martin and Lewis (1956).
15 E.g. Fabricant (1952).
16 Bird (1969) and (1970), pp. 76 and 126; Morss (1966), pp. 97–102.

cilable 'scientific results'.[17] For economists of public expenditure, the empiricism of the computer has been a most thoroughly explored blind alley.

II DEVELOPMENT AND STATE ACCUMULATION

Clearly, then, a theory of some kind is required to give coherence both to what is looked for, and to what is found, in the process of research. Thus one must enquire: which is the appropriate theoretical framework for the study of public expenditure in contemporary India? Social science is not a value-free activity entirely. One major point at which values make their mark is the choice of basic theoretical orientation.[18] The value underlying the present work is a belief that the material living conditions of the mass of the people in India should be rapidly improved. Such a value locates our study of public expenditure in the context of Indian development, and makes the appropriate theory one that links these two phenomena.

As a start, three concepts within the single word 'development' should be discriminated. Development in what may be called the passive sense is merely something that happens, a series of events to which one is related as a spectator or observer. Secondly, development has a 'passive teleological' sense, in which the series of events observed is a sequence which culminates in some natural end (for example, an acorn becoming an oak-tree). Thirdly, there is an active sense of development. Obviously, our concern with Indian development is not a concern to observe what happens to Indian society and the economy, nor even to observe Indian society and the economy evolving to some pre-ordained natural end. It is a concern to see Indian society and the economy actively developed, in the same sense as a business, an estate, a new town or, to put almost too fine a point on it, a colony is actively developed. In the economic aspect of active development, the theory that is needed is the theory of economic *dirigisme*, that is, of ways of forcing the pace of economic growth and, at the same time,

17 Burkehead and Miner (1971), p. 312.
18 Hutchison (1964), pp. 53–9.

moulding that growth into rationally pre-selected forms. It involves purposeful intervention in the economy, not merely the planning of the forms such intervention might take. [19]

The differences between the development of an estate or town and the development of a national economy are differences of scale and complexity, not differences of principle. But what this kind of comparison brings out is the immense ambition of the desire to plan and control an economy that serves, or fails to serve, six hundred million people. For development studies, in their aspiration to become a policy discipline, there is a single basic question, namely, can economic *dirigisme* on such an immense scale be achieved? It can be attempted, of course, in any society, capitalist or socialist. But can it be achieved in both, or in neither or in only one? And what are the conditions for success? These fundamental questions will not be settled by appeal to the example of India alone. Yet progress towards an answer does require a thorough knowledge of dirigistic experiments, to which, for India, it is the intention of this work to contribute.

The links between dirigistic development and public expenditure are, conceivably, several. But in India they took a concrete form, which may be termed the policy of state accumulation. This policy may be defined with the greatest simplicity as the pursuit of an end: national capital accumulation by a particular means – state action. This definition does two things. It interprets the aim of development as the continuous expansion of the stock of produced means of production. It also identifies the government plus public economic corporations as the developer, or the development agent. Under a state accumulation policy so defined, public expenditure is necessarily one of the major policy instruments that regulate the rate of state accumulation.

This can be shown formally by adapting an analysis of capital formation made by Sachs. [20] Although it is more useful to operate with a four-sector model (i.e. agricultural, private domestic non-agricultural, private foreign non-agricultural and public sectors), for the sake of simplicity assume only two

19 Gadgil (1972), p. 188
20 Sachs (1964), pp. 37–51.

sectors, a private sector and a public sector comprising public enterprises and a unitary government. If we assume away all borrowing and lending between these sectors and all capital transfers on public account (i.e. 'aid'), total national capital accumulation will be defined as

$$A \equiv I(d, f) + In + a(T + Y + P) \tag{1}$$

where A is total national net capital accumulation, $I(d, f)$ is private domestic and foreign net investment. In is the profits of non-departmental enterprises after allowing for capital consumption, T is government tax revenue, Y is government non-tax revenue, P is the operating surpluses of departmental public enterprises, and a is the coefficient of accumulation in the government sector. Public saving can be defined as

$$Sp \equiv (T + Y + P) - (C + Z) \tag{2}$$

where the first bracket on the right-hand side shows the components of total government sector's (or 'public authorities') revenue and the second bracket on the right-hand side shows the main components of public expenditure in the absence of inter-sector transfers, namely consumption of goods and services (C) and subsidy payments (Z). By substitution, the capital formation of the public sector can be defined as

$$Ip \equiv In + a(S + C + Z) \tag{3}$$

which can be re-written as

$$a \equiv \frac{Ip - In}{S + C + Z} \tag{4}$$

In the absence of foreign 'aid', inter-sector borrowing and lending and forced saving arising out of governmental money-printing, the value of $(Ip - In)$ must equal S, so that

$$a \equiv \frac{1}{1 + C + Z} \tag{5}$$

In the assumed circumstances, any increase in the size of current public expenditure $(C + Z)$ directly reduces a, the coefficient of accumulation in the government sector, *ceteris paribus*. Conversely, any reduction in current government spending will, *ceteris paribus* increase *a*, also the value of $(Ip - In)$ and S. It will, however, not necessarily increase A. Whether it does so or not will depend on whether, and if so how much, private and non-departmental public enterprises alter their investment in response to the government's spending cuts, which may fall on investment grants or economic infrastructure, which is regarded as complementary with the enterprises' own investment.

Apart from reducing current government expenditure, equation (5) indicates the two other major methods (apart from borrowing, accepting foreign 'aid' and printing money) by which public capital formation can be increased. They are the raising of additional tax or non-tax revenues and increasing the profits or operating surpluses of enterprises in the public sector. Thus, from the perspective of the requirements of dirigistic development, the planning and control of public expenditure (both current and capital) is one of the three fiscal supports for the policy of state accumulation, the other two being revenue-raising and the profitable management of public enterprises. It could be argued also to be the most critical support for that policy. For while, if public expenditure were satisfactorily planned and controlled, a poor performance in either revenue-raising or public enterprise management would not wreck the state accumulation policy, it is very difficult to conceive any method of gathering receipts for the public sector which could continuously out-pace the growth of public expenditure, once its leash had been slipped.

It is, therefore, no hyperbole to claim that the planning and control of public expenditure is a prerequisite for the success of a state accumulation policy. Public expenditure control implies the existence of some effective method of adjusting the trajectory of public spending, in a changing environment, in the pursuit of a previously planned target. Whatever this method is, it must embrace all types of public expenditure (and not merely that voted by the legislature) by all types of public authority. It must involve a survey of all public authorities' spending plans far enough in advance for adjustments to those plans to be practicable. It must involve scrutiny of the survey by a powerful central institution able to decide on adjustments to plans in the light of the latest medium-term economic forecast. It must involve effective curbs on subordinate institutions that will often try to depart from centrally-taken decisions without being able to show good cause. This, in turn, implies a continuous process of monitoring public expenditure and judging which departures from the decided-on path are permissible.

Our spelling out in this way the detail of what is involved in the adequate control of public spending is designed to suggest the immensity of the challenge to the intelligence of economists and administrators, to the organizing and persuading skills of politicians and to the collective self-discipline of the mass of the people, which a state accumulation policy presents. But, although the structure and dimensions of such a policy may now be clear, its justification in theory has not been mentioned. The reader may very well be asking himself, why should any government think of attempting it in the first place? To answer that extremely difficult question is the next task.

III THE RATIONALE OF STATE ACCUMULATION

Material development can be defined as the enlargement of surplus. The surplus is the residual from current production after deduction of what is required (in replacement investment and consumption) to maintain the existing production level in the next period. The larger the residual, or surplus, the more lavish can be the material foundations of cultural life. The dilemma of development is that one well established method of surplus enlargement is the accumulation of physical capital (buildings, vehicles, machinery and equipment) which itself pre-empts part of the existing surplus. There are other methods of surplus creation, such as bringing unemployed labour and land into use or the introduction of changes in technique which are not capital-augmenting. But their efficiency in expanding the surplus without capital accumulation has always been taken to be rather limited. Thus development usually involves directing an increasing share of the actual surplus into capital accumulation, as well as creating additional surplus in the ways described, and by squeezing consumption that is not 'replacement consumption.'

Is the state accumulation policy a 'progressive' one, and one that ought to be supported? Formally, a policy of capital accumulation that is undertaken by the state can be justified by listing the advantages which, hypothetically, the state enjoys over households to private firms in the role of accumulation agent. For example:

(1) States have powers to tax, to create money and therefore to guarantee their borrowing more substantially than can private agents. Taxation, money creation and state borrowing *could* be used to reduce inessential private consumption below what it otherwise might be, and thus create surplus in the state's hands for investment. If the inessential private consumption which is prevented with these fiscal instruments is the inessential private consumption of the rich; and if the state investment made possible by them benefits the mass of the people; then the distribution of income and assets in the economy will be improved. Of course the state's powers to tax, to create money and to borrow on good terms do not necessarily create additional surplus in the state's hands for investment. They may merely transfer part of the actual surplus from private to government hands – and even this may not be used for capital accumulation. It might be used to increase government consumption, and, therefore, total consumption. (Such a use would also improve the income distribution if the erstwhile surplus of the rich was used for public consumption which benefits the poor, e.g. basic education and health care expenditure).

(2) The hypothetical advantage of the state in finding surplus-creating uses for the surplus which it controls derives from a number of different considerations. The sheer volume of capital it commands may enable the state to do surplus-creating things which private agents could not do at all because of technical indivisibilities, or could undertake only with the loss of economies of scale. The state may also be less restricted in the choice of methods of surplus-creation because it is less risk averse, has a lower rate of time preference and is not constrained to ignore created surplus that cannot be internalized under existing private property rights. Strictly speaking, these advantages may be obtained by ensuring state direction of

investment. The assets may be owned and managed privately, with public subsidies as required.

(3) But if the state were not to own the assets bought with the finance capital it had acquired/created, it would be at a disadvantage compared to private units. Whereas the latter can retain profits to contribute to future finance capital, the state would not be in a position to do likewise, so that at every stage its finance capital would have to be created/aquired afresh. Even where there is no doubt about the state's ability to do this in full measure, it would be an unnecessarily costly and circuitous procedure. But where, as in most underdeveloped countries, the conventional instruments of public finance work poorly, the forgoing of public ownership involves a substantial limitation of the state's ability to accumulate capital. It is a strong advantage of widespread public ownership in poor countries with weak fiscal systems that public saving 'involves simultaneous generation and mobilization of investible funds', whereas 'private saving, particularly household saving often presents formidable problems of mobilization and adequate canalisation'.[21] Again, the formality of public ownership is not sufficient to ensure the generation and mobilization of surplus. Since state ownership usually involves state management to a greater or lesser degree, the state then has to organize production in a cost-minimizing way – a task for which it has no inherent advantages, and perhaps even disadvantages. (Further, from the previous argument, it may be using surplus for activities that create surplus which it cannot internalize.) However, public ownership creates a potential for state capital accumulation with a weak fiscal system, just as profit retention creates a potential for private capital accumulation with an imperfect capital market.[22]

So far, the arguments for state accumulation have been set out in terms of the state's advantages and disadvantages as an agent of capital accumulation compared with private units. But the state could be more than one atom, even a very large and powerful one, in the anarchy of accumulation. In theory, it can regulate the overall rate of capital accumulation. If a policy of maximizing the reinvestible surplus is

21 Planning Commission, 1974, p. 13.   22 Cf. Sachs (1964), pp. 49–50.

judged to be impossibly austere, some milder rule can be adopted, and an attempt made to have it applied throughout the economy.[23] In addition, the conjunctural need to adjust total finance capital to total purchases of capital goods may arise. The state could alter its own accumulation programme in the short run to secure the required adjustment.[24] Thus the rationale of a policy of state accumulation includes the argument that only the state has the potential ability to regulate the anarchy of accumulation. Since that is precisely the declared aim of macroeconomic planning, regimes where planning is taken seriously ought to rely on the purposeful control of an extensive state sector.[25]

It is very important, at this point, to be clear that the formal justifications for a state accumulation policy which have just been mentioned are couched in terms of the possibilities of state action, and not of the common characteristics of existing states. By speaking of the state's 'potential abilities' and 'hypothetical advantages', it is intended to emphasize that the specified abilities and advantages do not inhere in every state, simply by virtue of its being a state. One might easily conclude otherwise, however, from reading the most popular and influential account of capital accumulation in poor countries, that of Sir Arthur Lewis. Lewis holds that, in general, the agent of capital accumulation may be 'the state'; and, while not giving a full comparison between state and private groups as agents, he implies the overall superiority of 'the state'.[26] He acknowledges that a question mark attaches to the sociological basis of state accumulation. But in response he offers only the following curious formula: 'in these days, many [countries] (e.g. U.S.S.R., India) are growing a class of state capitalists who, for political reasons of one sort or another, are determined to create capital rapidly on public account'.[27] How a 'class' of state capitalists can be 'grown', and what sort of political compulsions are required to motivate them, are both left unanswered, but in a manner which suggests that neither need be an enduring obstacle for the dedicated social

---

23 Thirlwall (1972) pp. 215–16; cf. Little and Mirrlees (1974), pp. 114–19.
24 Little and Mirrlees (1974), p. 182.
25 Cf. Sachs (1964), p. 50.
26 Lewis (1954), p. 419.   27 Lewis (1954), p. 420.

engineer. That there might be some differences of consequence between India, where state and private capitalists co-exist, and the U.S.S.R., where they do not, apparently did not seem relevant to Lewis; otherwise he could scarcely have bracketed the two instances so casually.

The hidden assumption, that 'the state' universally yokes power to benevolence and rationality, is an unselfconscious transposition of the political vision of British democratic socialism to situations where it is even more inappropriate than in Britain. The British social democrats' vision was of a 'Supreme Economic Authority' whose wise and just policies generated their own broad popular support.[28] It not only suffused the advice of economists like Lewis and Little, but pre-disposed a section of India's post-independence leadership to accept their advice, since from the 1930s it had been part of their own mental furniture.[29] Yet, even for advanced capitalist countries, it is unrealistic, given the existing monopolies of capital and labour, to view government as the work of a meritocracy with a popular mandate. It is even less realistic in India, where both civil servants and politicians are more corrupt, and where the electorate is more illiterate. It is thus easy to see how the abstract and politically unspecified justification of the state accumulation policy, which Lewis uses, can be criticized as utopian. This is particularly so because Lewis diverts attention from the social base of the operators of the policy by identifying their *class* with their *function*.[30] Actual 'state capitalists' in India do not form a class (or part of one) in any meaningful Marxist sense. On the other hand, they do have symbiotic links with a private capitalist class. They are one of the 'professional groups who are not direct exploiters, but [are] integrated into the system of exploitation'.[31] It is, therefore, plausible to suggest that they will not make policy impartially in the common interest and that their administration of a state accumulation policy would be biassed in ways that favour the growth of private sector capital. Thus

28 E.g. Durbin (1949), pp. 41–7.
29 Desai and Bhagwati (1975), p. 219, note 3; Addy and Azad (1975), p. 130.
30 Lewis (1954), p. 420; cf. Plamenatz (1963), pp. 351–73.
31 Patnaik (1972), p. 215.

the potential advantages of state accumulation would never be realized.[32]

Those who attack the sociological naivety of the social democratic justification of the state accumulation policy often confer on that policy other justifications which, on examination, turn out to be no less naive. One familiar line of argument begins by postulating the state as the instrument of a dominant class, the so-called 'national bourgeoisie'. The national bourgeoisie, supported by progressive elements of the proletariat and peasantry, is held to be capable of directing a 'peaceful transition to socialism', by undertaking a policy of state accumulation and thereby short-circuiting the development of capitalism.[33] This thesis is logically weak. Lenin's policy of socialist state accumulation took as its premise the prior removal of the social dominance of feudal and capitalist classes. This premise, despite the anti-coloniai movement, has never been fulfilled in India. Therefore (since a national bourgeoisie *is* an exploiting class and not, like the proletariat, a 'class above classes'), a policy of state accumulation in India could not have the same consequences as it would under socialism.[34] The national bourgeois state can neither eliminate class conflicts, nor plan comprehensively to eliminate the crises of capitalist production.[35] But how a policy of state accumulation, operating within these limits, can eventually transcend them to usher in socialism peacefully is nowhere explained, and is, indeed, inexplicable.

Insisting on the Leninist premise for a state accumulation policy involves a different difficulty. To emphasize that 'the bourgeois state machinery, even under state capitalism, must first be destroyed' restores a certain consistency, but only by creating another dilemma. Why, it may be asked, is a policy of state accumulation in any way desirable *before* the Leninist condition is fulfilled? It is useless to argue that 'by creating the necessary material base [the policy] facilitates the transition to socialism once the working class seizes political power'.[36]

32 Cf. Holland (1972), p. 7.   33 Clarkson (1972), p. 623.
34 Habib (1975), p. 167.
35 Ulyanovsky and Pavlov (1973), pp. 96–8.
36 Chattopadhyay (1970), pp. 17–18.

Private capitalism could be given exactly the same justification: it might even do better in creating the necessary material base. In order to rule out the possibility of private capitalism doing better, or equally well, some argument must be put forward for the *superiority* of the state as an agent of accumulation. It is difficult to know what arguments would be regarded as acceptable for this purpose, without, at the same time, being open to the very objection which is raised against social democratic theorists, namely their idealization of the state.

It is commonplace to justify the state accumulation policy with references to the *in*ability of private capitalists to accumulate at the right speed and in the right sectors. This makes the state a superior agent of accumulation, so to speak, by default. In fact, this conventional *faute de mieux* defence of state accumulation is often shared by liberals and social democrats with their strongest critics.[37] This defence is only one half of an argument, in that the incompetence of private units is not established *relative to* the competence of the state. Only when that is done is a foundation laid for the claim that the growth of the private sector at the expense of the public is necessarily retrograde.[38] But the belief in the relative competence of the state is the central tenet of social democracy.

It is sometimes also argued that a state accumulation policy is desirable before the destruction of the bourgeois state machinery because it fights 'feudal and semi-feudal production relations, monopoly capitalism, and imperialism'.[39] Again it is unclear why state capitalism should make a better enemy to feudalism than would private capitalism – unless the *faute de mieux* defence of state accumulation is again being invoked. Further, why should state capitalism be preferred to foreign monopoly capitalism? It is taken to be so, but surely any conflict between them should, if the state is the instrument of a dominant bourgeois class, be regarded as an intra-capitalist quarrel?[40] It is also said to be a quarrel which the domestic

---

37 E.g. Bhagwati (1966), p. 170; Tinbergen (1967), p. 34; cf. Kalecki (1972), pp. 162–3; Ulyanovsky and Pavlov (1973), pp. 114–15.
38 Chattopadhyay (1970), p. 27; Nayar (1972), p. 52, note 63.
39 Chattopadhyay (1970), p. 36; cf. Ulyanovsky and Pavlov (1973), p. 115.
40 Warren (1973), pp. 42–4; Kalecki (1972), pp. 167, 168.

bourgeoisie loses, and that this defeat ultimately makes a state accumulation policy unworkable.[41] So it is doubly difficult to argue that a state accumulation policy is desirable as a bulwark against foreign monopoly capitalism.

One must conclude therefore, that neither the social democratic viewpoint, nor that of its sociologically oriented critics, provides an adequate rationale for the state accumulation policy. The former highlights its potential economic advantages, but neglects the social and political disposition of its operators. The latter repairs this neglect, and in doing so discovers that 'the political and social conditions for national state-capitalist expansion – requiring limitations on imperialist influence while retaining the conditions of capitalist exploitation – create an explosive contradictory regime'.[42] The former holds that a state accumulation policy can always succeed, provided only that it is fully understood and firmly willed by a government. The underlying assumption, that every state, regardless of its political and social environment, exercises untrammelled power in all relevant respects, is indeed evidence of a blandly technocratic attitude towards social change. The latter view, that a state accumulation policy can never succeed for long, even when fully understood and firmly willed by a government, *until* social revolution abolishes private property in the means of production, is valuable insofar as it challenges bland technocratism. But, in doing so, it should not be allowed to slide from historical analysis into dubious prophecy. The future is only relatively predictable, and then only from a solid and extensive knowledge of the past. This suggests that the best that can be done, *in principle*, is to investigate the history of the factors influencing state accumulation policies in particular cases, and then to use such history as the foundation for intelligent judgement of the future.

41 Chattopadhyav (1970), p. 37; Petras (1977), pp. 7–8; Patnaik (1972), p. 229.
42 Petras (1977), p. 13

2

Indian nationalism and the state accumulation policy

Having examined the notions of 'public expenditure control' and 'state accumulation' in the abstract, they must now be located in the concrete context to which our empirical evidence relates. This context is the political economy of India in the 1960s. The theme that underlies our characterization of the Indian political economy is that class analysis must be supplemented by an understanding of the phenomenon of nationalism, if over-simple conclusions are to be avoided.

One fundamental error which continues to plague class analyses of India must be firmly rejected right at the start. That error is the view that the state is *merely* the instrument of a *single* dominant class. Rejection should be based on two separate grounds. First, in many less developed countries, and certainly in India, the empirical analysis of class shows that there is no *single* dominant class. Rather, several distinct classes with conflicting economic interests are co-dominant. Even with the most aggregative class analysis of India, the monopoly bourgeoisie, landlords, rich peasants and other groups like the bureaucracy and the armed forces (which are not strictly classes on Marxist criteria) would have to be separately distinguished as co-dominant classes and groups. This alliance of social co-dominance is uneasy, and short-run and even medium-term class analysis for India consists of charting the shifts in status, power and influence among the parties to this alliance.[1] Second, even if it were correct to speak in social terms of a single dominant class (say, the mythical 'national bourgeoisie' or the

1 E. g. Toye (1977); cf. Kidron (1965), p. 128, n. 1.

Kaleckian notion of an 'intermediate régime' based on the dominance of the lower middle class[2]), it would scarcely be in a position to use the state merely as an instrument of its dominance. Essentially, this is because the colonial state was fashioned under *external* pressures, for purposes *exogenous* to the interests of the indigenous society, and cannot be assumed, therefore, to be readily adaptable to the pursuit of its interests by a socially dominant class, even if such a class could be shown to exist.[3] In comparison with the European paradigm, the state apparatus inherited by independent India was overdeveloped in relation to the social and economic strength of any indigenous class. So it had, and still retains, some power to act independently of the specific interests of any domestic class.

Some writers go further than this, ascribing to state sector employees, civilian and military, the social force to act with almost complete autonomy. This bureaucratic group has been termed 'a class-conscious stratum . . . functioning as an independent class . . . with its own political economic project [of national state capital accumulation]'.[4] Whatever the aptness of this conception for other post-colonial societies, it exaggerates the autonomy of the Indian state. Its autonomy of action is definitely limited by its need to maintain a balance between the conflicting interests of the classes which, in uneasy coalition, share social dominance.[5]

In addition, the Indian state's limited freedom of manoeuvre *vis-à-vis* internal hegemonic struggles does not in any way make it immune from external pressures. These external pressures on the overdeveloped state arise from the rapid and uneven outward penetration of the capitalist mode of production from its European places of origin. In the colonial period, capitalist penetration had been experienced as invasion and domination, a tidal wave of outside interference and control. The Indian reaction had been the ambivalent response of nationalism, felt as the twin imperatives 'at once to resist [capitalism, in so far as it implies European domination] and somehow to take over

2 Kalecki (1972), pp. 162–9; Post and Wright (1978), pp. 649–51.
3 Martinussen (1976), p. 5; Alavi (1972), p. 147.
4 Petras (1977), p.3.
5 Cf. Martinussen (1976), p. 5, n. 3.

its vital forces for [the non-European elite's] own use'.[6] The bureaucratic group which inherited the colonial state found itself with a certain limited freedom within the domestic area to realize this double-edged response. There is motive enough to induce the bureaucratic group to attend to this task, since the preservation and strengthening of the sovereignty of the nationalist state are the conditions of their own self-perpetuation as a group.

It is worth distinguishing the above interpretation from others apparently similar. Writers in the utilitarian tradition account for economic nationalism in two ways; it derives either from an intellectual error, or from the fact that the private interests of bureaucrats are best served by nationalist policies.[7] Writers in the historical materialist tradition sometimes seem to be suggesting that bureaucratic strata have the power to choose which 'political economic project' they wish to advance.[8] The above interpretation stresses what has been called 'the fatal impact' of European capitalism on peripheral peoples and civilizations as the determining factor of the form of non-European nationalism. It would dismiss the other three accounts as, respectively, idealistic, hedonistic and voluntaristic errors.

It follows that non-European nationalism has different meanings from the nationalisms of European history. Nationalism in India is not the same slow, interpenetrating development of capitalism and consolidation of state sovereignty which occurred in pre-industrial Europe. Nor is it a programme of political self-determination for groups united by language and culture, of the kind so widely espoused in nineteenth- and early-twentieth-century Europe. By contrast, it is a struggle to appropriate an externally designed and imposed state apparatus, and thereafter to preserve a modified version of it in indigenous hands.

This interpretation again appears close to theories of a modernization imperative.[9] It certainly shares with such theories an emphasis on the determinism of long-run historical tendencies. Where it differs is in avoiding the teleological

6 Nairn (1975), p. 12.
7 Johnson (1967), p. 68; Bird (1970), p. 127, n. 19.
8 Petras (1977), p. 3.   9 E. g. Nayar (1972).

element in the concept of modernity, which implies a steady and successful achievement by non-European countries of the ideals of European civilization. Quite to the contrary of these ideals, the actual history of the spread of capitalism has been characterized by uneven development, international conflict and the rise to power of embodiments of unreason and barbarism. National sovereignty is pursued by ex-colonies like India because they have to exist, if they are to exist, in an international arena in which the ultimate rule of action in foreign relations is *sauve qui peut*.

The only way to preserve national sovereignty in such a dangerous environment is to provide the nation with those types of property, and those types of skills, that will serve to defend it against those developed countries whose destructive impact has already been experienced so painfully. Initially this requires learning how to copy the relevant property and skills of those developed countries whose domination is feared. This process of defensive copying by post-colonial society may be termed 'mimetic nationalism'. Mimetic nationalism is a phenomenon which has frequently been noted although not, perhaps, under that particular label.

Sometimes it is remarked disparagingly, as by Trotsky, who claimed that 'the backward nation . . . not infrequently debases the achievements borrowed from outside in the process of adapting them to its more primitive culture'. [10] This makes it clear that the mimesis is not, indeed could not be, exact replication. As it has been more recently explained, 'unable to literally "copy" the advanced lands (which would have entailed repeating the stages of slow growth which had led to the breakthrough), the backward regions were forced to take what they wanted and cobble it on to their own native inheritance of social forms'. [11] The motivation behind mimetic nationalism is also clear to those who stumble upon it without utilitarian blinkers: 'the largest [poor] countries seem to be engaged in duplicating work for the [purpose] of neutralizing the political effects of more powerful alien achievements'. [12]

This kind of 'nationalism' has, as a consequence, a number of unusual features. First, the process of nationalist struggle

10 Davey (1975), p. 109.   11 Nairn (1975), p. 11.
12 Melzer (1974), p. 3.

actually stimulates regional linguistic and/or religious patriotism. The cultural impact of British rule had already done much
to prepare the ground. [13] By 1920, the National Congress sought
to harness this regional patriotism both by reorganizing itself
linguistically and demanding reorganization of British India
on linguistic lines. The arrival of independence made manifest
the contradiction – a nationalism which coexists with a low
level of national integration. [14]

The second unusual feature arises because mimetic nationalism tends to achieve mobilization by means of populist politics. Especially when pre-capitalist economic formations have
failed to crystallize strong class identities, the overdeveloped
state apparatus is directed by a political 'united front', a comprehensive but loose coalition which is quite heterogeneous in
terms of class. Thus the managers of the united front are not
tightly constrained to develop their nationalism as a disguise
for a particular set of class interests. Limited scope for the
exercise of 'great leadership' exists, and whether it is exercised
by a Bose, a Gandhi, a Patel, or as happened, a Nehru, is a
matter of real historical consequence. Nehru's personal responsibility for setting up the Indian state accumulation policy
cannot be glossed over.

Thirdly, while mimetic nationalism may launch itself on a
wave of radical anti-imperialism, including the nationalization
of imperial assets, this posture is maintained more in word
than in deed. Before long, former colonial or semi-colonial
states take financial assistance from multiple sources. That they
become 'the clever calves who suck two cows' is not necessarily
the outcome of particular internal class conflicts. [15] Yet the fate
of a state accumulation policy can often be vitally affected, in
the short run, by the willingness of foreign sources to provide
finance capital.

These remarks about mimetic nationalism should certainly
not be interpreted as an attempt to advance a new single-factor
hypothesis of Indian development, or to propagate a new kind
of reductionism in which an abstract force is set up as the sole

13 Clark (1970), pp. 9–15; Rudolph and Rudolph (1969), p. 1039; States Reorganization Commission (1955), pp. 10, 35.
14 Desai (1975), pp. 30–5.
15 Kalecki (1972), pp. 167–8; Warren (1973), p. 13.

engine of contemporary history. Their intention is merely to take a more comprehensive view, and one that includes a little more of the complexity of the real world, than one often finds in the standard approach to class analysis. Specifically, it aims to break with class analyses of post-colonial societies which assume that these societies are self-contained entities within which one must be able to find the same classes which Marx identified, engaged in the same conflicts as were to be found in nineteenth-century capitalist Europe. In one important respect, this assumption is similar to that underlying the much-mocked Rostovian view of these societies as sequentially experiencing a uniform process of 'modernization': both adopt an atomistic rather than a global perspective. The result in both cases is an inability to cast any light on the differences between the role of the state and of nationalism as between today's fully capitalist and today's not fully capitalist societies.

In this century, capitalism is global, and ultimately the only satisfactory analysis of it is global also. Since capitalism as a system of production and social organization was not originally indigenous to India, the object of analysis at the national level in underdeveloped countries is the reception of capitalism, either via the pressures of imported technology or directly by the internationalization of consumption tastes and capitalist social and political institutions. For the colonial period, the colonial state was one very obvious channel for the reception of capitalism, and the theory of the overdeveloped post-colonial state is a way of emphasizing the continuity of that channel in the immediate post-independence period. This theory should not, however, be read as implying that the post-colonial state must remain permanently overdeveloped in relation to indigenous social classes, long after the removal of the imperial power from the stage. The penetration of capitalism intensifies the initially weak struggles between indigenous classes, and in the course of these struggles state institutions are modified. With the removal of the imperial power, the degree of overdevelopment of the state reduces, the possibilities of 'great leadership' are foreclosed and the vigour of populism, anti-imperialism and mimetic nationalism wanes. They are therefore transient forces. But they were powerful in the historical period with which we are concerned, and their strength even now is far from exhausted.

Beneath the surface of the political and economic events which form the focus of this work, there are signs in India of an increasing divergence of interest between the co-dominant social classes. In particular, the power of rural landlords and rich peasants to block policies which encroach on their interests (such as land redistribution, extra agricultural taxation, unfavourable grain procurement prices, and institutional reforms in the villages) has been increasingly openly asserted.[16] The evidence for the assertion of power by the rural upper class is sufficiently strong and relates to a sufficiently long period to justify speaking of it as a long-run trend. However, one is reluctant to endorse the conclusion that the state accumulation policy was inevitably frustrated by this trend alone, or, even more narrowly, by the 'failure to squeeze agriculture'. It is probably not the case that Indian agriculture in 1960 was in a very squeezable condition.[17] In addition, it would probably be agreed that the medium-term effects on the net marketed surplus of purely institutional reforms in the agricultural sector are extremely difficult to quantify: that there would have been a substantial increase must still be regarded as not proven. Thus, to link the shift in power from urban to rural dominant classes so directly with the frustration of the state accumulation policy begs some important questions and fails to do full justice to the international dimension of India's experience.

II PRE-HISTORY OF INDIAN STATE ACCUMULATION POLICY

The early history in India of the state accumulation policy has often been told.[18] So a further detailed account would be out of place here. However, certain aspects of that history illuminate the relationship between classes, state and mimetic nationalism which has so far been discussed in very broad terms. These aspects have not been sufficiently emphasized by previous writers, and, because of their significance for a proper understanding of India's state accumulation policy in the 1950s and 1960s, they are worth pointing out, even at the risk of some repetition.

16 Mitra (1977), pp. 92–103 and 170–83; Frankel (1978), pp. 113–55, 187–200, 335–40.
17 Toye (1978), p. 224.
18 E.g. Sachs (1964), pp. 106–25; Chattopadhyay (1970); Martinussen (1976).

The nationalist tradition holds that British *laissez-faire* policies were the cause of India's failure to develop economically, and that this fact gave the anti-colonial struggle its 'progressive' character. It is fair to say that the potentialities for development in nineteenth-century India, and, therefore, the scope and the sophistication of the policies that would have been needed to realize them, remain very controversial among Indian economic historians. This is not the place to attempt an arbitration. For the more limited purpose of clarifying the history of the state accumulation policy, it must be emphasized that, until the state apparatus was on the verge of transfer to Indian nationalist hands, the British administration in India was more interested in the possibilities of state entrepreneurship than the Indian nationalists themselves.

Certainly, even before 1914, the British adherence to *laissez-faire* was not total and rigid. Rather in the manner of Moghul mercantilism, the British had experimented with state ownership of large industrial units, such as coal mines and ironworks. The motive was to try and ease some of the supply difficulties of the state-owned railways. But when the government found itself facing the demand for fresh capital to maintain and expand its units, it shied away. It would not confront the anticipated charge that public money was being used to increase competition for British manufacturers.[19] So the state-owned units were sold off to private entrepreneurs, some to flourish, and others to be quietly closed down. Chatterton's state-owned consumer goods factories in Madras are perhaps better known. This personal and local experiment was, on the whole, successful. But it was censured on grounds of *laissez-faire* principle by the Secretary of State, Lord Morley, in 1910, after which the remaining factories closed down. This censure also led to the closing of a state-owned cotton-seed oil factory in the United Provinces. In this episode, British dogmatism, and its ill-effects, are seen most clearly. Shortly afterwards, however, a partial retreat from dogmatism took place. The start of the 1914–18 war quickly exposed the full extent of India's reliance on industrial imports, and the glaring gaps in her indigenous production capabilities. The Indian Industrial Commission of 1916–

19 Sen (1966), pp. 31–5; pp. 41–5; cf. Spencer (1959), p. 39.

18 responded by recommending a range of state aids for industrial development, including state 'pioneer' factories, though not going so far as state ownership on a normal basis. But, by this time, economic policy could no longer be isolated from larger political decisions which were made under the shadow of nationalist opposition. The Industrial Commission's plan for an Imperial Department of Industries was swallowed up in the Montagu–Chelmsford decentralization of 1918, so that promotion of industrial growth became a duty of the new provincial governments. Lack of revenue kept provincial efforts miniscule. The provincial pioneer factories of the 1920s made about a dozen different types of simple consumer goods, of which some succeeded commercially, but rather more failed from technical problems, marketing difficulties or surrender in the face of complaints from competitive private enterprise.[20] Once the war was over, and provincial autonomy and certain protective tariffs had been conceded, financial stringency inhibited any further British official experiments with state entrepreneurship.

Meanwhile, it is quite clear that Indian nationalist opinion was very far from advocating a state accumulation policy. Its position (as set out by the Indian Industrial Conference, 1905–12) was that state powers of tariff-making, procurement and development banking should be used to aid *private* industrial growth. At this time, state entrepreneurship was definitely favoured less by nationalists than by British officialdom in India.[21] One nationalist publicly tried to defend Lord Morley's policy when his colleagues on the Industrial Commission were condemning its 'deadening effect'![22] Another example of the nationalist disdain of state enterprise is the attitude of Sir M. Visvesvaraya. As Dewan of Mysore (1914–18) and Chairman of the Bhadravati Ironworks (1923–29), he established a major industrial enterprise in the state sector, and managed it with considerable success in adverse trading conditions.[23] Yet when, in 1934, he came to write India's prototype development plan, despite its extreme emphasis on industrialization, the division of investment between private and public sectors was an issue

20 Sinha and Khera (1962), p. 143; Clow (1928), pp. 94–103.
21 Rider (1971), pp. 177–82, 190–2.   22 Malaviya (1918), pp. 292–3, 314.
23 Visvesvaraya (1951), pp. 77–93.

left completely unresolved.[24] He saw the role of the government as one of encouraging corporate and individual enterprise, advising India 'to proceed along the lines practised in such capitalist countries as France and the United States of America'.[25] His later efforts aimed at promoting industry (vehicles and aircraft manufacturing schemes in the late 1930s) also centred on the private sector.

Nehru did, however, succeed in 1931 in having the Karachi Congress resolve that the State 'shall own or control key industries and services, mineral resources, railways, waterways, shipping and other means of public transport', as well as extending tariff protection to indigenous industries.[26] But the socialism which he had absorbed on his visit to Europe in 1926–27 was of a mild and timid variety – a peculiar blend of British municipal socialism and Russian communism without the coercion – and the Karachi resolution was even milder and more timid.[27] In addition, most other Congressmen, and particularly Gandhi and Patel, were completely out of sympathy with both models and Nehru, when he came under pressure in the mid 1930s, was prepared to soft-pedal his socialism to preserve the nationalist united front.[28]

In defining a state accumulation policy, the critical issue is the balance between state ownership and state control (which of course exists even under 'night watchman' capitalism). No attempt was made to specify this balance until the National Planning Committee was set up in 1938 under Nehru's chairmanship. So it is no exaggeration to maintain that Indian nationalists 'until the mid-1930s . . . had no clear conception of the part the government was to play in the process of industrialization'.[29] The reason for this is that a state accumulation policy could only become attractive to nationalist sentiment once the *transfer of the state apparatus to Indian control* was practically assured.

Nehru's basic views on economic policy are clear enough. His final goals were the maintenance of Indian sovereignty and the increase of popular welfare. His proximate goal was indus-

24 Visvesvaraya (1934), p. 297. 25 Visvesvaraya (1934), pp. 221–2, 240.
26 Shah (1949), p. 27. 27 Gopal (1975), pp. 113–15, 125–6, 136–7, 152.
28 Gopal (1975), pp. 209–20. 29 Shirokov (1973), p. 56.

trialization, which, he believed, would secure *both* his final goals simultaneously. Planning was not a way of choosing a development path; it was a method of clarifying the practicalities of industrialization.[30] This complex of aims and beliefs is the economic strategy of 'mimetic nationalism'. Its characteristic is to measure progress by the degree of 'ownership and control by nationals' (individually and collectively) of desirable types of 'modern property', defined 'by imitation and emulation of the economic structure of established nation-states'.[31] The question of whether ownership and control by nationals of 'modern' property should be weighted in favour of collectivism or individualism is, for nationalists, a subsidiary issue.

The purest Indian expression of mimetic nationalism is to be found in Visvesvaraya's volume on economic planning. The essence of the doctrine is encapsulated in the following characteristic passages:

Industries and manufactures supply the elements needed to make a people self-sufficient and self-reliant and develop their organic life as a nation ... Industrial life connotes production, wealth, power and modernity ... The principal nations of the world have all been concentrating on industries and manufactures with a view to strengthening their economic position ... No modern nation whose national policies are not guided by the two forces of industrialism and nationalism has gained military power or become rich and prosperous ... Industries flourish under any civilized *national* government, whether that government is semiautocratic ... or oligarchic ... or under one-man dictatorship ...

Training in defence is the first step in the building up of national life ... No nation can regard itself as safe that is not prepared to defend itself ... the supervision and ultimate control of the defence forces should be completely Indianized within, say, fifteen years.

It is necessary that Indians should ... assimilate the beneficial experience of other countries in order to raise their own level of working capacity and material prosperity.[32]

These sentiments are echoed again and again in Nehru's own writings and speeches, but with the addition of his own strong preference for collective rather than individual owner-

---

30 Nehru (1961), p. 420; pp. 432–3; Nayar (1972), pp. 113–38.
31 Johnson (1967), p. 67.
32 Visvesvaraya (1934), pp. 220–2, 256–7.

ship of industry.[33] He tried to ensure that this preference was embodied in the decisions of the National Planning Committee. But within the N.P.C. a marked difference of opinion existed over whether 'basic industries' other than defence industries ought to be state owned. The N.P.C. as such never resolved this issue in the affirmative, despite Nehru's own later statement to the contrary.[34] Nehru did obtain the agreement of a bare majority of N.P.C. sub-committee chairmen in February 1940, but the full N.P.C. never pronounced a verdict before the various disruptions of wartime overtook its activities. Because of the disruption and incompleteness, it is impossible to ascribe to the N.P.C. a coherent attitude towards the policy of state accumulation. The outbreak of war saved Nehru from having to confront the opposition which the right-wing of the Congress, led by Gandhi, was raising against the work of the N.P.C.[35]

The Tata-Birla or Bombay Plan of 1944, written by eight big businessmen, four of whom had served on the N.P.C., serves as another exceptionally vivid statement of the nationalist consensus on economic policy. The Second World War, like the First, had emphasized the serious lacunae in India's range of industrial production. Accordingly, it is not surprising to find that the Bombay Plan puts industry's investment share even higher than the actual Second Five-Year Plan; and that the rationale of rapid industrialization in terms of *national security* is stated with exceptional clarity. But the commitment to ownership of industry by the state was hedged around carefully with qualifications. State control (presumably an improved version of the existing wartime economic controls) was held to be more important than state ownership as a general rule. Where state control was considered to be ineffective without state ownership, the candidate industries for state ownership given in the Plan were two that were already state-owned – defence and communications. The Plan certainly contemplated state ownership for new industries, but with the proviso that, once flourishing, they could be sold to the private

33 Desai and Bhagwati (1975), p. 218, notes 2 and 3.
34 Shah (1949), pp. 41, 50, 59, 100, 124, 140, 244; but cf. Nehru (1961), p. 422; Chattopadhyay (1970), pp. 19–20; Spencer (1959), p. 45.
35 Gopal (1975), p. 247.

sector. State ownership did not however require state management; management could be supplied by existing private firms of managing agents. The authors were not prepared to believe that the question of ownership, or their criteria for determining it, were matters of high principle. On the other hand, now that the transfer of power from British to Indian hands was so plainly on the cards, they were not prepared to offer outright opposition to state ownership either. What the Bombay Plan suggests is a compromise, by which industries would be divided half-and-half between the private and the public sectors.[36] Although the nationalist big bourgeoisie had softened its attitude towards state ownership in this Plan, one cannot argue that business espoused a state accumulation policy because it realised its own weakness *vis-à-vis* foreign capital. On the contrary, one can infer that it felt strong enough to offer only a limited acquiescence in the policy – provided that withholding of full support for it did not prevent a national industrialization drive.[37] This interpretation is consistent with statistical evidence that Indian capital decisively overshadowed foreign capital in India on the eve of independence.[38]

Calculated hesitation towards a state accumulation policy is also evident in the Report of the Interim Government's Advisory Planning Board. This Report argued that large-scale state ownership actually might *prevent* industrialization at the required speed. Accordingly, it proposed for state ownership a list of industries even shorter than the list in S.N. Agarwal's Gandhian Plan. These were only to be state owned if private capital was not forthcoming. Even this timidity did not save the Report from dissenting notes by the Board's chairman, K. C. Neogy, and another member, G. L. Mehta.[39] Nor had the case for a state accumulation policy gone by default, thanks to Professor K. T. Shah. As chairman of the N.P.C. sub-committee on Public Finance, he had already pointed out that 'apart from other considerations, questions of finance and the necessity for increasing revenue for the nation-building activities of the State made it essential' for key industries to be state-owned,

36 Thakurdas (1945), pp. 58, 94–8; Shirokov (1973), p. 57, n.3.
37 Kidron (1965), pp. 103–12, cf. pp. 72–3.
38 Shirokov (1973), p. 49.
39 Roy (1965), pp. 59–62, 56.

rather than just state-controlled.[40] Shah repeated this argument in his note on the Advisory Board's Report, together with arguments for a state accumulation policy based on macro-planning and distributional grounds.[41] He got little support, even from 'industrializers'.

The history of the debate on a state accumulation policy is quite consistent with the actions actually taken after independence by the Indian government. With the perspective just presented, the strategic economic policy decisions of the 1950s appear as an epilogue to that history, rather than as a drama in their own right.

The principle of an industrializing course was adopted nearly unanimously. The controversy of the time centred on the size of total investments, not their pattern or the desirability of their expected results. The industrialization strategy itself was regarded as conventional wisdom that was the product of a long maturing national consensus of politicians and academics.[42] Its widespread, uncritical acceptance undoubtedly rested on something more fundamental than the short-term influences which have been in the past cited as explanations. Export pessimism, often cited as the rationale of the industrialization strategy, may have existed, but it was not generated by any thorough preliminary study of export prospects – for none was done.[43] Optimism about agriculture may have bred complacency, but again no proper study of agricultural prospects was made.[44] Mahalanobis certainly had advice from the U.S.S.R., but it was to moderate his enthusiasm for ideas which were basically formalized versions of Nehru's own, and which he had shared with Nehru since the days of the N.P.C.[45]

The firmness of the industrialization commitment contrasts markedly with vacillation over the role of the state in industrialization. Until the deaths of Gandhi and Patel, it was by no means assured that Nehru's socialism would win a clear run even as official Congress Party doctrine.[46] As is well-known,

40 Shah (1949), pp. 188–9.
41 Roy (1965), pp. 61–6.
42 Deshmukh (1957), pp. 69–77; Gadgil (1972), pp. 3–4; 42; Clarkson (1973), pp. 722–3.
43 Bhagwati and Chakravarthy (1971), p. 12.
44 Byres (1972), pp. 223–47.
45 Nayar (1972), pp. 144–5; Shah (1949), pp. 112, 119.
46 Kidron (1965), pp. 83–8.

even at the high tide of enthusiasm for the 'socialist pattern' in 1956, the role of the state remained vague, the elaborate attempts at precision only emphasizing the underlying fluidity. The second Industrial Policy Resolution of 1956 closed to private enterprise without any qualification *only four* industries, all of which had obvious strategic importance.[47] For all other industries, the Resolution was consistent with any combination of public and private enterprise which the government cared to decide upon. The scope for pragmatism without formal breach of the Resolution was extensive. This latitude was certainly also used, particularly to secure the services of foreign private oil companies.[48]

Despite the pragmatism of government policy on the role to be played by the state in industrialization, after 1955 substantial public investment went to create a heavy industry complex in the public sector. By 1970, a further seventy central government enterprises had been added to twenty-one that existed at the start of the Second Plan, mainly in the iron and steel, heavy and precision engineering, chemical and transport industries.[49] The amount invested in them had risen from 0.8 to 43.0 billion rupees at current prices. This, and related investment in state government departmental enterprises, probably increased the proportion of the national capital stock in public ownership from about 15 per cent to about 35 per cent in the mid 1960s.

But far from being the first phase of controlled advance to a society on a 'socialistic pattern', this public sector growth was tolerated because it could be seen from a nationalist viewpoint as a vital step in the consolidation of independent India's international position. This, for India as for all nations, rests squarely on her ability to dispose of modern *material de guerre*. Nehru's statements are notoriously opaque, but a powerful case has recently been documented from them that the military advantages of the industrialization strategy were always in the forefront of his thinking.[50] One finds for example, that Nehru's defense of the Avadi resolutions on the 'socialist pattern of society' uses the theme: 'we have to fit India into the nuclear

47 Planning Commission (1956), p. 46.
48 Chattopadhyay (1970), pp. 21–3; Kapoor (1974), pp. 25–65.
49 Cf. Martinussen (1976), p. 14.
50 Nayar (1972), pp. 113–43; Maxwell (1972), p. 268.

age, and do it quickly'. This, and many other similar examples, could be cited in support of the judgement on Nehru's work that 'nationalism and socialism were the intellectual driving forces . . . [but] of these nationalism was by far the most powerful most of the time'.[51]

At almost the start of the industrialization drive, in 1957–58, the consequent acute scarcity of foreign exchange induced the government to impose stringent quota restrictions on imports. These restrictions provided strong protection for all forms of production in India with which, otherwise, imports would have competed. Behind the barrier of quotas an extensive range of new, but inefficient and internationally uncompetitive industries grew up, in the public and private sectors alike. This growth in the number and variety of domestically produced products was not viewed with alarm. On the contrary, the advent of each new import-substitute was welcomed as a further step towards national self-reliance, in accordance with the nationalist view that 'India should not import products which she can with some effort manufacture for herself'.[52] In the effort to avoid the Scylla of indiscriminate importation, mimetic nationalism headed straight for the Charybdis of indiscriminate import substitution.

The concrete context in which a state accumulation policy, itself falteringly supported by the government, was supposed to work was composed of an industrialization drive aimed particularly at basic and heavy industries, and a foreign trade regime which provided incentives for indiscriminate import substitution. It is the attempt to operate a state accumulation policy within the boundaries specified by mimetic nationalism which provides the framework for the ensuing studies of Indian public expenditure in the 1960s.

The state accumulation policy has its own political constituency in India, the 'Left' who advocate economic growth through state capitalism and non-alignment in foreign affairs. Their opponents of the 'Right' support private enterprise capitalism with a large, but subsidiary role for the state, and closer alignment to advanced capitalist countries. What unites both Left and Right is agreement on the need for Indian eco-

51 Tyson (1966), pp. 21, 19.   52 Visvesvaraya (1934), pp. 376–7.

nomic independence, the central nationalist objective.[53] The Congress government naturally emphasized the point of agreement in its policy making, and tried to blur the choice on the issues on which the two wings conflicted. Indeed, how could it be otherwise while the Congress Party remained the only political grouping capable of supporting an all-India government? The retention by the Congress as a party of a great deal of the allegiance it received as an anti-colonial movement was achieved by avoiding domestic divisions on issues of principle, a meticulous attention to the balanced distribution of governmental favours amongst the co-dominant social classes, and more recently by judicious acts of violence and repression. To survive in this form, Congress has had to remain extraordinarily catholic, and aim to comprehend as many different ideologies and interests as will tolerate each other's company.[54] The periodic suggestion that it was about to become 'a body of tightly-knit devotees, activists, militants in a cause' has proved illusory.[55] Its leadership has largely been recruited from the dominant classes and groups.[56] It has drawn the finance to pay its candidates' election expenses from large firms in the organized sector, and the votes it needs to elect them from the vote-brokers of the countryside.[57] In electoral terms, its support has been more heterogeneous than any other party.[58] It has also been the only party whose main support does not cluster in merely one or two geographical areas of the country. As the party of consensus *par excellence*, the Congress policy priorities were mimetic nationalism first and state accumulation a rather poor second.

To claim that mimetic nationalism shaped India's economic strategy implies the denial of the view that international conflict is fully explicable in terms of class conflict. This denial is justified because the two treatments of international conflict as an epiphenomenon to class divisions both ignore important facts. Can the entire population of poor countries be treated as an overseas extension of the proletariat of advanced capitalism, with nationalism its revolutionary ideology? If so, why is non-European nationalism so frequently associated

53 Kidron (1965), p. 128, n. 1.   54 Baran (1973), pp. 369–70.
55 Cf. Morris-Jones (1967).   56 Roy (1966–67), I, p. 19; IV, pp. 371–6.
57 Forrester (1968), pp. 1087–93.   58 Sheth (1971), p. 284.

with internal reaction?[59] Is nationalism the ideology of capitalist latecomers?[60] If so, why, does it flourish regardless of the internal class structure?[61] Whichever particular class interest one tries to connect with non-European nationalism, its variety and ubiquity is inadequately explained. And quite apart from the discrepancy with fact, it is doubtful whether a theoretically consistent explanation of international conflict in terms of class division is possible.[62]

The implication of our emphasis on nationalism is that government policy is directed towards creating an industrial base that will supply *material de guerre*, extending political and economic control over peripheral land areas and increasing the manpower available for the preservation both of external defence and internal order. This will be so regardless of the professed welfare and other objectives of those who announce state policy.

III BACKGROUND TO POST-INDEPENDENCE DEVELOPMENT POLICY

For the reader who is not closely acquainted with the vicissitudes of planning and development in contemporary India, it may be helpful to be told something of the broad economic and political background against which the ensuing detailed discussion of Indian public expenditure is set. There are many different ways in which this could be done, as exemplified by the work of Malenbaum, Chaudhuri and Frankel, for instance.[63] The most straightforward approach is to adopt the official chronology of the planners as the framework on which to present the major indicators of economic progress in the post-independence period. This is a useful first step, but a limited one. Taken on its own, it over-emphasizes the importance of the planning process itself as a determinant of economic progress and by implication draws attention away from other determinants. There are at least two other chronologies which seem to demand consideration. One is the chronology of foreign exchange control, which represents the influence of external

---

59 Cf. Warren (1973), p. 11.   60 Petras (1977), p. 12.
61 Cf. Warren (1973), p. 43.   62 Berki (1971), pp. 80–105.
63 See Malenbaum (1971); Chaudhuri (1978); Frankel (1978).

conditions and the policy response to them. The other is the chronology of internal political events, which influence the institutions and climate of opinion within which planning has to operate. It is advisable to think in terms of a number of chronologies superimposed one on another, rather than a single periodization of Indian development, particularly one which ministers to the official view that planning itself somehow *causes* development.

i   The chronology of planning

The duration of each of the series of Plans which was initiated in India in April 1951 is as follows.

First Five-Year Plan		1951–56
Second Five-Year Plan		1956–61
Third Five-Year Plan		1961–66
First Annual Plan	the 'plan	1966–67
Second Annual Plan	holiday'	1967–68
Third Annual Plan		1968–69
Fourth Five-Year Plan		1969–74
Fifth Five-Year Plan		1974–79

On this basis, the time with which this book is particularly concerned, the decade of the 1960s, seems to fall naturally into three sub-periods. They are (i) the period of the Third Five-Year Plan, (ii) the period of the 'plan holiday' during which the operation of five-year plans was suspended, and three 'annual plans' substituted and (iii) the so-called resumption of planning after 1969, when the abortive draft Fourth Five-Year Plan issued in August 1966 was officially replaced by a new Fourth Plan to be implemented between 1969 and 1974. Between the first and second sub-period comes the caesura of the severe drought and harvest failure of the year 1965/66, conditions which persisted in the following year and which were given as the justification for switching economic policy making on to the exclusively short-term basis of the annual plans.

Not only were all of these plans drawn up using different analytical techniques to solve the problems of economic planning,[64] they also reflected a changing emphasis in overall policy strategy. The First Plan is best seen as a collection of projects, mainly infrastructural and agricultural. The Second Plan represents the start of the industrialization drive, including the production of a wide range of new intermediate and capital goods. The Third Plan continued the essential strategy of the Second, but with more effort devoted to problems of industrial and agricultural linkages on the one hand, and to problems of foreign trade stagnation on the other. The three years of annual planning show that priority in policies had shifted from growth and structural change to consolidation and stabilization in the face of production shortfalls and accelerating inflation. There-

TABLE 2.1. *Growth of net national product at 1960/61 prices, 1950/51 to 1973/74*

	Pre-plan year	End year of plan	Per-centage change	Annual growth rate (per cent)
First Plan	1950/51	1955/56		
N.N.P. (Rs. crores)	9 078	10 860	+19.6	+3.6
N.N.P. per head (Rs.)	252.9	276.3	+ 9.3	+1.8
Second Plan	1955/56	1960/61		
N.N.P. (Rs. crores)	10 860	13 263	+22.1	+4.0
N.N.P. per head (Rs.)	276.3	305.6	+10.6	+2.0
Third Plan	1960/61	1965/66		
N.N.P. (Rs. crores)	13 263	15 082	+13.7	+2.6
N.N.P. per head (Rs.)	305.6	311.0	+ 1.7	+0.4
Annual plans	1965/66	1968/69		
N.N.P. (Rs. crores)	15 082	16 991	+12.7	+4.0
N.N.P. per head (Rs.)	311.0	328.0	+ 5.5	+1.8
Fourth Plan	1968/69	1973/74		
N.N.P. (Rs. crores)	16 991	20 034	+17.9	+3.3
N.N.P. per head (Rs.)	328.0	347.2	+ 5.9	+1.2

Note: Net national product is measured 'at factor cost', that is, disregarding the price effects of indirect taxes and subsidies.
Source: Calculated from C.S.O. (1975), Table A.1 and C.S.O. (1976a), Table 1.

64 See Bhagwati and Chakravarthy (1971); Rudra (1975).

after, the resumed five-year plans aimed to resume growth with more sophisticated attempts at inter-sectoral balance and with greater concern for the objectives of employment and equitable income distribution.

The most familiar, though not necessarily the most informative, indicator of the success of each plan is the growth rate of real output over the plan period. That rate is given in Table 2.1 opposite, along with the growth rate of real output per head of population.

From Table 2.1 it is clear that growth in the absolute level of real net national product and in the level per head was fastest during the Second Five-Year Plan. The comparisons are distorted somewhat by the exceptionally low figures for 1965/66, which artificially detract from the achievements of the Third Plan and give an exaggerated picture of growth during the 'plan holiday'. But, even allowing for this, the overall picture of the Indian economy is one of sluggish growth, with the speed of growth becoming slower over the years rather than faster.

The data in Table 2.2 show output growth in real terms, with purely monetary fluctuations removed by the device of pricing all output at a single set of prices (those of 1960/61). However, this device should not lead us to ignore monetary fluctuations, which were present throughout, and of differing intensity in the different plan periods. These fluctuations show up in Table 2.2, where the index of wholesale prices for all commodities

TABLE 2.2   *Indicators of price level changes, 1950/51 to 1973/74*

	Pre-plan year	End year	Percent change	Average annual growth rate (%)
First Plan	79.9†	73.9	−6.0	negative
Second Plan	73.9	99.8	+35.0	+6.0
Third Plan	99.8	131.6	+31.9	+5.5
Annual Plans	131.6	165.4	+25.7	+7.6
Fourth Plan	165.4	254.2	+53.7	+8.6

Note: All figures represent average value of index for the year.

    † Figure relates to the year 1952/53.

Sources: Calculated from data in Ministry of Finance, *Economic Survey*, for the years 1967/68 and 1975/76.

is used as the indicator. The evidence is of a deflation of prices during the First Plan, during the period of recovery from the Korean War, followed by an average inflation of 5–6 per cent during the next two plans which accelerated thereafter until it was running at an average rate of $8\frac{1}{2}$ per cent during the Fourth Plan. The consumer price index for industrial workers gives almost identical results. [65] The implicit price deflator of the national accounts is not available on a comparable basis for the 1950s, but after 1960/61, it yields the following inflation rates.

$$
\left.
\begin{array}{ll}
\text{Third Plan} & 6.3 \\
\text{Annual Plans} & 6.9 \\
\text{Fourth Plan} & 7.4
\end{array}
\right\}
\begin{array}{l}
\text{per cent} \\
\text{per annum}
\end{array}
$$

These rates confirm the finding of a steady acceleration of inflation from 1960 onwards, although the pace of acceleration appears to be less. Thus what we see is a strengthening of inflation at the same time as the growth rate of real output is gradually slowing down. The phenomenon of 'stagflation', stagnant real growth combined with the depreciation of the currency, becomes increasingly prominent as the years pass.

ii   The phases of external economic policy

The regulation of the external sector of the Indian economy exhibits a slightly different chronology from that of the official planning efforts of the government. The chronology of external economic policy has been recently worked out in some detail. [66] The picture that emerges is one of five distinct phases. In brief, they are as follows.

(a) *1950–56*
   During this period, few special administrative restrictions on trade or payments were required to equilibrate the foreign exchange rate. The machinery for imposing quotas on imports still existed as a legacy of the 1939–45 war, but it was not a crucial instrument of economic control.

65 Simha (1974), p. 349.
66 Bhagwati and Srinivasan (1975), pp. 27–30 and passim.

(b) *1957–62*

Following a severe balance of payments crisis in early 1957, highly restrictive import quotas were used as the chief method of balancing the international accounts, together with increased inflows of foreign 'aid' capital. The licensing of imports was linked to the setting of physical output targets in the plans, and the licensing of investment as an instrument in support of the plan targets.

(c) *1962–66*

The foreign trade regime remained as in phase (b) above, except that export subsidies were introduced to counter the disincentive effects of an overvalued foreign exchange rate on exports, import duties were increasingly used to capture for the government the premium attaching to imports, and industrial licensing procedures began to be slightly more liberal.

(d) *1966–68*

The suspension of foreign 'aid' in late 1965, following the Indo-Pakistan war in September 1965, combined with very low levels of foreign exchange reserves, exposed the government to foreign pressure to devalue the rupee, which it did in June 1966. With the devaluation, export subsidies were eliminated and import duties reduced.

(e) *1968–70*

The attempted liberalization of the foreign trade regime in phase (d) did not, however, proceed any further, and after 1968 export subsidies and import premia reappeared, returning institutions and policies to the same sort of position as during phases (b) and (c).

The variations in the level of 'aid' inflows and in the level of foreign exchange reserves over the period of the first four plans are given in Table 2.3. It is evident that before the 1966 devaluation foreign payments were balanced at the existing exchange with the help of import controls and two non-sustainable sources of finance: year-by-year increases in the size of the inflow of external assistance and the further progressive depletion of the stock of foreign exchange reserves.

Both of these sources had been effectively exhausted by the

TABLE 2.3: *'Aid' inflows and foreign exchange reserves 1950/51 to 1970/71* ($ mn.)

	Total external assistance	Total reserves	Outstanding obligations	Net reserves position
1950–51	n.a.	2161.3	27.5	2133.8
1956–57	202.1*	1430.3	127.5	1302.8
1961–62	718.7*	624.3	250.0	374.3
1965–66	1509.6	625.8	287.5	338.3
1967–68	1498.0	718.1	450.0	268.1
1970–71	1038.1	976.5	—	976.5

Notes: Rupee figures converted at the pre-devaluation rate of $1 = 4.76 Rs.
Sources: Ministry of Finance, *Economic Survey* for the years 1957/58, 1967/68 and 1971/72.

mid 1960s. The very low level of net foreign exchange reserves in 1965/66, the suspension of 'aid' in late 1965, and the inherent difficulties of generating foreign exchange through exports with an administered exchange rate, boxed the government into a position from which it was persuaded it might escape by devaluation and liberalizing the foreign trade regime. However, because exportables were in short supply owing to harvest failures and the growing industrial recession, the initial measures of liberalization failed to produce any favourable impact on the underlying balance of payments, and were quickly dropped. At the same time, the promises of resumed 'aid' on a greater scale than before (the *quid pro quo* of devaluation and liberalization) were never honoured. By the end of the decade an overvalued rupee bolstered by quantitative restrictions on imports had reemerged, while the depleted foreign exchange reserves were rebuilt by cutting back the demand for capital goods, about half of the value of which was at the time still imported.

iii   The chronology of politics

Pandit Nehru, who had become the first prime minister of Independent India in 1947, remained in that office until his death in May 1964. In retrospect, the 1950s appear as a period of relative political calm and stability. Public attention was focussed on the successes and failures of national economic planning. The political milestones of the era were the meetings and resolutions that generated the guidelines for each stage of the national planning effort. Political history centres around the documents issued by the Planning Commission, and their reception by the government and the Congress Party: the periodic deliberations of the National Development Council, in which chief ministers of state governments confronted the ministers of the Centre; and the resolutions of the All-India Congress Committee such as those on the 'socialistic pattern of society' (at Avadi, 1955) and cooperative joint farming and democratic decentralization (at Nagpur, 1959). During the 1950s, Nehru held the initiative for most of the time in managing government, party, and the country, even when the policies he espoused failed to make any headway.

By the early 1960s, the question of how much longer he could hold on to the initiative was clearly on the agenda. The question mark arose, in part, simply because time tends to run out on every well-established political leader, as the ranks of the disappointed and disgruntled are swollen and as the rousing manifestoes of yesteryear are brought into painful contact with the real world. Apart from these considerations, the Congress Party, because of its history as an anti-imperialist movement, had stood extraordinarily high in popular esteem in the elections of 1952. In the subsequent elections of 1957 and 1962, almost inevitably its electoral strength was eroded – not perhaps seriously yet, but enough to give its second and third rank leaders cause for some anxiety about the future. In addition, even the official enunciation of 'socialistic' policies was enough to crystallize opposition on grounds of interest and ideology both outside and inside the Congress Party. The major interests which felt themselves threatened, although in fact they had so far suffered very little damage, were the larger land-owners, money lenders and traders in the rural areas, and (to a lesser extent) the industrial haute bourgeoisie. [67]

Nehru's Achilles' heel, however, proved to be in the field of foreign affairs. His handling of the dispute with China over

67 Frankel (1978), pp. 201–48.

the Sino-Indian border has been shown to have been extremely chauvinistic, indeed much more consistent with attitudes of British imperialism than with the principles of *Panch Sheel* endorsed at the 1955 Bandung Conference.[68] In 1962, this dispute erupted in armed conflict when a Chinese punitive expedition invaded Indian territory, an invasion for which India was militarily almost completely unprepared. A considerable effort was made to prevent the consequent immediate upsurge in defence spending from wrecking the central development schemes of the Third Plan, with some success. But the damage to Nehru's standing as a national leader done by the military defeat could not be remedied. Although he secured the additional tax revenues needed to bolster up the Third Plan by appeals to patriotism, the whole strategy of 'socialistic' planning which he had pioneered came under attack. It appeared to have failed on the very terms of national security on which he had originally commended it.

Nehru's last effort to retain his preeminent position and out-manoeuvre his opponents inside the Congress party was the so-called 'Kamaraj Plan' of August 1963, in which he succeeded in securing the resignations of Morarji Desai, S. K. Patil and Lal Bahadur Shastri from their ministerial portfolios. Shastri, however, who was less rightist than the other two, was soon re-introduced to the Cabinet as Minister without Portfolio when Nehru fell ill in early 1964. On Nehru's death, Shastri was effectively chosen as his successor by the 'Syndicate', a group of senior chief ministers of states who preferred the weaker, more centrist Shastri in that office, rather than the proud, domineering Morarji Desai. A sincere and honest apparatchik who had been promoted throughout his career by Nehru, Shastri remained until his sudden death in January 1966 the creature of the Syndicate.

The change of Prime Minister paved the way for changes of emphasis in economic policy and the institutions of economic policy making. The industrialization drive, with the public sector as the leading agent of accumulation, was never really a part of Shastri's basic political commitments. Political protests against the accelerating inflation, India's heavy reliance on United States food aid and a belief in the superior efficiency of

68 Maxwell (1972), pp. 179–273.

private compared with public enterprise inclined Shastri to try and switch resources into agriculture in the hope of being able to improve the consumption of 'the common man'. In addition, the organizational links between the Planning Commission and the prime minister that existed in Nehru's time began to be severed, starting a process of reducing the political influence of the Commission that continued throughout the rest of the 1960s and was never effectively reversed. Power in economic policy making shifted to the prime minister's own office, to the central ministries with developmental responsibilities and, further, to the chief ministers of the states. The Planning Commission's initial memorandum on the Fourth Plan, due to start in 1966, immediately ran into considerable dissent, which prevented it from ever getting launched – the Fourth Plan of 1969–74 being entirely different in conception.

During Shastri's brief tenure, foreign pressure combined with internal pressure and his own policy predilections to bring about a change in economic strategy. In late 1965, the World Bank's Bell Mission to India recommended a shift in investment priority to agriculture, aiming at large output increases from giving an advanced technical package of inputs to the richer farmers in irrigated areas. It also recommended greater incentives both for richer farmers and for domestic and foreign private investors in industry, the liberalization of the foreign trade regime and the devaluation of the rupee. At the same time, territorial conflicts with Pakistan erupted into military clashes, at which point the U.S. suspended its aid to India and Pakistan. Implicitly, the condition for the resumption of U.S. aid was the re-orienting of economic policy on the lines of the Bell Report. Before his death, Shastri had gained acceptance of all of the required changes except devaluation, and he was moving toward that by replacing T. T. Krishnamachari as Finance Minister with Sachindra Chaudhuri, who was known to favour a change of parity.

Mrs Gandhi's election as Congress leader, and thus prime minister, in early 1966 made little impact on the new direction of economic policy, despite her reputation as a left-winger and a supporter of planning and the public sector. The devaluation of the rupee was done in June 1966. The controversy over the size and composition of the Fourth Plan was allowed to continue until after the elections held in early 1967. The results of those elections, discussed in detail later, led to the replacement of Sachindra Chaudhuri as Finance Minister by Morarji Desai, the leading right-wing Congressman, whose ambition for the Congress leadership had been frustrated first by Shastri and then by Mrs Gandhi. The Planning Commission was reorganized as a technical advisory body only, and deprived of the financial instrument of specific grant-aid which it had used to back up its view of planning priorities in the days when it had effectively made policy. The start of the Fourth Plan was officially postponed until 1969.

The gradual decline in the popularity and political authority of the Congress Party continued also in the late 1960s. Struggles for office between factions, lacking any rationale of programme or public purpose, intensified within the Congress Party, and between it and its rivals, both at the central and at the state government level. Mrs Gandhi, threatened by the Syndicate's desire to use Morarji Desai as their stalking horse inside the Cabinet, gradually edged towards a more anti-imperialist stance, closer economic and military cooperation with the U.S.S.R. and accommodation with the Communist Party of India. Economic policy remained paralysed as the Syndicate and Desai attempted to oust Mrs Gandhi from the prime ministerial office. Mrs Gandhi defended her position by opposing the Syndicate's candidate for President of India, dismissing Desai from the Cabinet and nationalizing the fourteen largest commercial banks in July 1969. Her tactical alliance with the more progressive elements in the Congress Party was a source of considerable political strength, and enabled her to emerge with the larger part when the organization split into two sections at the end of 1969. Her victory was finally consolidated when her section of the old Congress Party humiliated the Syndicate's in the 1971 polls.

The radical, populist rhetoric which she had used in this struggle for power could not, however, yet be tested decisively to see what substance it had. Almost before the 1971 election was over, events in Pakistan embroiled India in the December 1971 war for the liberation of Bangladesh, and the question of how far Mrs Gandhi was either able or willing to 'abolish poverty' was deferred until a time beyond the immediate scope of this book.

3

The interpretation of Indian public expenditure statistics

Having said something, however brief and inadequate, about the broad economic and political background to post-independence development policy, one more preliminary is necessary before confronting the empirical evidence of the behaviour of public expenditure. The statistical material to be presented on the subject, and the implications of using one data set rather than another do not always immediately suggest themselves, even to readers who have been trained to be sensitive to such things. If the reader is to have some confidence in the solidity of the conclusions of the later chapters, he must first be reminded of the problems inherent in getting meaning out of public expenditure statistics, and satisfied that these problems have been handled (they will never be solved) in the most reasonable way. The present chapter is an attempt to do this. As it will appear, the choice of definitions is never straightforward, but need not be arbitrary. It raises often large and fundamental questions, such as the nature of government, the causes of economic growth and the value of education. These questions have been discussed here not exhaustively or for their own sake, but only as far as is necessary to decide which of the possible alternative frameworks for recording public expenditure has, on the balance of advantages, the greatest relevance for understanding the working of a state accumulation policy.

I PRIMARY DOCUMENTS AND SECONDARY RECLASSIFICATIONS

Our main focus of interest will be governmental fiscal activity, more especially on the expenditure side, and yet no direct use will be made of the documents on budgets and accounts which

have an operational role in the fiscal cycle. Our main source
will be the various re-classifications of accounts and budgets,
produced, on a number of differing bases, by either the government or quasi-governmental bodies. It is thus necessary to
explain:

(a) why reclassifications are preferable to the 'primary' budgeting and accounting documents;
(b) the rationale of the different possible reclassifications;
(c) why one of these, based on national accounting conventions, is more suitable to the present purpose than the
others;
(d) the differences between the existing attempts at national
accounting reclassifications.

Because of the costs of statistical production, there are
relatively few pure sets of social statistics. Most social statistics are by-products of some existing social process, and can
only be interpreted with knowledge of that process. The primary budgetary documents, i.e. those with an operational role
in the fiscal cycle, are drawn up for only one purpose, to gain
legal authorization for the government's annual expenditure
and taxation proposals and to check *ex post* whether the legally
authorized limits were exceeded. This purpose governs the
form of the annual Financial Statements, Demands for Grants,
Budget Memoranda, Estimates of Plan Schemes and Revenue
and Finance Accounts of the central and state governments
in India. But the legal requirements of a particular parliamentary system will not, except as a result either of coincidence
or elaborate contrivance, produce information in a form suitable for economic and political analysis. Expenditure will be
excluded if it does not require parliamentary sanction; pure
accounting transactions will appear as 'expenditure'; expenditure will be analysed by spending department and category of
input rather than by function and type of output. These defects
are shared by all abridgements of the primary documents –
the 'budget-in-brief' pamphlets and the budgetary data in the
various state and central government economic surveys, statistical abstracts and statistical histories. [1]
There is also a near-universal tendency for primary budget

1 Cf. C.S.O. (1966); Government of Rajasthan (1970).

documents to become archaic. The reasons for this, however, differ according to the kind of polity in which the budgetary process takes place. They are quite different, for example, as between the U.K. and India. The colonial and post-colonial situation has been the important determinant in the Indian case. In the British period, the colonial power took a broadly static view of the functions of government, which meant that for a long time the original form of estimates and accounts kept more or less in line with the reality of government policies. At the same time, there was no domestic political forum attempting to scrutinize and use the information presented, and so no demand for a more realistic or informative presentation. With independence, the lack of a domestic political forum was remedied. But the bureaucracy retained a deep respect for the formal conventions of British style budgeting, guarding them brahminically as a sacred inheritance at the very time that they came to lose their relevance to actual conditions more rapidly than ever before.

Thus it could be authoritatively reported in 1968 that 'in recent years there has been an enormous expansion in the activities and functions of Government ... [but] although attempts have been made to amend the structure of accounting heads from time to time, the essential framework has remained more or less intact'.[2] In its century-long existence, the account-framework has, indeed, undergone only a few experiences of minor surgery. Some changes were made in 1937 to accommodate provincial autonomy; in 1950 the double accounts system was introduced; and since then the only concession to development planning was the alteration in 1961–63 of certain major heads of account to permit their grouping in semi-functional form.[3]

The unfortunate consequence of archaic primary budget documents is that the government's problems in following any consistent line of policy become more severe. The information that is readily available becomes less and less comprehensive, increasingly loaded with irrelevant detail and more tortuous in interpretation as attempts are made to incorporate new developments into the straight-jacket of an obsolete

2 A.R.C. (1968a), p.9.
3 Premchand (1966), pp. 529–32; (1969), pp. 93–100.

framework. In the end, this 'information' becomes so obscure
that its meaning can only be teased out by those who, by training and practice acquired in long years of compiling it, can
act as specialized interpreters of its lore and lack of logic.
Even although it is able to draw upon the services of such
specialized interpreters (who are, of course, its own employees)
a government in this position will find that it needs, if it is to
follow through any consistent line of policy, secondary analyses
of the primary documents. The government, or quasi
government institutions such as the central bank, eventually
begin to produce these secondary analyses. Characteristically,
and in contrast with the primary documents, secondary
analyses play no part in the political process that legitimates
governmental acquisition and disposal of resources. They
show how the information in the primary documents must
be re-arranged to be consistent with information on other
economic magnitudes – the government's deficit or surplus,
the public sector component of the development plan or the
national accounts aggregates. It is these secondary analyses
that are normally treated as original sources by economic
researchers, a sensible practice given the near-impossibility of
avoiding error in the use of the primary documents.

The production of secondary analyses should not be
thought of as the ideal solution to the problem of supplying
financial information relevant to policy. In theory, it would
be preferable to have a single accounting system embodying
a hierarchy of different classifications, one of which is
designed for purposes of accountability and the rest designed
to meet different informational needs. Using a computer, it
would then be possible to produce any one of a number of
different arrangements of the basic data at will.

It would also be misleading to infer from what has been said
above that the production of secondary analyses of budget
material in India is in fact the result of internal government
pressures for information more directly relevant to its policy
objectives. It is difficult to escape the impression that in India
the motive has been, in part, mimetic. The desire is to imitate
the best practice of advanced countries, without too much
regard for whether achievement of chosen objectives is
actually aided thereby. This impression is not equally strong

in relation to all the different secondary analyses: it is much stronger for the reconciliations with national accounts aggregates than for the reconciliations with Plan and money supply statistics. The former, at any rate, seem to be produced in an institutional vacuum, it being no one's responsibility to ensure that the information they contain is properly integrated into the decision-making process. Although it is frequently claimed by the civil servants responsible for producing the secondary analyses that their primary purpose is to educate politicians about the consequences of their decisions, there is little evidence that any such educational effect does exist, or that the existing political system gives much scope for it to develop.

II SCHEMES OF RECLASSIFICATION: A CRITIQUE

Two of the main types of secondary analysis of budget material can be mentioned fairly briefly, because, for reasons that will be explained, they are not particularly useful in providing time series data on public expenditure and its economic components.

At the end of the 1960s, proper reconciliations of budget documents with planning figures of plan outlay and resources began to be produced, on the recommendation of the Administrative Reforms Commission.[4] This was a long overdue step forward in rationalizing the financial side of the planning process. On the other hand, such reconciliations are not very helpful in the analysis of public expenditure, because, as is well known, 'plan outlay' (like 'plan resources') is an administrative and not an economic concept. Plan outlay is not government development expenditure, since it excludes development expenditure arising from schemes accepted in previous plans, and development expenditure on schemes undertaken in the present plan period but not deemed eligible for plan grants. Nor is it that part of government investment included in the present plan, because plan schemes usually include both capital and current elements.[5] Plan outlay simply means that part of public expenditure which, at the end of the long and heavily political planning negotiations

4 A.R.C. (1968a), pp. 28–9.
5 Venkataraman(1968), pp. 69–7; Chanda (1965), pp. 220–1.

between the Planning Commission, and central and state government departments, has been agreed to be eligible for payment of plan grants. As such, they are of no very great interest from the purely economic viewpoint.

Secondly, the Reserve Bank of India publishes its own analyses of the central government budget, the railways budget, the finances of state governments, the union territories and of local authorities. The Bank's work stems from its responsibility for the control of inflation and the repercussions of this on the balance of payments. Its aim is to derive from its fiscal analyses the size of the overall surplus or deficit on government account, as a measure of the impact of government operations on the money supply. But it is possible to measure the overall surplus or deficit without throwing up as a by-product statistics which are useful for the analysis of public expenditure. The reasons for this are as follows. First, the Bank's coverage is weak where no possibility of a surplus or deficit exists. In the case of local authorities, the information is drawn from a series of (slightly different) sample surveys, excluding from their scope *panchayati raj* institutions and covering only years 1962/63, 1964/65, 1965/66, and 1966/67.[6] Second, the measurement of government surplus or deficit does not require any departure from the existing system of double accounts (which is misleading from an economic point of view), or any uniformity of functional classification between the central government and the states. Third, although uniformity between states in any one year is usually achieved, a number of changes in the definition of particular expenditure items were made during the 1960s. Only one of these changes alters the concept of surplus and deficit employed, but all of them interfere with strict intertemporal comparisons of expenditure components. Lack of comprehensiveness, lack of uniformity and lack of definitional stability through time rather badly weaken the usefulness of the Reserve Bank of India's data for general fiscal analysis, although on some important questions it is still the best available, if handled with sufficient caution.

The type of secondary reclassification of expenditure which

6   R.B.I. (1970), p. 1471.

we use most extensively is the economic classification of government transactions. What are the reasons for relying so heavily on expenditure information in this form? The reasons can be summarized under the following headings:

(i) Relatively comprehensive definition of the government sector;

(ii) Uniformity of treatment of different levels of government;

(iii) Improved conceptual linkage with macroeconomic aggregates;

(iv) Elimination of double-counting in measuring expenditure;

(v) A superior measure of government capital formation.

Although this is an impressive list of advantages, it is not contended that even the economic classification is absolutely adequate for the purpose of illuminating the fiscal aspects of state accumulation. To explain its advantages more fully and thus also pinpoint the remaining deficiencies, each of the above headings requires more detailed examination.

i Definition of 'government'

On the neo-classical view, there is no problem in defining the government sector of the economy. Governments spend on 'public goods' (justice, police, arms) because their benefits cannot be confined to those who are willing to pay for them, on 'merit wants' because in some cases individuals cannot be the best judges of what contributes to their own welfare, and on transfers to correct income distribution or unwanted fluctuations in the overall level of economic activity, financing all this expenditure by politically determined levies. Meanwhile, in the non-government sector, firms and households exchange factor services and the production made possible thereby. Obviously, there is no place for state accumulation in this vision, and the adoption of a state accumulation policy opens up the question of where the boundary of the government sector lies. Do public enterprises form part of it or not? Are they non-government because, like firms, they produce output for sale in the market, or are they government because their market operations are limited by 'social obligations' and other less explicit forms of government influence?

In India, the resolution of this problem has been to divide public enterprises into two groups, 'departmental' and 'non-departmental'. The first are assimilated into the government sector on the grounds that they are less like firms, while the second are assimilated into the corporate sector, because they are more like firms. The departmental enterprises are those set up under the auspices of, and run subject to the direct supervision of, ministries of the central or state governments. They are not incorporated, but owned and controlled by government departments. They do not hold or manage financial assets and liabilities, apart from their working balances and business accounts. The central government's departmental enterprises are the railways, posts and telegraphs, overseas communication service and defence manufacturing establishments. Those of the State governments are irrigation and electricity schemes, forestry and logging and certain road and water transport services. Some types of departmental enterprises are undertaken jointly – mainly multi-purpose river schemes and government printing presses. By contrast, the non-departmental enterprises have three different institutional forms – government companies, in which at least 51 per cent of the paid-up share capital is held by the government; subsidiaries of government companies; and statutory corporations established by special legislation. Their sphere of operations covers air transport, a whole range of concerns in the heavy industrial sector such as steel, engineering, petrochemicals, and fertilizers, and financial and trading activities in insurance, banking, foreign trade, food-grain procurement, etc. The variety of operation is so great that it does not lend itself to neat summary.

The Indian practice of defining the government sector (or, as it is called, the 'public authorities') to include the departmental enterprises is, to some extent, a fiction. For the purpose of getting empirical evidence on the progress of state accumulation, it is necessary to have accounts which show the operation of the public sector as a whole, that is, of the 'public authorities' as at present defined plus the non-departmental enterprises.

ii Uniformity of treatment

Apart from the departmental enterprises, the term 'public authorities' or government sector covers all the three main levels of government in India – the union or central government, the governments of all the states and Union Territories and the sub-state local governments such as municipalities and the various *panchayati raj* institutions. Clearly, if the relationship between the three levels of government is to be seen correctly, and if the data for all three levels are to be capable of aggregation in a correct picture for all-India, the principles according to which data are organized must be the same at each level. It is tempting to do otherwise, since the activities of the three levels differ considerably, and different data breakdowns would better highlight the major functions and transactions of each. But to study public expenditure at any level in isolation is unnecessarily arbitrary, given that activity at any level is part of a larger inter-related system. It is certainly desirable to disaggregate data at least to the state level, but this is conditional on having correctly aggregated data in the first place. This requires uniformity of classification at all levels, which is the great advantage of a consistent use of national accounting concepts over, e.g., the Reserve Bank of India type of analyses.

iii Linking public expenditure with macroeconomic aggregates.

The term 'public expenditure' has no unique, accepted meaning, so that variations in its usage (usually relatively minor) occur both between countries and from time to time in the same country. The reason for attempting a definition is that the government (itself, as we have just seen, not a homogeneous entity) influences by its manifold transactions, with varying degrees of directness, the disposition of available economic resources. Measuring the growth and composition of public expenditure is designed to indicate the extent and nature of this influence, as exercised on the disbursement side of government operations. Although 'public expenditure' is not a term in the national accounts lexicon, if the impact of government spending on the economy is to be measured it is preferable that it be defined in relation to national accounting categories, since these are the categories commonly used for the analysis of the total economy, notwithstanding all their well-known defects.

The major economic distinction of the various impacts that government spending can have is between spending that is 'exhaustive' of available resources, and that which is 'non-exhaustive'. The first directly appropriates part of the supply or output available in the current accounting period, and is therefore the government's direct share in the total of national expenditure. Exhaustive expenditure then breaks down by use – according to whether it is for consumption, gross domestic fixed capital formation or changes in stocks. Non-exhaustive spending, on the other hand, merely transfers purchasing power to other sectors of the domestic economy, or abroad. Public debt interest, grants, subsidies, net sales of assets, etc, have only an indirect impact on the economy by altering the income constraint on non-government demand for current output. The advantage of an economic reclassification of expenditure is that it allows these various types of impact to be distinguished. Of course, we cannot concern ourselves with each and every one of them. Since our focus is mainly on the question of the government as an agent of accumulation, we are interested primarily in the government's impact on capital formation and consumption. But it must be emphasized that the government's activity in these areas cannot be measured unless the conceptual basis of the expenditure statistics we use is identical with that used by national accountants who measure the total capital formation and consumption in the whole economy. Further, the actual government accounts, in India as elsewhere, do not provide expenditure statistics on this basis, because they were designed for the quite different purpose of ensuring the legality of expenditure in accord with certain parliamentary procedures. It is an elementary point, but one too often ignored by economists themselves.

There is one respect, however, in which the Indian economic expenditure reclassifications are not entirely consonant with the conceptual basis of the national accounts. They are reclassifications of cash accounts. Cash accounts represent the state of receipts and disbursements, that is the actual payments for goods and services, without regard to when ordered, received or consumed. Cash accounting is essential to meet the prime requirements of government solvency, for receipts must be adequate to cover payments. By contrast, accrual accounts represent the state of income receivable and bills payable in respect of goods and services received, without regard to when ordered, paid for or consumed.[7] We are not concerned here with the question whether the cash or accrual basis is in some sense better for government accounts, on which differences of opinion flourish.[8] The point is that the national accounts are themselves drawn up on an accrual basis, in terms of receivables and payables, and that therefore 'magnitudes in government accounts corresponding to national income concepts should strictly speaking also be measured on an accrual basis if like is to be compared with like.[9] The data difficulties involved in converting cash to accrual figures are so formidable that no single scholar could possibly make the conversion in any reasonable time period. Until an accrual basis is adopted by the government as a matter of policy, we can only work, *faute de mieux*, with reclassifications of cash expenditure statistics.

iv Elimination of double-counting

In what sense do the actual government accounts involve the double-counting of expenditure? What constitutes double-counting depends on what one is trying to count. For some analyses of production we may wish our totals to be gross of inter-industrial supplies, but not in estimating national product, where the inclusion of inter-industrial supplies constitutes double-counting. Similarly, for some analytical purposes we may wish to have figures for gross public expenditure, which is what appears in actual government accounts. But this is not so when we are concerned with the economic impact

7 U.N. (1970), p. 43.
8 Cf. U.N. (1970), p. 43; Matthews (1973), pp. 237–8.
9 Chelliah (1968), p. 30.

of government spending on the rest of the economy, either through exhaustive or non-exhaustive spending as previously defined. For this purpose, it must be noted that certain expenditures appear in the actual accounts which do not have an economic impact independently of and separate from certain other expenditures which also appear. These must be netted out because, if that is not done, the total of 'public expenditure with an economic impact' will be over-estimated. Or, to put it another way, the totals of public expenditure will be higher than the total of 'public expenditure with an economic impact', and it is only with the latter that economists need trouble.

Of all the expenditures which appear in actual government accounts, the following are those which must be eliminated if double-counting in the above sense is to be avoided.

(1) *Transfers within the government sector.* Intra-government sector transfers compromise transactions (a) between 'funds' and (b) between different levels of government. Category (a) arise in the absence of a consolidated fund into which all revenues are paid regardless of source and from which all payments are made regardless of purpose. Of course, India has a Consolidated Fund, but in addition various other types of fund also coexist with it, and a certain amount of borrowing and lending takes place between the different funds. These inter-fund adjustments will all be recorded in the accounts. So will the transactions between different levels of government, such as borrowing and lending and the making of grants which arise from a disparity between the expenditure responsibilities on the one hand and the revenue possibilities on the other of the central and local levels of government.

From the viewpoint of the government sector as a whole, both of these types of transactions amount simply to a shifting of money from one pocket of a purse to another pocket of the same purse. They have no economic impact separate from that of the expenditure of the recipient fund or level of government, which will also be recorded in the accounts. These intra-government sector transfers, therefore, ought to be excluded from an economic concept of public expenditure. To include them is, in the national accounts framework, double-counting. Also, since the total of public expenditure, defined to include them, would fluctuate according to the size and frequency of these pocket-to-pocket shifts, synchronic and diachronic public spending comparisons would lose all their economic meaning.

(2) *Operating expenditure of public enterprises.* If public enterprises are to continue to function, their operating expenses must be covered either by the proceeds of the sale of the goods and service that they produce, or by subsidies out of general revenue. In the first case, the sale proceeds will, sooner or later, enter the national accounts as the consumption expenditure of households. In the second case, the subsidies will be automatically included as a part of public expenditure if this is defined by the national accounts categories which have been listed already. There is no reason to include public enterprises operating expenses in the total of public spending.

(3) *Expenditure matched by certain types of charges.* We have so far examined the problem of quasi-commercial activity in the public sector only in its major manifestation, that of public enterprises. There is a minor variant of the same problem when the government proper undertakes quasi-commercial activity. The government itself sometimes provides goods and services which are not collective in nature, in that it is technically quite possible to exclude from their benefits individuals whom, for some reason, it is desired to exclude. Further, the principle of exclusion is often the commercial one of individuals' willingness to pay a charge related to the cost of providing the goods and services in question. An example would be the public operation of fee-paying schools or medical services.

If the arguments for ignoring the operating expenses of departmental public enterprises in calculating public expenditure are sound, they will apply with equal force to the quasi-commercial charges. These may be defined as charges which (a) are clearly and directly linked to the acquisition of specific goods and services and (b) are consistently related to the cost of their provision. It will be clear from (b) that not all government charges are quasi-commercial, and that consequently there is no justification for calculating public spending net of all types of charge. Whereas purchases of goods and services are calculated net sales of goods and services, interest payments are net of commercial interest receipts, additions to stocks and assets are net of disposals, etc., an important range of government charges are not netted off from public expenditure, but appear on the revenue side of the account as income from property and fees and miscellaneous receipts.

Strictly speaking, a definition of public expenditure that is consistent with the national accounts requires more than simply the exclusion of transactions of types (1)–(3) from actual government accounts. It also requires the addition of certain types of expenditure which do not have a counterpart in monetary transactions. The best known example is that of imputing a rental cost for buildings which the government has built for itself. In practice, as with other types of national accounting imputations, this bristles with difficulties and is often, for that reason, omitted. The amounts involved can be quite large relative to total public expenditure, and the margin of error in the estimates is usually large also. This leads to an unsatisfactory situation where total public expenditure can fluctuate quite noticeably over time simply because statisticians make different estimates of the true cost of imputed rents. For these reasons, no imputation is attempted in the statistics used here.

v The measure of government capital formation

The nearest the actual government accounts come to providing a measure of government capital formation is by means of its system of double accounts. (This is not to be confused with a system of double entry book-keeping. That the Indian public authorities practice single entry book-keeping is entirely irrelevant to this discussion.) The system of double accounts is the division of all receipts and payments between two accounts, one 'current' and the other 'capital', both of which are required to balance.

The principle on which 'capital' items are to be distinguished from 'current' is rather hard to discern, even in an ideal system of double accounts. According to the United Nations' manual of government accounting, the distinction is 'similar to the one used in commercial practice to distinguish between charges that relate to operating accounts and those that affect balance sheet accounts, [which] should be recognized as different from the classification by economic nature'. As an example, it is claimed that expenditure to establish a military installation, which would be current consumption in the economic reclassification of expenditures 'may be treated as a capital outlay in the accounts'. [10] This certainly cuts across the U.N.'s own earlier advice. Arguing in 1951 against the adoption of double accounts as a device to rationalize government debt creation (by implying that all 'capital' expenditure could be financed by government borrowing quite safely), it was urged that double accounting should be adopted 'where it will contribute to an analysis of the economic significance of government activities'. [11] But if, as is currently claimed, the distinction between the two accounts differs from that between consumption and investment expenditure, it is difficult to see how the system could illuminate the question of economic significance. The attempt to define items of government spending as 'capital' by analogy with commercial accounting practice simply breaks down to the extent that the purpose of government activity differs from that of commercial firms. In all those areas of operation where the government does not (like a firm) seek to maintain a stock of resources as the basis for deriving its own periodic income, what substance can be given to the notion of a government balance sheet? The government, *qua* agent of accumulation, in part creates assets for the purpose of raising *national* income, and so its expenditures should be classified to make them intelligible within the framework of the national accounts.

But, in the Indian practice of government accounting, neither the earlier nor the later U.N. advice is followed. The allocation of items between the two accounts follows no single, clear-cut principle. It is true that the bulk of government consumption spending falls into the current('revenue') account, while the bulk of government investment falls into the capital

10 U.N. (1970), p. 63.
11 U.N. (1970), p. 44.

account. But there remains an important minority of items which have been officially allocated to the 'wrong' account, from the point of view of the consumption/investment distinction. Doubtful items have, from time to time, been allocated to one account or the other by the Comptroller and Auditor-General of India on the basis of an administrative case law which does not lend itself to any kind of logical reduction.[12] Nevertheless, simply because the primary budget documents are drawn as double accounts, many analysts of Indian public finance continue to treat the existing distinction with great respect, as if expenditure on revenue or on capital account did have a precise economic meaning.

Account	*Economic impact*	*Expenditure type*
A Current	A.a. Exhaustive	A.1. Consumption
	A.b. Non-exhaustive	A.2. Interest on public debt
		A.3. Subsidies
		A.4. Current transfers (other)
B Capital	B.a. Exhaustive	B.1. Gross fixed capital formation
		B.2. Net changes in stocks
	B.b. Non-exhaustive	B.3. Net purchases of existing assets
		B.4. Capital transfers (other)

If it is desired to persist with the current/capital distinction, it can only be meaningfully done on the basis of the above breakdown. Even on this basis, the capital account is far from showing the flows which ought to be represented in a set of national government balance sheets. This is because fixed capital formation and the purchases (less sales) of existing assets are recorded, while the consumption of capital is left unrecorded. But our argument is that gathering the information to write a government balance sheet is the pursuit of a misconceived ideal, and that dividing expenditure into two

12 Gupta (1970), pp. 169–70; Premchand (1966), pp. 148–9; Caiden and Wildavsky (1974), pp. 89–90.

accounts adds almost nothing to our knowledge once an expenditure classification as shown in the third column has been carried out.

Thus far, however, we have not confronted the question whether the national accounts categories of expenditure are themselves really meaningful. This we must now do, given that considerable reliance is placed in Part Two on expenditure statistics classified by these categories. It may be objected that this is an unsound method, since national accounts concepts are not 'appropriate' to the conditions that obtain in South Asia. Professor Myrdal, particularly, has been a protagonist of this view. Put as briefly as possible, the doctrine of inappropriateness states that national accounts concepts were elaborated by the governments of advanced capitalist countries aiming at short-run demand management, and were chosen to be appropriate to that objective. If, however, the policy objective is one of long-run growth, they are inappropriate unless one accepts the validity of post-Keynesian growth models such as those of Harrod and Domar.[13] This line of generalized criticism, which is reiterated by Myrdal, is weak and superficial, an excellent example of what has been called Myrdal's 'show of iconoclasm'.[14] On the one hand, it exaggerates the snugness of fit between concepts and policy in advanced capitalist countries, while on the other it carries the implication that national accounting will be impossible in India until we have a fully-fledged theory of economic growth capable of replacing Harrod–Domar.

Any searching criticism of the conventions of the national accounts must start from their philosophical roots in the utilitarian theory of the market. Government has no obvious place in this theory, and no place can be created for it without setting up internal contradictions in it. Utilitarians want to argue that governments provide services which generate utility, in the sense that, if they could be offered as private goods, they would find ready buyers; while at the same time it is clear that there can be no market test of the value of government services.

This difficulty is met by treating government services as a

13 Cf. Oshima (1965), pp. 8–9; Seers and Jolly (1966), pp. 196–7.
14 Byres (1969), p. 178.

final good, but valuing them at the cost of their inputs.[15] Such a compromise immediately produces another dilemma. If a government becomes more efficient in its use of inputs of labour or land, the value added by government declines, *ceteris paribus,* and with it the measured national income, while increased inefficiency will raise value added by government, and thus national income.[16] Myrdal is oblivious of this fundamental difficulty, seeming indeed to deny its existence by saying that 'meaningful estimates of inputs and outputs, both actual and planned, can be ascertained in the public sector'.[17]

But how does the dilemma of incorporating government in a utilitarian market theory affect the concept of government capital formation? Some authorities regard this concept as unproblematical. If government services are a final good, 'it is only logical to include all government capital formation in gross domestic capital formation'. If they are an intermediate good, 'court houses and military installations are included' as capital formation 'where blast furnaces ... are considered part of capital formation on the analogy of private capital formation though pig iron is strictly an intermediate product'.[18] But these conclusions rest on a particular interpretation of what it is that the government, *qua* consumer, purchases from itself, *qua* producer. Is the government, *qua* consumer, deemed to purchase from itself government services (e.g. administration services or defence services), or, along with the services of its own employees, real assets (e.g. court houses and military installations)? If it is the former, then the real assets bought by the government are part of gross domestic capital formation. But if it is the latter, they are merely part of the government's consumption.[19] In other words, the question of the content of government capital formation cannot be settled within the logic of the national accounts conventions themselves.

Nor, *pace* Myrdal, is an answer to be had merely by asking what is convenient from the point of view of Keynesian demand

15 Van Arkadie and Frank (1969), pp. 184–7; Van Arkadie (1973), pp. 23–4.
16 Ward (1974), p. 51.
17 Myrdal (1968), p. 2506.
18 Van Arkadie and Frank (1969), pp. 186, 188.
19 O.E.C.D. (1972), pp. 101–2.

management policy. Keynes wished to distinguish investment from consumption because his thesis was that they had quite distinct determinants. But, as Hicks has pointed out, in the case of government demand, the distinction is much less important since, with the exception of the investment demand of public enterprises, both consumption and investment expenditure come from the same source, and are decided upon together in the light of government policies. It follows that 'the line between them is inevitably an arbitrary line [and that] useful and intelligible accounts could be constructed with the line drawn in several different places'.[20] Drawing of the line in several different places is exactly what one finds on examining the national accounts conventions of advanced capitalist economies. In the U.K., all durable assets purchased by government, except (most of) those with military uses, are treated as fixed capital formation.[21] But in the U.S. 'no capital formation is recognized for ... the general government'.[22] In the sphere of capital formation, the claims that national accounts concepts are monolithic, and shaped to the pursuit of Keynesian stabilization objectives, are quite incorrect.

The Indian practice in defining the content of government capital formation has varied, and at present seems to differ from both that of the U.K. and the U.S. In 1969, the Indian Central Statistical Organization published *Estimates of Capital Formation in India, 1960/61 to 1965/66* in which the U.K. definition was used. By 1973, however, this had been altered in that 'capital expenditure in Defence ... [was] reclassified as "capital formation", instead of classification under "current expenditure" followed earlier'.[23] Since the capital formation series published in 1973 correspond exactly with that published in 1971, except where the estimates are stated to be 'provisional', it seems safe to conclude that the new definition also applied in 1971, despite the fact that this is not made clear in the definition of 'gross fixed capital formation' supplied at that time.[24]

20 Ohlsson (1953), p. 247.
21 Maurice (1968), pp. 11–12.
22 Ruggles and Ruggles (1970), p. 53.
23 C.S.O. (1973), p. 31.
24 C.S.O. (1971), p. 47.

Myrdal's argument for the inappropriateness of national accounts in less developed countries does not relate to the arbitrariness of the definition of government capital formation of the kind that is pointed out above. That he seems content to ignore. Instead it rests on the proposition that in South Asian economies 'the basic distinction between investment and consumption does not hold [since] higher consumption forms "investment" – that is, raises production – and at the same time remains consumption'.[25] Clearly, this is quite a different line of criticism. The question of how to draw the boundary line between investment and consumption across the government's real asset purchases pre-supposes a valid distinction between consumption and investment, which Myrdal denies. Nor is Myrdal merely raising the question of whether some present consumption spending should properly be thought of as intangible investment, for that, too, presupposes a valid consumption/investment distinction. In claiming that this dichotomy can, and ought to be, abolished, he has taken up an extreme position which is not defensible, and has advanced invalid reasoning to back up his charge of inappropriateness.

To arrive at the conclusion that consumption and investment are indistinguishable, he assumed that the conventional definition of investment is 'any expenditure that raises production', and then suggests that in poor countries almost all consumption expenditures raise production. The trouble with this argument is that it is based on a false assumption. The conventional definition of investment in national accounting is as residual: it is the portion of the income generated in one time period (normally, a year) that is not spent on goods and services which are used up, extinguished or destroyed within that time period. In physical terms investment is the goods produced in the year which, at the end of the year, are still available, either as stocks or fixed structures, to satisfy future consumption needs. It is clear that this Keynesian definition ·neither asserts that investment is in fact productive, nor does it deny that consumption may have consequences for future production. On the first point, the carried over

25 Myrdal (1968), p. 1916.

stocks may deteriorate and go to waste; the carried over new fixed structures may lie idle, or work flat out to produce nil or negative value added. No definition can guarantee that investment will not be infructuous, and disappoint the expectations on which it was made. On the second point, the definition of consumption leaves its productivity effects an open question. To say of goods and services that they are extinguished or destroyed by use in an accounting period is not to deny that these acts of extinction or destructive use can have consequences for production in future periods.

To claim, with Myrdal, that most consumption is productive is not a formal contradiction of the conventional definition of consumption. The claim, however, does have other weaknesses. The proposal is that 'the new term "investment in man" should include not only the consumption of educational and health facilities but practically all essential consumption'.[26] This formulation disguises two important aspects of the productivity effects of consumption. It obscures differences in the time-profile of these effects. A unit of resources devoted to extra nutrition will raise production now but not in the future, while the same unit devoted to education will actually reduce production now in the expectation of raising production by a much greater amount in the distant future. By lumping together under the label 'productive consumption' expenditures whose effects on production have completely contrasted time-profiles, Myrdal obscures the fact that, in choosing between types of consumption, the basic choice between benefits now and benefits later remains. The 'discovery' of productive consumption does not abolish this choice. The other aspect which Myrdal's formulation does not sufficiently emphasize is that increments to existing types of consumption have very small productivity effects. It is only when quite different types of food, education and health care are consumed that large productivity effects will ensue.

If, for the sake of argument, we grant Myrdal's premises, his conclusion that consumption and investment are indistinguishable does not follow. He has not abolished the distinction, but merely complicated it to the point where the

26 Myrdal (1968), p. 1550.

two original categories become three – productive consumption, unproductive consumption, and productive non-consumption (i.e. investment in the conventional sense).[27] Policy still requires a choice of some mixture of these three categories. Even if the second is disregarded as being possible to eliminate and undesirable without qualification, a policy choice remains between productive consumption and conventional investment. If the consumption/investment distinction had no validity, this policy choice would be inconceivable. Since it is not, Myrdal's attack on national accounting must be rejected.

Unfortunately, a rebuttal of Mydal's more extravagant views does not dispose of the question whether certain expenditure now called consumption should be treated in the accounts in the same way as conventional investment. The most popular candidate, in the poor country context, for treatment as 'intangible investment' is educational spending.[28] The proposal here is for a reform of the investment/consumption distinction – a reform which Myrdal, arguing from the alleged all-pervasive nature of productive consumption, holds to be impossible.[29] The proposal is to redefine 'investment' in a way that is relevant to long-run growth: consumption now becomes a residual, namely all those expenditures within the accounting period which do not contribute to the economy's future growth potential. All that do become 'investment'. The fundamental objection to such a change is that it assumes that we have a theory of long-run growth as soundly based as the Keynesian theory of short-run income determination. What grounds are there for making such an assumption? The association between educational spending and increased labour productivity (to the extent that it has been established empirically at all) rests on evidence from advanced capitalist countries. Moreover, there are well-known difficulties to frustrate calculations of 'returns' to educational spending in countries where a colonial pattern of reward differentials still remains. Existing empirical techniques are not good enough to quantify the links between today's educational (or for that matter, health) spending, and tomorrow's economic growth.

27 Cf. Stanfield (1973), p. 22.
28 Cf. Seers and Jolly (1966).   29 Myrdal (1968), pp. 1916–7.

As to which kinds of education are growth-promoting, we remain in the realm of qualitative judgements. Seers and Jolly may be correct in their appreciation of the importance of any kind of education to growth in East and Central Africa. On the other hand, for Asia, quite contrary views are put forward.[30] If the compromise view is taken that some forms of education do add to growth while others do not, how should the two kinds be separated? In Ceylon, the practice of treating the training of accountants, tradesmen, etc., as intangible investment, but not any other kind of education, was abandoned because in the end such arbitrariness was considered to be indefensible. Until the problem of identifying educational spending which does yield output beyond the accounting period is solved, no one can say how misleading the conventional notion of investment is from the long-run growth perspective.

Other considerations which bear on the debate about 'intangible investment' are relatively minor in comparison with the weak theoretical and empirical links between intangible investment and growth. From a statistical viewpoint it is objected that the recognition of intangible investment would add a great deal to the element of imputation in the national accounts, and would thus make them less reliable overall. Logic would require estimates of intangible investment to be made for households, firms and non-profit institutions as well as the government. It would also require an estimate of the flow of present services from the past additions to the intangible asset stock, which in turn would require estimates of the rate of depreciation of the intangible assets. If national accountants blanch at imputation on this scale, so do individual scholars faced with the task of adjusting past capital formation series in line with such a reform.[31] For India, where standard breakdowns of conventional investment are only just beginning to be published, it might seem better to improve the measure of the narrower concept, rather than make less precise estimates of a broader concept. But, basically, pleas to reform the national accounts to make them 'appropriate' to conditions in poor countries are disguised claims

30 O.E.C.D. (1972), pp. 87, 134.
31 Cf. Reynolds (1971), pp. 518–20.

that some new growth theory can be made the basis of development policy. The proposal that education should be classed as 'investment' assumes that the augmentation of labour skills plus increments to physical assets are the keys to long-run growth. To those who do not accept that growth has yet been satisfactorily attributed to any small number of 'key factors', such reform programmes will appeal little, even without taking account of the statistical objections.

But to national accounts theorists such a reform does have a particular ideological appeal. It is odd, but true, that the conventional concept of investment is the Marxist one of material means of production, despite the fact that immaterial services are included in the value of total product.[32] The recognition of intangible investment would eliminate this, and thereby improve the consistency of utilitarian accounting. But concepts become hypostatized.[33] It is but a short step from saying that in one economic aspect tangible and intangible investment are similar to the erroneous conclusion that in all aspects of social reality they are identical. On the contrary, tangible capital lends itself far more readily than intangible capital to concentration of ownership. There is a fairly low ceiling on the amount of intangible capital that any one individual can acquire and will wish to acquire. This explains the different historical roles which have been played by tangible and intangible capital in the process of accumulation in advanced capitalist countries. The demand for large-scale government intangible investment arose as part of a political struggle against the economic power of the owners of tangible capital, precisely by those who were excluded from such ownership. Thus if one needs economic categories relevant for broader sociological analysis, it is fortunate that existing national accounts concepts inconsistently retain a Marxist notion of investment.

On a more pragmatic level, the aim of this work is to explore in quantitative terms the consequences of the attempt to use the state as the engine of accumulation in India. Obviously in the first instance we want to look at physical capital formation, because that is the meaning given to accumulation both by writers on state capitalism in the Soviet Union

32 Ruggles and Ruggles (1970), p. 42.   33 Dobb (1937), p. 43.

and by non-Soviet exponents of state accumulation as a development strategy. This does not debar questions about the relation between the state's role in accumulation in this sense and its role in the accumulation of intangible assets. But the taking of government expenditure on education and health as an indicator of the latter can only be done subject to the severe cautions which we have already given.

III INDIAN VERSIONS OF THE NATIONAL ACCOUNTS RECLASSIFICATION

It remains to be seen to what extent the economic (in the national accounts sense) expenditure reclassifications that have actually been produced in India do allow one to produce a picture of the government sector which is complete, integrated and diachronically comparable.

It is well known that the earliest Indian economic classifications of government budgets were prepared in the late 1950s and early 1960s by the central government Finance Ministry and two non-government bodies, Punjab University and the National Council of Applied Economic Research. The central Finance Ministry has maintained a continuous series for the central government budget since 1957, expanding the economic classification into an economic-cum-functional one since 1967. The two non-government bodies, however, after completing pioneering studies of both central and state government budgets, have retired from the field as work on state government budgets was gradually taken up by the statistical bureaux of the states (hereafter S.S.B.s).

The work done by the S.S.B.s in producing economic classifications seems to be very little known, even by well-informed sources inside India.[34] It may therefore be useful to give some account of it, both to set the record straight, and because the record itself provides an apt illustration of the problems of statistical policy in less developed countries. The 1960s saw a rapid rise in the number of S.S.B.s producing economic classifications of state expenditure. A detailed check-list of economic/functional classifications produced by the S.S.B.s and inspected by the author is given in Appendix A. In 1960, this

---

34 Anon (1973), p. 885; Premchand (1969), p. 124, note 17.

work was done only in Assam, and there in a truncated form.
By 1970, an economic classification for at least one year had
been produced by all S.S.B.s except those of Bihar, Himachal
Pradesh and West Bengal, and by all the statistical bureaux
of the Union Territories except those of Delhi, Chandigarh,
Pondicherry and Goa, Daman and Diu. Further, in Andhra
Jammu and Kashmir, Madhya Pradesh and Orissa, the S.S.B.s
had followed the central Finance Ministry's 1967 initiative
by preparing an economic-cum-functional classification
for at least one year.

But, even though the S.S.B.s have been much more active
than they have been given credit for, it is necessarily decentralized activity, and the statistics produced show many of the
classic defects of statistical decentralization. The speed with
which individual S.S.B.s took on this new responsibility varied,
generating output that is, from the all-India viewpoint,
uneven both quantitatively and qualitatively. Quantitatively,
the staggered start on the work has prevented all but few states
completing a series of five or more consecutive years. The
bulk of the S.S.B. classifications, and certainly the more reliable ones, relate to the late 1960s. They might have been
usable for intertemporal comparisons, but in fact they cannot
be matched up with the pioneering studies done by Punjab
University and the N.C.A.E.R. at the end of the 1950s.[35]

The unevenness of the S.S.B. work is also qualitative. Even
by the end of the 1960s, not all classifications were prepared
according to the standard methodology. They are, therefore,
non-comparable on a cross-section basis, apart from the fact
that in no single year is a classification available for every state.
The Central Statistical Organization, discharging its responsibility for evolving a national statistical policy, has been pursuing a standard methodology as a policy objective. In 1968,
the C.S.O. prepared a model economic and functional classification (called 'the Madras model' because it used Government
of Madras revised estimates for 1965/66) which was circulated
to all S.S.B.s in the hope of persuading them all to adopt it. The
main incentive to change was the C.S.O.'s ability to offer S.S.B.
personnel a good level of technical training in the task of economic classification – but using the 'Madras model' as the

35 Rangnekar and associates (1958); N.C.A.E.R. (1960) and (1961).

vehicle for instruction. But how has the pursuit of standardization actually worked?

Two states, Andhra and Assam, did switch immediately to the Madras model. As a result, of course, discontinuities appear in their time series.[36] But no other states did likewise. So the two states which did incur the short-run costs of change have made very little difference to the balance of support of the two different methodologies. The long-run benefits of standardization, which are supposed more than to offset the short-run costs, are still merely a prospect of the future.

If the process of standardization is too slow, however, it will be out-paced by the evolution of statistical norms. This has indeed happened already to the attempt to standardize the principle of the functional classification. The methodology of the functional classification, as well as the economic classification, has differed between states. The Madras model's four-function division of expenditure into (i) general, (ii) community, (iii) social and (iv) economic services represents what was regarded as 'best practice' in these matters in 1958, when the United Nations issued its manual on methods.[37] But without the 1958 best practice ever having been uniformly adopted, scholarly notions of best practice are beginning to change. The four-function division has been persuasively criticized on the grounds that functions (ii) and (iv) do not represent mutually exclusive categories of expenditure.[38] The dilemma for the designers of a national statistical policy is whether now to change the standard model. The point is that, if the pace of standardization is slow enough, national uniformity and the use of current best practice become alternative policies, rather than goals capable of simultaneous achievement.

In sum, then, the work of the S.S.B.s on expenditure classifications has been weak for three reasons.

(1) The incentives at the command of the C.S.O. have not been strong enough to induce all S.S.B.s to give the work the same degree of priority. Accordingly, there is wide inter-state variation in how much of the work has been done, and, in a few states and Union Territories, nothing has been done at

36 Government of Andhra Pradesh (n.d., ? 1970), preface and p. 5;
  Government of Assam (1970), preface and pp. 17–24.
37 U.N. (1958).   38 Matthews (1973), pp. 244–7.

all. From the all-India viewpoint, coverage is simply patchy and sporadic.

(2) Where the work has been done, it suffers from the defects inherent in a decentralized statistical system. These defects have been well described as 'duplication of effort, and inconsistency or non-comparability among similar parts of related systems ... [confronting] users with apparently conflicting sets of data, with no way to bridge the gap except through elaborate reconciliation tables which explain the conceptual and statistical differences'[39] Different methodologies prevent cross-section comparison, and, in the short-run, the switch to a standard methodology, when it does take place, makes the change-over state's time series discontinuous.

(3) As seen by the statisticians, their problem is the meagreness of the resources put at their disposal. There is a sense in which this is correct. Given the present inefficient organization of statistical production, a greater resource input would result in more and better quality statistics – for example, it would speed up the process of standardization and mitigate the uniformity *versus* best practice dilemma. However, on a wider view, meagreness of resources for statictics is not merely an exogenous constraint. Politicians and bureaucrats either do not understand, or understand but regard as redundant, the use of statistical information as an aid to rational decision making. They regard the statistics produced with the current level of resources as extensive and refined enough to meet all requirements except that of prestige. As previously implied, the motive for undertaking expenditure classification at all is, in part, a mimetic one.[40]

Were it necessary to rely on the S.S.B.s' spending classifications, the analysis of Indian public expenditure could only remain fragmentary and obscure. Fortunately for the economic classification, such reliance is not necessary. For while the C.S.O. has been supervising the S.S.B.s' work, it has been doing very closely related work on its own. This is one more illustration of the duplication of effort that occurs in a decentralized statistical system. The C.S.O.'s own work on expenditure classification arises from the central government's decision

39 Ruggles and Ruggles (1970), p. 61.   40 Cf. Anon (1967), p. 1198.

to produce a set of national accounts which increasingly conforms to the recommendations of the United Nations Statistical Office as set out in the 1968 System of National Accounts.[41] The basic format is a production, income and capital account for all-India, plus a consolidated account of India's transactions with the rest of the world. The accounts are compiled by first making up the same set of accounts for the three sectors of the economy recognized for the purposes of social accounting – households, businesses and the public authorities. As far as the public authorities are concerned, 'a detailed economic and functional classification of the budgets of Central and state governments as well as local authorities is necessary in order to get data in respect of all the flows which are needed in order to prepare income, outlay and capital finance accounts as recommended by the S.N.A.'[42]

This work has resulted in the publication, by the C.S.O., of the set of consolidated national accounts, accounts for the public authorities at the all-India level and tables on all-India saving and capital formation.[43] In later chapters of this work we rely heavily on these sources for data. But, in addition, when it is necessary to disaggregate the data below the all-India level, it is possible to do this by consulting the C.S.O.'s unpublished working sheets. The unpublished working sheets permit, subject to qualifications to be shortly noted, a disaggregation of the all-India public authorities' accounts into separate accounts for central government and Union Territories (taken together) and for each of the individual states (including all the local bodies in that state).

We have already specified the detailed advantages which accrue from analysing budgetary transactions within the framework of national accounts concepts and definitions. We now take these advantages as given, and discuss the relative merits of national accounts expenditure data produced on the one hand by the S.S.B.s and on the other by the C.S.O. The comparison involves four main topics, coverage and consistency, the economic classification, the functional classification and the treatment of local authorities.

41 U.N. (1968); O.E.C.D. (1972), p. 173.
42 O.E.C.D. (1972), p. 183.
43 C.S.O. (1971, 1973, 1975, 1976a and 1976b)

a   Coverage and consistency

We have already described the main defects in coverage of the
S.S.B. classifications. The C.S.O. classifications stand in startling contrast. They have very few, and then very minor, defects
of geographical and temporal coverage. Broadly speaking, they
cover all states having statehood at the relevant time, for all
years between 1960/61 and 1969/70 inclusive. The blemishes
that there are arise either because, for one or two states for
one or two years, 'revised estimates' rather than 'accounts'
data is analysed, or because the coverage of local authorities
is weak (though progress is made on eliminating some of the
weakness through the decade). The S.S.B. classifications, of
course, do not cover local authorities at all – a point discussed
at greater length at (d) below.

We have already discussed the methodological differences
that plague the work done by the S.S.B.s. Again, in strong
contrast, the C.S.O. has followed one method throughout.
Thus the comparisons that are necessary for both cross-
section and time-series analysis are relatively straightforward.
This consistency holds not only for the treatment of expenditure of the different state governments, but for all the governmental bodies included under term 'public authorities'.

b   The economic classification

When it comes to the degree of detailed information available from their respective economic classification, however,
the work of the C.S.O. compares unfavourably with that of
the S.S.B.s. In the S.S.B. economic classification, the information is arranged in the form of six accounts. The first three
of these six are accounts of transactions in commodities and
services: the current account for Government Administration
(I); the current account for departmental commercial enterprises (II); and the capital account for both Administration
and commercial enterprises (III). The last three accounts are
statements for both Administration and commercial enterprises of changes in financial assets (IV) and liabilities (V)
and a cash and capital reconciliation account (VI) deriving
from the balancing items in accounts III–V. The C.S.O.
national accounts expenditure data relate only to trans-

actions in commodities and services, capital and current.
This means the the C.S.O. figures can be rearranged to provide broadly the same information as can be found in S.S.B.
model economic classification accounts I–III.

The result of these information deficiencies in the C.S.O.
economic classification of expenditure is to prevent interstate
comparison of:

(i) methods of financing capital expenditure – owing to
the absence of accounts IV and V;
(ii) financial investment and net lending to the rest of the
economy;
(iii) financial assistance received from various central sources,
and given by the state government to its own local bodies.
This is because the transferred portion of income and
excise taxes is not separately identified by the C.S.O.;
and central lending to the state government is included
along with other items (such as inter-state debt settlement,
remittances, etc.) in a single item on the receipts side of
the capital account. The C.S.O. data, therefore, cannot
be used directly as a guide to the size and nature of the
flows of finance between the different levels of governments.
For flows of finance between central and state governments, the best source remains the figures by the Reserve
Bank of India, although these too, as has already been
mentioned, present difficulties for inter-temporal comparisons.[44]

c   The functional classification

The most serious limitation imposed by use of the C.S.O.
data is undoubtedly the absence of any functional classification of expenditure. The reason for this omission is that a
functional breakdown of expenditure is not required for the
income and outlay and capital accounts of the public authorities, in the form in which this information is currently being
published by the C.S.O. It is, however, required if the C.S.O.
is to publish its national accounts in the form recommended
in the U.N. 1968 System of National Accounts (S.N.A.). Tables
4, 13, 21 and 22 of the S.N.A. can only be completed once a

functional classification is available. Since the progressive move towards the S.N.A. format is an Indian policy objective, it may be assumed that the preparation of a functional classification is now being undertaken, although not yet completed. The completion of this work should make possible a major improvement in our understanding of Indian public spending.

In the meantime, the position remains highly unsatisfactory. Information may be sought from data published by the Reserve Bank of India, which again applies only to central and state governments (not local authorities), which uses the so-called 'semi-functional' scheme of expenditure classification introduced in 1962 (an improvement on the old classification but still a long way from being a true functional scheme), and which nevertheless still has discontinuities which interfere with intertemporal comparison.[45]

d   Treatment of local authorities

Whereas the S.S.B. analyses of expenditure confine themselves to the expenditure of state governments only, the C.S.O. analyses are for the public authorities as a whole, i.e. the expenditure of central, state and local governments (as well as their departmental commercial enterprises). This comprehensiveness is a great advantage, but it also brings with it two problems of interpretation.

The first concerns the expenditure of the Union Territories, which are a collection of smallish areas in India that are judged unsuitable for incorporation in existing states or for elaborate and relatively autonomous administrations of their own, as are enjoyed by the states. Their governments are therefore simpler and more open to the influence of the central government than are those of the states. During the 1960s, some Union Territories (U.T.) which had previously been funded through the central government budget were allowed to establish their own budgetary mechanisms. It therefore is preferable to include U.T. expenditure with that of the central government. A minor distortion still remains, because of the annexation of Goa, Daman and Diu from Portu-

45 Toye (1973), pp. 267–9, 275.

gal in 1962, and the establishment of the city of Chandigarh as a U.T. rather than as part of Punjab in 1967.

The second problem concerns the treatment of local authorities that operate within the area administered by state governments. These local authorities are both traditional (municipal corporations, municipalities and port trusts) and the *panchayati raj* institutions (*zila parishads, gram panchayats,* etc.) established in the wake of the Balvantry Mehta Report.[46] The C.S.O. data identifies their expenditure as a separate aggregate for 1960/61 to 1964/65, but then merges it into the totals for the individual states for 1965/66 to 1969/70. The latter method of treatment is the more useful. It reflects both the constitutional form and political reality of the relationship between state governments and local authorities. State governments delegate to local bodies (who have no constitutional standing) some of the functions which are constitutionally theirs, and assign for purposes of local finance, in whole or part, taxes which appear in the states' list in the constitution.[47] In practice, too, because of the *panchayati raj* institutions' heavy dependence on conditional grants from the state governments, 'the scope for local initiative is limited . . . to minor matters'.[48] Apart from this, it is important to note that the functions and expenditure of local bodies vary very considerably from state to state.[49] In this situation, the exclusion of local bodies' expenditure from inter-state expenditure comparisons would simply produce arbitrary and misleading interstate comparisons. To quote one authority, 'comparisons of state government expenditures are treacherous [because] in State A the government may perform functions that in State B are left to localities'.[50] Accordingly better comparisons result if state government and local bodies' expenditure is combined.

To do this, the aggregate local bodies' expenditure figures for 1960/61 to 1964/65 in the C.S.O. data must be allocated to the states. It cannot be ignored on *de minimis* grounds,

46 Planning Commission (Committee Plan Projects) (1957).
47 Ministry of Finance (1955), p. 14.
48 Raj (1971), p. 1611.
49 Venkataraman (1965), pp. 56–7 and 57, note 1.
50 Maxwell (1969), pp. 2–3.

because it accounts for one fifth of all expenditure at the state level and below. Nor can it be allocated in equal shares between the states because of the great inequality known to prevail in 1965/66. Our procedure was to allocate the local bodies total to states according to the percentage shares of each state in 1965/66. This is a crude procedure because it assumes constant shares by states during a period when democratic decentralization was proceeding at different speeds in different states. But it was the most convenient method that did not appear to lead to gross distortions of the true positions.

It should be obvious from this discussion that, if an all-India perspective is desired – that is, some grasp of the national position plus some understanding of inter-state variations – the national accounts data produced by the C.S.O. will be vastly more informative than any attempt to patch together conclusions from the data produced by the various S.S.B.s. The C.S.O.'s advantages of coverage, consistency and comprehensiveness far outweigh the information loss arising from an abbreviated economic classification and the absence of a functional classification. But the C.S.O. would have done still better to have allowed the S.S.B.s entirely to follow their own devices, and to have devoted the manpower resources saved thereby to producing their own urgently needed functional classification of the budget data they have already classified by economic category.

Part two
Empirical evidence

4
The fiscal performance of the public sector

The Third Plan noted that 'careful attention must be given to factors which will increase the capacity of the public sector to expand still more rapidly . . . As the relative share of the public sector increases, its role in economic growth will become even more strategic and the state will be in a still stronger position to determine the character and functioning of the economy as a whole.'[1] The public sector was seen as 'producing large surpluses for development', and therefore being 'one of the most important factors determining the rate at which the economy can grow'.[2] This was a more positive and confident statement of the state accumulation policy than those in either the First or the Second Plan. The First Plan had only said that 'in promoting capital formation on the required scale . . . the state will have to play a crucial role. This need not involve complete nationalization of the means of production . . . [but it] does, however, mean a progressive widening of the public sector and a re-orientation of the private sector to the needs of a planned economy.'[3] The public sector, according to the Second Plan, had 'not only to initiate developments which the private sector is either unwilling or unable to undertake; it has to play the dominant role in shaping the entire pattern of investments in the economy'.[4]

By the time of the Fourth Plan, however, a change of emphasis can be detected. In specifying the aims and objectives of planning, the statements in previous Plans were quoted selectively. Additional prominence was given to the themes of

1 Planning Commission (1962), p. 14.
2 Ibid., p. 50.
3 Planning Commission (1952), p. 9.
4 Planning Commission (1956), p. 22.

complementarity of public and private sector activities and the scope for private sector development. This was at the expense of the usual homage to the role of the public sector.[5] It was further noted that 'the original expectations of an expanding public sector yielding, in due course, substantial resources for its continued development, have not been realized'.[6] As a result special attention to operational efficiency and economic discipline in the public sector and to the coordination of the various public sector activities was called for. After these implied criticisms, it is perhaps not surprising that the endorsement of the future of the public sector is vague and tautological: 'a matter of crucial significance will be the emergence of the public sector as a whole as the dominant and effective area of the economy [which] will enable it to take charge more and more of the commanding heights' of the economy.[7]

This decline, in the planners' official policy pronouncements, from confidence in, to confusion about, the state accumulation policy, accurately reflects the increasing failure to make

TABLE 4.1 *Public expenditure growth in relation to the growth of output, prices and population, 1960/61 to 1968/69*

	Linear trend annual growth rates		
	1960/61 to 1964/65	*1964/65 to 1968/69*	*1960/61 to 1968/69*
1 Total expenditure of public authorities	16.8	9.4	*12.9*
2 N.N.P. at current prices	11.2	11.0	*11.0*
3 Index of wholesale prices	6.2	8.0	*8.0*
4 Total population	n.a.	n.a.	*2.2*

Sources

1 Calculated from C.S.O. unpublished data.
2 Calculated from data in C.S.O. (1971).
3 Calculated from Ministry of Finance, *Economic Survey, 1971/72*.
4 Census of India (1971).

5 Planning Commission (1970), pp. 3–4.
6 Ibid., p. 14.
7 Ibid., p. 28.

the policy work in the decade 1960 to 1970. In order to document the effective breakdown of the state accumulation policy, we rely mainly on national accounts data for the government sector or 'public authorities'. Supplementary data are used where appropriate for two purposes. The first is to show the functional breakdown of public authorities' spending: the second is to provide information on the non-departmental enterprises which, together with the government sector or public authorities, comprise the public sector.

I GROWTH OF PUBLIC AUTHORITIES' EXPENDITURE

It is all too common, both among officials and, less excusably, among scholars, to confine an assessment of fiscal performance to a calculation of the increase in money expenditures or revenues in a given period. But such a calculation, on its own, says nothing whatever about fiscal performance. The first thing that must be done is to relate changes in money expenditures, as in Table 4.1, to simultaneous changes in national output, the level of prices and population.

Total public expenditure at current prices grew over the period 1960/61 to 1968/69 at almost 13 per cent a year compound. Since net national product at current prices grew by 11 per cent a year compound over the same period, a strong *a priori* presumption is established that the relative share of the public authorities in the economy expanded. (There are logical problems in measuring the public authorities' relative share, which will be mentioned shortly.) Also, since prices rose by about 8 per cent compound and population grew at 2.2 per cent compound, the whole decade saw an increase in the *average* level of real public expenditure – although this says nothing about the distribution of the increment.

Looking at average annual growth rates can also be deceptive, because they can mask sharp changes in the tempo of growth. As Table 4.1 makes clear, the growth of public expenditure was anything but steady and continuous throughout the decade. From a compound growth rate of nearly 17 per cent in the first half of the decade, the fall to a rate of $9\frac{1}{2}$ per cent in the second half makes a remarkable contrast. Given the relatively much more gentle deceleration of money net output and acceleration of inflation, and assuming steady population growth, two conclusions may be drawn. The expansion of the public authorities' relative share in the economy and the rise in the average level of real public expenditure were both phenomena exclusively of the period before 1964/65. After 1964/65, both of these changes were partially, but not completely reversed because public spending failed to keep pace with either money net output or with the combined effects of inflation and population growth.

There is no ideal measure of the government's relative share in the economy. Public expenditure has two distinct economic effects: part of it directly absorbs currently available resources, while part merely redistributes purchasing power in the non-government sector. The latter ('non-exhaustive' spending or transfer payments) should not be included in public expenditure when expressed as a percentage of G.N.P., since transfer payments of all kinds are excluded in the calculation of G.N.P. On the other hand, if the government's share in the economy is measured by the ratio of only 'exhaustive' expenditure to G.N.P. all indirect influences of government on the disposition of resources are ignored. Both measures, $G/GNP \times 100$ and $N + G/GNP \times 100$ (where G is exhaustive and N is non-exhaustive spending) are imperfect in logic. But in India, as in

TABLE 4.2. *The share of the government sector in the economy: 3 measures, 1960/62 to 1968/70.*

	(1) $\dfrac{G}{GNP} \times 100$	(2) $\dfrac{N + G}{GNP} \times 100$	(3) $\dfrac{T}{GNP} \times 100^{*}$
1960–62[**]	13.0	15.4	10.8
1962–64	15.7	18.6	13.0
1964–66	15.7	18.4	13.3
1966–68	13.8	17.5	12.8
1968–70	13.9	19.2	13.1

Source: C.S.O. (1971).
Notes: [*] T = total tax revenues of public authorities.
   [**] Figures represent an average of two accounting years, i.e. 1960–62 is an average of the figures for 1960/61 and 1961/62, and so on.

many poor countries, the transfer payments element in total public expenditure is relatively small, and it happens that the two measures show, subject to one qualification, the same changes over time. Table 4.2 shows the two measures so far discussed, plus a third, that of total tax revenues as a percentage of G.N.P. Measures (1) and (3) show a close similarity in the phasing of expansion and partial relative contraction. Measure (2), total expenditure as a percentage of G.N.P. shows two differences: (a) a slightly earlier peak of expansion and (b) an apparent resumption in the expansion of the government sector, reaching a new peak in 1968–70. The latter is the result of a huge increase in the government's net purchase of assets at this time, presumably reflecting the compensation paid for the nationalization of fourteen domestic banks in 1969.

Similar timing in the expansion and partial contraction of 'real' public expenditure per head is also evident from the figures in Table 4.3. To get at these figures, the rather crude deflator of the wholesale price index was used, and population expansion was assumed to be steady and continuous. The

TABLE 4.3. *Changes in real public expenditure per head.*

Year	(a) $\dfrac{(N + G) \times 100}{\text{Price index}}$ (Rs. crores at 1960/61 prices)	(b) Estimated population (millions)	(c) $\dfrac{(N + G) \times 100}{\text{Price index} \times \text{population}}$ (Rupees at 1960/61 prices)
1960/61	2109	439.1	48
1961/62	2289	448.8	51
1962/63	2710	458.7	59
1963/64	2983	468.8	64
1964/65	2969	479.1	62
1965/66	3045	489.6	62
1966/67	2924	500.4	58
1967/68	2968	511.4	58
1968/69	3202	522.7	61

Sources
  (a) Calculated from C.S.O. unpublished data and wholesale price index in Ministry of Finance, *Economic Survey, 1971/72.*
  (b) 1961 population figure in 1971 Census compounded at 2.2 per cent per annum.

results, which are admittedly only an approximation, show a rapid rise in real public spending per head to 64 rupees by 1963/64, a peak which was not regained by 1968/69.

The observed fluctuations in the government's share in the economy coincide with (a) the change from expanding national income per head to contraction and subsequent partial recovery and (b) the change from a structure of output increasingly favouring industry to a structure shifting back again in favour of agriculture. Broadly speaking, the first half of the decade manifests rising income per head, some slight growth in the industrial sector's share in output, growth in the relative share of the government in the economy and rising real levels of public expenditure per head. In the second half of the decade, all these developments are reversed, then resume again too weakly to attain their mid-decade peak levels.

That this set of statistical facts is not formally inconsistent with Wagner's law of expanding state activity should not be given much significance. An increasing government share in national output has been the secular experience of many now developed economies.[8] But it would be wrong to conclude from this, taken in conjunction with the Indian evidence, that India since independence has been undergoing some kind of inevitable universalistic 'development' process which automatically expands the government share. The explanations offered by Wagner of the phenomenon which he correctly identified are unsatisfactory, even in relation to the 'developing' nations of his own time. Certainly one of the major expansionary forces behind public sector relative growth in advanced capitalist economies – growing social security systems redistributing income by public transfers – has been absent in India. Another expansionary force – the nationalization of private sector assets – has appeared only sporadically, and not, as Wagner predicted, as a response to increasing market failure promoted by economic growth. When poor, post-colonial economies, like India's, show a Wagnerian trend in expenditures, the direction of causation is the exact opposite of that formulated by Wagner. The forces of output expansion and industrialization do not operate, through the demand side, to expand the

8 Bird (1970), p. 75.

government's share. That share, on the contrary, is deliberately expanded by the government with the objective of stimulating the accumulation of productive capital.

II CHANGING COMPOSITION OF PUBLIC EXPENDITURE

On the one hand, public spending is the sum of a set of programmes directed to different purposes, such as defence, education or agricultural development. On the other hand, it is the addition of a set of inputs or resources (such as manpower, buildings or second-hand assets) which are absorbed by the programmes in different combinations. An analysis of public spending by programme is the 'functional' classification of expenditure, while an analysis by types of input is the 'economic' classification. Although the two classifications are conceptually distinct, they are not independent of each other, since they are simply two facets of the same reality.

The unpublished C.S.O. data on which we have relied thus far does not have an accompanying functional breakdown. Thus we are forced to adopt the unsatisfactory alternative of using the functional breakdown of other data which rest on a different conceptual basis. These are taken from the Ministry of Finance's annual *Economic Survey*. They differ from the C.S.O. data in that

(i) they take no direct account of spending by public authority other than the central and state governments;

(ii) they include in the category 'development outlay' the Plan expenditure of the railways and non-departmental undertakings out of their own resources, as well as loans by the central and state governments to local bodies, non-departmental commercial undertakings (including Electricity Boards) and other parties.

At the same time, they differ from the Reserve Bank of India's statistics on central and state government finances, in that, for example, they exclude transfers to the Special Development Fund through which United States P.L. 480 foreign aid is mediated. It follows that the aggregates of public expenditure given in the *Economic Survey* are not the same as those used heretofore, being both larger initially and showing a faster rate of

TABLE 4.4. *Budgetary transactions of central and state governments expressed as percentages of total outlay, 1960/61 to 1969/70*

	1960/61	1961/62	1962/63	1963/64	1964/65	1965/66	1966/67	1967/68	1968/69	1969/70
Development spending	67.4	66.7	63.7	59.5	61.8	62.1	55.6	57.0	57.7	56.6
of which										
(a) *Plan*	41.8	40.2	42.0	39.1	42.7	40.9	35.2	32.4	34.8	29.5
of which										
1 Agriculture and allied sectors		5.27	5.15	4.84	5.30	5.48	5.44	4.93	6.67	4.39
2 irrigation and flood control		3.77	3.40	2.81	3.14	3.11	2.43	2.24	2.39	2.63
3 Power		4.96	5.42	6.00	6.43	6.47	6.57	6.07	5.70	6.39
4 Industry and minerals		6.94	7.60	8.00	7.95	8.76	8.37	7.32	7.24	5.80
5 Village and small scale industries		1.33	1.18	1.00	1.00	0.94	0.69	0.67	0.65	0.50
6 Transport and communication		10.55	11.13	10.73	10.64	8.46	6.90	6.10	6.27	5.52
7 Education and scientific research		2.76	2.97	2.87	3.38	3.52	1.68	1.84	2.18	1.36
8 Health and family planning		1.93	1.92	1.49	1.59	1.73	0.94	1.13	1.29	1.04

9 Other miscellaneous*		2.60	2.37	2.12	2.21	2.35	2.18	2.07	2.15	1.84
10 Adjustment		+0.10	+0.8	−0.8	+1.0	0	0	0	+0.3	0
(b) Non-Plan	25.6	26.4	21.6	20.4	19.1	21.2	20.4	24.6	22.9	27.1
Non-development spending of which	32.6	33.3	36.3	40.5	38.2	37.9	44.4	43.0	42.3	43.4
(c) Defence (net)	11.0	11.1	14.1	19.0	17.0	15.8	14.8	15.0	15.1	14.9
(d) Debt service	4.5	4.8	5.2	7.1	7.4	7.5	8.5	8.9	8.7	8.8
(e) Tax collection charges	2.7	2.4	2.0	1.8	1.7	1.8	1.6	1.8	2.0	1.9
(f) Police	3.7	3.9	3.7	3.2	3.3	3.4	3.4	3.9	4.0	4.2
(g) Others**	10.7	11.1	11.3	9.4	8.7	9.4	16.0	13.5	12.4	13.5

Source: *Economic Survey*, for the years 1962/63, 1963/64, 1964/65, 1965/66, 1967/68, 1968/69, 1969/70 and 1971/72: percentages calculated from sundry tables of absolute values given therein.

Notes: *includes water supply and sanitation; housing, urban and regional development; welfare of backward classes; social welfare, labour welfare and craftsmen training, etc.

**includes general administration, pensions and privy purses, famine relief, food subsidy, grants and loans to foreign countries and non-developmental loans to other parties.

growth, because of the wider definition implied by (ii) above.
Further, as will become clear, the classification provided is not
a complete functional classification. A number of important
functional categories are separated out from non-development
outlay, and *Plan* development outlay can be broken down into
nine groups of development heads. But no sub-division of
non-Plan development outlay appears to be possible, although
one is clearly needed by development head for a comprehensive
analysis. Finally, the breakdown of Plan development outlay
is based on later figures, revising slightly downwards for the
early years of the decade, a discrepancy reflected in the 'adjustment' item in Table 4.4.

Despite the various deficiencies which have been mentioned,
Table 4.4 is a pointer towards a number of tentative conclusions. The first is that, before 1965/66, while the economy
was still expanding and the government's share in it increasing, the growth rate of non-development spending was higher
than that of development spending. At this time the major
contributor to the higher growth rate of non-development
spending was defence, the budget for which was roughly doubled in real terms. From the viewpoint of the chosen development policy, the desirable situation would be just the opposite.
Yet, on the other hand, it is not strictly possible to regard the
additional resources devoted to defence as a diversion from
other government programmes. To do so is to assume that the
same *total* volume of resources would have been available for
government spending in the absence of the strong additional
demands from the defence services. This is not a safe assumption.

One can, however, examine the consequences of two opposite assumptions. If defence spending had been held constant
in real terms in the first half of the decade, and the additional
expenditure which was in fact devoted to defence had been
devoted instead to development programmes, then (obviously)
the government's share in the economy would have been
exactly what it did in fact grow to, but the growth rate of development expenditure would have exceeded the growth rate of
non-development spending. At the end of the period, the
proportion of total government spending for development
would have risen from 67 to 70, instead of falling to 62 per

cent. Although a highly satisfactory outcome, it seems doubtful, on political grounds, whether the government would ever have mobilized the full increment of resources without the stimulus of a national emergency. The more likely case is to imagine defence spending constant in real terms, and the extra resources which were in fact mobilized for defence being allowed to stay in the private sector. The consequences of this would have been a government share in the economy of about 17 per cent, against the actual 19 per cent in mid-decade; and an equipro-portional growth of development and non-development spending. If it is now admitted that defence and development did to some extent compete for resources in the government's hands, it is clear that the very rapid expansion of the defence budget must have prevented a *rise* in the ratio of development to non-development spending that would otherwise have occur-red. This conclusion reflects quite well on the development orientation of government expenditure under the Third Plan. The emphasis was placed strongly on *Plan* development expen-diture which grew faster than total spending *despite* the very rapid growth in defence programmes.

By 1965/66, the growth of total public expenditure in real terms had slowed down considerably, falling to an average annual rate of only 1½ per cent between 1964/65 and 1968/69. In this situation, the problem of whether the extra resources the government was raising should be regarded as specialized, for political reasons, to a particular spending programme, ceases to have its former importance. Once there are tight limits on the amount of overall real growth, one need no longer be so cautious about regarding changes in programme shares as a redistribution of available resources between competing programmes in response to changing government priorities.

The changes in programme priorities in the second half of the 1960s were, in fact, quite startling. Non-development con-tinued to grow faster than development spending. But this was no longer due to the expansionist impulse of the defence programme. Defence's share in total spending fell from 17 per cent in 1964/65 to 15 per cent in 1969/70, while defence's share in non-development spending fell from 44 to 34 per cent between the same dates. This makes it easy to accept the view that, from the mid sixties, 'the constraints on developmental

expenditure do not arise from increased defence spending'.[9]
The burgeoning elements of non-development spending after
1965–66 were twofold. The most important was expenditure
on famine relief measures and food subsidies, the impact of
which was felt particularly strongly in 1966/67 and 1967/68
following the monsoon failures of the previous two years. Less
important, but also significant, was increased expenditure on
police. Police spending rose as a percentage of total expenditure from 3.3 per cent in 1964/65 to 4.2 per cent in 1969/70,
and as a percentage of non-development spending from 8.6
to 9.7 per cent over the same period. It appears that the government's response to the internal economic crisis was a markedly
'colonial' one – large-scale measures to alleviate immediate
popular distress coupled with increased attention to its capabilities for maintaining internal 'law and order'.

Given the slow rate of overall expenditure growth in real
terms and the faster growth on non-development than development spending, it is no surprise to discover that development
spending itself remained virtually static in real terms. But
whereas, during the Third Plan, Plan development spending
grew faster than non-Plan, after 1965/66 the reverse happened.
While development spending failed to grow in real terms,
Plan development spending was held constant *in money terms* at a
time of price inflation of an average of 6 per cent a year. Thus
in real terms, Plan development spending suffered a marked
decline, thereby releasing resources for non-Plan development
spending.

It is not possible to present a complete picture of the effects
of these changes on individual heads (i.e. categories) of development, since the *Economic Survey* provides an expenditure
breakdown by development head only in respect of Plan development outlay. It must always be borne in mind that any cur-
tailment in Plan development outlay may be partly, fully or
more than fully compensated for by an increase in non-Plan
development outlay under the same development head. However, offsetting increases outside the Plan are more probable
in relation to some heads or categories of development than
others. If the changing balance between Plan and non-Plan

9 Subrahmanyam (1973), pp. 1155–8.

development spending is accompanied by a change in the balance between centre and state government spending, it is quite probable that heads of development where a large slice of spending is the responsibility of the state governments would show growing shares of non-Plan spending to compensate for shrinking shares of Plan spending. The heads of development where state governments exercise a major responsibility are agriculture and allied sectors, irrigation and flood control, education and scientific research and health and family planning. Plan development outlay on each of these heads decreased as a percentage of total expenditure. But it is doubtful that development outlay (i.e. both Plan and non-Plan) on these heads as a percentage of total expenditure also decreased. It is much more likely that it stagnated in real terms but that an increasing proportion was administered outside the framework of the Plan.

The most dramatic decline in Plan development outlay as a percentage of total expenditure occurs in respect of transport and communications. Plan development outlay under this head was $10\frac{1}{2}$ per cent of total expenditure in 1964/65, but fell steadily to $5\frac{1}{2}$ per cent in 1969/70. The programmes involved – railways, post and telegraphs and civil aviation – are all central government responsibilities, so that there is no possibility of compensating increases in non-Plan development outlay on state government account, nor is there any reason for expecting them on central government non-Plan account. Although, given the defective nature of the evidence, no certainty is attainable, it seems probable that transport and communications was the head or category of development which experienced the severest effects of the restraint on development expenditure. Outlay under this head almost certainly contracted in money terms, so that, in real terms, its contraction was even greater. As we shall see, this had very important repercussions on the growth and structure of Indian industrial output, and was at the heart of the breakdown of the policy of state accumulation.

Even for those programmes where development outlay was more or less maintained in real terms, the shifting of an increasing part of them outside the framework of the Plan was not a matter of merely administrative interest. Planning, if it has any virtues, does so precisely because of the comprehen-

TABLE 4.5 Public authorities' expenditure by economic category expressed as percentages of the total,

	1960/61	1961/62	1962/63	1963/64	1964/65	1965/66	1966/67	1967/68	1968/69	1969/70
1 Government consumption of which	51.5	51.6	50.7	54.7	53.6	55.0	54.4	55.1	58.3	55.3
1a Compensation of employees	34.3	34.8	31.6	30.5	31.9	32.4	33.1	34.8	36.8	35.2
1b Net purchase of goods and services	17.2	16.9	19.1	24.1	21.7	22.7	22.3	20.3	21.4	20.1
2 Interest on public debt	2.8	3.1	3.7	3.4	3.3	4.2	5.1	4.8	4.6	4.5
3 Subsidies	4.4	4.7	5.0	4.3	3.9	4.6	9.0	7.0	5.4	4.8
4 Current transfers	8.2	8.4	6.9	6.0	6.3	6.5	7.0	7.5	8.2	8.4

5 Gross fixed capital formation of which	33.9	32.2	31.3	30.4	31.2	30.1	26.6	24.0	24.9	21.1
5a Departmental enterprises	20.8	19.4	19.3	19.0	19.5	18.7	16.0	14.1	14.6	12.0
5b Administration	13.2	12.8	12.0	11.4	11.7	11.4	10.6	9.9	10.3	9.0
6 Changes in stocks	1.2	−1.2	1.5	0.1	1.1	0.1	−2.6	0.9	−2.2	−0.7
7 Net purchases of assets	−3.4	−0.3	−0.1	−0.2	−0.2	−1.5	−0.4	0	−0.1	5.6
8 Capital transfers	1.4	1.4	1.0	1.3	0.8	1.0	1.0	0.8	0.8	1.1

Sources: 1960/61 to 1968/69: based on data in C.S.O. (1971), Tables 8 and 10. 1969/70: based on C.S.O. unpublished data.

siveness of its approach and the centralization of decision making which it encourages. It is a sad commentary on the Fourth Five-Year Plan, which was intended to restore Indian planning to its pre-1965/66 position, that in its first year of operation, 1969/70, Plan development outlay constituted a markedly smaller part of total government expenditure than was the case in the three preceding years of 'plan holiday'. This proves how much easier it is to begin plan holidays than to end them.

III   THE DECLINE OF PUBLIC SECTOR CAPITAL FORMATION AND SAVING

If we now turn from the functional classification given in the *Economic Survey* to the economic classification of public expenditure on a national accounts basis, as prepared by the C.S.O., the tentative conclusions already arrived at are strengthened. The distribution of expenditure during the Third Plan between government consumption, assorted varieties of transfer, gross fixed capital formation and other capital transactions is remarkably stable during the period of real expenditure growth, except for the sudden expansion of net purchases of commodities and services in 1963/64 resulting from rapid rearmament (see Table 4.5). After 1964/65, when the annual average rate of real expenditure growth had fallen to about $1\frac{1}{2}$ per cent, considerably more dramatic changes occurred in the relative importance of the various economic categories. The effects of the double monsoon failure are clearly visible in 1966/67 and 1967/68, when subsidies took 9 and 7 per cent of total expenditure, compared with an average of 4–5 per cent under the Third Plan. In the last three years of the 1960s, compensation of government employees begins to take a larger share of the total than at any time in the previous seven years, the joint result of an ever-expanding bureaucracy and generous grants of additional dearness allowances. The cost to the exchequer of bank nationalization is evident in the transformation of net purchase of assets from a small negative item to a large positive one in 1969/70.

To make room for all these expanding items beneath a virtually static ceiling on real expenditure, the axe had to fall, and fall it did – on gross fixed capital formation. Even under the Third Plan, gross fixed capital formation had failed to grow quite as fast as total expenditure. But after 1965/66 hardly any growth at all was permitted, even in money terms, while, on the same basis, total expenditure grew by 9 per cent a year. Consequently, the share of expenditure devoted to gross fixed capital formation fell from 30 per cent in 1965/66 to 21 per cent in 1969/70. Here is one more stark reflection of the official plan holiday between 1966 and 1969, and the failure of the official resumption of planning in 1969/70 to reverse the trend of the previous three years. It is worth noting that the check to gross fixed capital formation after 1965/66 was more harshly felt by departmental enterprises than government departments proper. This confirms the earlier indications that the transport industries, particularly railways, were the worst sufferers in the government investment famine. From the evidence both of the economic and the functional classification, it would appear that, at least after 1965/66, neither capital formation nor development expenditure nor Plan development expenditure was a priority in the government budget. On the contrary, 'in effect, capital expenditure has been the residual component in total government sector operations'.[10]

Consequently, when the trends in public authorities' capital formation are viewed in conjunction with trends in other relevant magnitudes (Table 4.6), the picture is one of movement in the *opposite* direction from that which is required if the government is to act as the engine of a capitalist industrialization. It is clear that, after the end of the Third Plan, public authorities' gross fixed capital formation failed to keep pace either with the overall growth of the economy or with the growth of total gross fixed capital formation. The public authorities, of course, do not constitute the whole of the public sector. But even when account is taken of the investment that was done by the non-departmental public enterprises, the capital formation of the whole public sector shows the same failure to keep pace with G.N.P. and with total gross fixed capital formation. Thus the Indian strategy of enlarging the role of the public sector in investment was allowed to falter. The government

10 Edwards (1969), p. 12.

TABLE 4.6 *Public authorities' gross fixed capital formation in relation to G.N.P. and total gross fixed capital formation, 1960/61 to 1969/70.*

	1960/61	1961/62	1962/63	1963/64	1964/65	1965/66	1966/67	1967/68	1968/69	1969/70
1 Public authorities' G.F.C.F.* (Rs. cr.)	716	753	899	1042	1167	1257	1223	1210	1258	1296
2 As a percentage (a) of G.N.P. at factor cost	5.1	5.1	5.7	5.8	5.5	5.7	4.8	4.1	4.1	3.8
(b) of total G.F.C.F.	33.2	31.2	33.7	33.1	31.9	30.4	26.6	23.8	23.4	22.2

Note: * G.F.C.F. means gross fixed capital formation.
Source: C.S.O. (1976a), pp. 6, 34 and 69.

TABLE 4.7 *Public sector gross fixed capital formation in relation to G.N.P. and total gross fixed capital formation, 1960/61 to 1969/70*

	1960/61	1961/62	1962/63	1963/64	1964/65	1965/66	1966/67	1967/68	1968/69	1969/70
1 Public sector G.F.C.F. (Rs. cr.)	1055	1107	1312	1562	1824	2046	2047	2012	2111	2190
2 As a percentage (a) of G.N.P. at factor cost	7.5	7.5	8.3	8.7	8.6	9.4	8.1	6.8	6.9	6.5
(b) of total G.F.C.F.	48.9	45.9	49.2	49.6	49.8	49.5	44.5	39.6	39.3	37.5

Source: C.S.O. (1976a), pp. 34, 69.

adopted a 'Mexican' policy of letting the balance between public and private investment swing back in favour of the private sector.[11]

There were two sources of pressure on the government to let this happen. One was the gradual slackening of the inflow of foreign aid to India after 1965. The other was the contraction of public saving in the late 1960s. As Table 4.8 shows, after 1964/65, the level of public savings underwent a substantial absolute decline at current prices, falling from 598 Rs. crores in that year to 360 Rs. crores in 1967/8. Thus public savings between 1964/65 and 1967/68 fell dramatically as a share of national expenditure, of total national savings, of public authorities' net receipts and of public authorities' gross fixed capital formation. In 1968/69 and 1969/70, these downward falls were reversed, but in no case were the previous peak values (in 1964/65) regained. It may not be unreasonable to expect some diminution in the government's ability to finance its own investment from public savings, when that investment is being rapidly *expanded*. But in India in the late 1960s, a falling share of public savings in the finance of government investment is combined with a falling level of government investment in real terms. In other words, despite the 'plan holiday' and the severe cutback in investment which it entailed, the government's requirement from sources of investment finance not under its own control (i.e. domestic borrowing and foreign aid) increased both relatively and absolutely.

This picture is in no way materially altered by extending the discussion to the public sector as a whole. The performance of the non-departmental public enterprises in terms of profitability was extremely poor in the 1960s. As a result, the dividends which they were able to contribute to the national exchequer were, despite their upward trend, miniscule in comparison with the totals of public authorities' saving, as is shown in Table 4.9.

The share of public sector capital formation that was financed by public sector saving (see Table 4.10) rose somewhat in the Third Plan period. It then plummeted to its nadir in 1967/68, and subsequently by 1969/70 returned to the same value as that for 1960/61. This is hardly a dynamic performance.

11 Cf. Reynolds (1971), pp. 538–9.

Table 4 Public authorities' saving in relation to G.N.P., total saving, current receipts and own investment, 1960/61 to 1969/70

	1960/61	1961/62	1962/63	1963/64	1964/65	1965/66	1966/67	1967/68	1968/69	1969/70
1 Public authorities' saving (Rs. cr.)	298	366	408	513	598	542	408	360	543	626
as a percentage of:										
2 G.N.P. at factor cost	2.1	2.5	2.6	2.9	2.8	2.5	1.6	1.2	1.8	1.9
3 Total saving	22.4	28.6	26.4	28.1	29.6	21.2	13.1	11.9	17.3	15.6
4 Public authorities' total current receipts	17.4	18.8	17.6	17.4	19.2	15.6	10.5	8.7	11.8	12.2
5 Public authorities' G.F.C.F.	41.6	48.6	45.4	49.2	51.2	43.1	33.4	29.7	43.1	48.3

Source: C.S.O. (1976a), pp. 2, 6, 66–7, 69.

TABLE 4.9 *Public enterprises' net trading profits and dividends contributed to the exchequer, 1962/63 to 1969/70.*

(Rs. crores)

Public enterprises:	1962/63	1963/64	1964/65	1965/66	1966/67	1967/68	1968/69	1969/70
a Net trading profit/loss	(—)9.1			10.3	(—)21.6	(—)34.7	(—)26.9	(—)8.7
b Dividends Paid	2.1	2.8	3.9	2.8	7.4	10.2	11.7	12.7

Sources: Ministry of Finance, Bureau of Public Enterprises, *A Handbook of Information on Public Enterprises 1970*, pp. 52 and 90. For 1969–70, Ministry of Finance, Bureau of Public Enterprises, *Annual Report on the Working of Industrial and Commercial Undertaking of the Central Government, 1969–70*, pp. 15, 29, 111 and 172.

TABLE 4.10 *Percentage of public sector capital formation financed by public sector saving, 1960/61 to 1969/70.*

	1960/61	1961/62	1962/63	1963/64	1964/65	1965/66	1966/67	1967/68	1968/69	1969/70
Public sector saving (Rs. cr.) as % of	309	363	408	539	611	592	407	355	522	645
Public sector G.F.C.F.	29.2	32.8	31.1	34.5	33.5	28.9	19.9	17.6	24.7	29.4

Source: C.S.O. (1976a), pp. 33–4.

Formally, public saving is the excess of current receipts (defined as those receipts which leave the government's assets and liabilities position unchanged) over current expenditure in the national accounts sense. Thus a decline in public saving results from poor performance in raising current receipts, failure to limit current expenditure, or some combination of both of these factors. In India since 1965/66, both factors have been at work, and so the problem is one of judging the relative degree of emphasis to be placed on each.

The Indian performance in raising current revenue for the government sector certainly cannot be characterized as uniformly poor. Between 1952 and 1962, the buoyancy of the Indian tax system was greater than that of any other country in Asia.[12] One result of this was that, until 1963/64, government current receipts steadily and appreciably increased as a percentage of national income (Table 4.11). The revenue motive was the dominant one in fiscal policy, 'the Finance Ministers at the Centre and in the States often adopting a more or less purely revenue approach to taxation'.[13] Since the increments to revenue resulted largely from successive increases in tax rates and the extension and multiplication of tax bases, their side-effects, in terms of economic impact, equity and administrative soundness were often damaging to the tax system as a whole. Damage of this kind is very hard to avoid in a tax system whose revenue productivity is being rapidly expanded, but can be limited by a continuous effort at repair and reform. Despite the quasi-Kaldorian experiments of the late 1950s and subsequent reports of mixed value by various official committees of enquiry, this sort of effort has been conspicuous by its absence in India. However, if one leaves such considerations aside and adopts only the revenue criterion, even after 1965/66 the government did succeed in keeping current receipts more or less constant as a fraction of national income. As one authority has remarked, 'in view of the severity of the drought of 1965 and 1966 and of its adverse effect on the level of domestic activity and on the balance of payments, the surprising feature is that there was no significant decline in any of the major components of total tax revenue'.[14] This comment,

12 Chelliah (1966), p. 35.
13 Chelliah (1967), p. 921.
14 Edwards (1969), p. 11.

TABLE 4.11 *Government current receipts in relation to national income 1960/61 to 1968/69.*

	1960/61	1961/62	1962/63	1963/64	1964/65	1965/66	1966/67	1967/68	1968/69
1 Current receipts (Rs. cr.)	1708	1950	2313	2860	3109	3476	3876	4120	4458
2 1 as a percentage of N.D.P.	12.8	13.8	15.4	16.6	15.4	16.7	16.1	14.4	15.4

Source: C.S.O. (1971), pp. 2 and 15.

TABLE 4.12 *The structure of government current receipts, 1960/61 to 1968/69.*

(Percentages)

Receipts	1960/61	1961/62	1962/63	1963/64	1964/65	1965/66	1966/67	1967/68	1968/69
1 *Entre-preneurial and prop-erty income*	10.9	11.4	10.7	12.1	9.8	9.9	9.5	9.5	11.1
a Operating surplus	5.6	6.5	6.0	6.3	4.2	4.2	3.6	2.6	3.2
of which: railways	2.3	3.0	2.9	3.3	1.8	1.7	1.3	0.5	1.0
b Income from property	5.3	4.9	4.7	5.8	5.6	5.7	5.9	6.9	7.9
of which: interest receipts	2.8	2.7	2.6	3.7	3.6	3.9	4.0	4.8	6.0
2 *Direct taxes*	24.6	24.0	24.8	24.7	24.6	22.3	21.5	20.8	20.3
a Corporation tax	6.5	8.1	9.6	9.6	10.1	8.8	8.6	7.5	7.2

b Land revenue	5.1	4.5	4.6	3.8	3.5	2.9	2.0	2.2	2.4
c Other	13.0	11.4	10.6	11.3	11.0	10.6	10.9	11.1	10.7
3 *Indirect taxes*	*60.9*	*61.0*	*60.9*	*59.9*	*62.1*	*65.4*	*66.9*	*67.5*	*66.7*
a Customs	10.0	10.9	10.7	11.7	12.8	15.5	15.1	12.4	10.0
b Excise	27.4	27.7	28.5	27.3	28.1	28.5	28.3	30.8	32.7
c Sales tax	9.6	9.5	9.3	9.6	10.3	10.9	11.8	12.8	13.0
d Stamps	2.3	2.3	2.0	1.9	2.0	1.9	1.8	2.1	1.9
e Other	11.6	10.6	10.4	9.4	9.9	8.6	9.9	9.4	9.1
4 *Miscellaneous receipts*	*3.6*	*3.6*	*3.6*	*3.3*	*3.5*	*2.4*	*2.1*	*2.2*	*1.9*

Source: C.S.O. (1971), p. 17.

however, loses its force as agriculture gradually recovered by
the end of the 1960s, and current receipts as a share in national
income failed to resume their earlier upward climb.

The changing structure of current receipts (Table 4.12) is
revealing for two reasons, one theoretical, the other practical.
There is a theory of fiscal development, pioneered by Hinrichs,
which argues that, as economic growth occurs, the share of (a)
tax receipts in total receipts and (b) indirect taxes in total taxes
first of all increases, then reaches a maximum value and begins
to decline. The empirical basis of this theory is an international
cross-section comparison and a time-series analysis of Japanese
public finances.[15] If such a theory were accepted as valid, it
might also be taken to have policy implications. It might come
to be believed that conforming to the 'normal' tax structure
for the existing level of income was a pre-condition for further
income growth; or alternatively that the revenue structure need
not be a central policy concern because income growth would
'automatically' produce the required changes. It is therefore of
interest to note that the Indian evidence on income growth and
revenue structure changes conflicts with the evidence adduced
by Hinrichs. During the period of economic growth, that is
up to the end of the Third Plan, the tax receipts/total receipts
ratio and the indirect taxes/total taxes ratio remained virtually
constant. It is evident that the increase in these two ratios did
not take place until 1964/65 and after, once the economy was
heading into a deep recession and partial recovery thereafter.
Nor can this set of facts be described as the operation of the
Hinrichs relationship with a lag. The rising share of taxes in
receipts and of indirect taxes in tax revenue are both directly
attributable to the recession itself – through its effect in diminishing the base of income and corporation taxes and depress-
ing the government's income from property and the products
of its entrepreneurship. Similar arguments hold for Hinrichs'
proposition that indirect taxes on foreign trade contribute
a decreasing share in indirect taxes as the economy grows.
However plausible this may sound, the opposite was in fact
true of India in the 1960s. The economic growth of the Third
Plan sucked in imports of capital goods, components and

15 Hinrichs (1966).

raw materials over high tariff walls, while the 1965 cut-off of 'aid' at a time when foreign exchange reserves were very low led the Indian government to adopt a trade liberalisation policy, which in turn produced a declining trend in the yield of customs duties.[16]

Practical interest in the changing structure of current receipts arises because it highlights two sources of revenue which, despite the government's generally adequate performance in revenue-raising, were insufficiently exploited. Moreover, both of these sources are, as we have seen in our earlier discussion of the rationale of state accumulation, particularly crucial to the success of a policy of government-promoted capital accumulation. The state capitalist can theoretically accumulate faster than the private capitalist because of his ability to tax. Looking first at the taxation of the agricultural sector, we find in India that land revenue has grown very little in absolute terms and forms a secularly dwindling proportion of current receipts. The basis on which land revenue is levied has remained unchanged for many decades, and cesses on land revenue have been sporadic and small. Further, the product of other forms of taxation of agricultural incomes is small and geographically skewed towards the plantation states of Assam, Kerala and Tamil Nadu. Meanwhile, agricultural incomes have by no means been stagnant. Without venturing here into the subject of agricultural taxation, it may be asserted that if all income and wealth were taxed without regard to sectoral source, at prevailing rates, a non-negligible addition to current revenues would be forthcoming. But the government was never prepared to attempt even such a modest reform as this.

IV STAGNATION OF PUBLIC ENTERPRISE SURPLUSES

The second source of revenue which is being exploited below its potential is the operating surpluses of the departmental public enterprises. This is particularly damaging to the policy of state accumulation because these, and the surpluses of non-departmental enterprises, are theoretically *the* dynamic element in the process of accumulation, if we leave aside the possibility

16 Lakdawala and Nambiar (1972), pp. 39–40.

of credit financed capital creation. At the beginning of the 1960s, the doctrine that public enterprises should be planned to operate on a no-profit, no-loss basis was being abandoned, and the respectability of a policy of planned public enterprise profits was established in official eyes. Yet, by the end of the decade, the money contribution of public enterprises to current receipts was no higher than at the time of the Third Plan, despite considerable inflation in the interim. Yet the bulk of the investment in these enterprises is relatively recent. The public sector in India is not, like the public sector in several European countries, the inheritor of declining industries from which the private sector can no longer extract a profit, except in the case of unprofitable textile mills.

Of course, one must beware of asserting that, even with newly established ventures, a profit *must* be forthcoming if the investment is to be worthwhile in terms of national welfare. The equating of prices with marginal variable costs, the economist's welfare maximizing rule, can under certain assumptions produce public enterprises deficits, and price discrimination is often practised to minimize deficits. But since, in India, no attempt is made to calculate marginal variable costs, and cross-subsidization within enterprises is endemic, it would be the purest accident if the low and declining levels of surpluses turned out to be theoretically justifiable on microeconomic resource allocation arguments.[17] Yet if the microeconomic calculus is ignored, as it was in India by and large,[18] on the ground that it is irrelevant or unimportant, one is thrown back more strongly on to macroeconomic considerations, which point to the need for increasing public enterprise surpluses, with the aim of raising the level of national saving, after allowing for any reduction of personal and corporate saving as a result of higher prices charged to users of public enterprise goods and services.

It is possible to pinpoint some of the policies that have produced the poor financial performance of the departmental public enterprises. For this purpose, a broad distinction can be made between those of the states, of which the most impor-

17 Prest (1969), pp. 70–4.
18 U.N. (1979), p. 29–30.

tant are irrigation and electricity schemes and those of the central government, of which the most important is the railways. In irrigation and electricity, preference was given to large, high cost projects, such as multi-purpose river schemes and extensive rural electrification. These involved considerable managerial failures, such as lengthy administrative delays, poor construction planning and excessive stock holding. But, in addition, and more seriously, there has been either inability or unwillingness on the part of the authorities to insist on a remotely economic level of to consumers charges[19]. Where this situation is explicitly defended, it is on the basis of the need, in the interests of agricultural growth, to encourage the consumption of irrigation water and electricity. There may be other factors obstructing more widespread water application than the lack of a price incentive, however, and electricity can be consumed for many purposes besides agricultural operations. Further, there is little empirical evidence to show the precise production response to such measures. But the income distribution consequences of such a policy are easier to predict. A deficit on irrigation and electricity schemes represents a transfer of income to the existing consumers, the rural rich, from those who will pay the subsidies from general revenue: since increments to general revenue largely come from extra indirect taxes on articles of mass consumption, this kind of transfer in all probability makes the distribution of income more unequal.

The central government's policies with respect to the railways have been different. The large amount of investment since independence has been directed more to replacing and expanding the rolling stock than towards lengthening the route mileage, in other words towards capital formation which should have been quick-yielding in revenue terms. Again, there has been no reluctance to raise tariffs across the board at regular intervals. But, in spite of this, and the decision (difficult to defend in economic terms) to reduce the required depreciation provision from 3.7 to 3.2 per cent of capital-at-charge in 1967/68, the railways were able to contribute only $4\frac{1}{2}$ per cent of their capital-at-charge to general revenue in that year.[20]

19 Hone (1968b), pp. 1151–4.   20 Anon (1969), pp. 351–3.

Part of the railways' problem seems to arise from the persistence, despite some modification, of the traditional rate structure for different types of freight. High rated goods (high-value freight moving in small consignments) are particularly vulnerable to competition from road transport, while the goods for which road transport is still unsuitable (low-value, bulk shipments) are low-rated.[21] It also seems that passenger traffic is subsidized to some extent from freight receipts.[22] It is not so obvious in the case of the railways that its pricing policies have the simple result that 'public wealth makes an inadequate profit, and subsidizes the earnings of private wealth instead'.[23] There probably is an element of subsidy to private sector firms who are bulk users of industrial raw materials like iron and steel, coal, cement and petroleum, and (before their nationalization) to private traders in food grains. But, as noted, there is probably a subsidy to passengers, not all of whom will be engaged on business journeys. Further, another contributory factor to the railways' poor financial performance has been its chronic inability to control its operating costs, which are swollen by its lavish employment of labour. A profitable price policy without better cost control would make consumers of railway services shoulder the cost of the railways' employment policy – not a bad thing, perhaps, but the reverse of a subsidy to the earnings of private wealth.

The situation of the non-departmental enterprises is different again. Despite the vast variety of the economic tasks which they undertake, their aggregate performance in producing a reinvestible surplus is dominated by the performance of one industry – steel. The steel industry accounted for more than half of the total investment in the non-departmental enterprises to 1970, and its huge and persistent losses approximately balanced (more or less, in bad years or good) the profits made by a number of more competently managed non-departmental enterprises. The failure here, then, is a failure of government entrepreneurship. The problems of establishing and managing a complex of modern steel plants have over fifteen years outrun the entrepreneurial capabilities of the public

21 Owen (1968), pp. 38–40.
22 Prest (1969), p. 50.
23 Mirrlees (1968), p. 80.

sector. That is not to say that these problems will never be solved. But it does hold out the prospect that a great deal of the initial investment will prove to be infructuous, given that steel plants do not have infinite lives, and, even if they did, they would soon face technological obsolescence.

Apart from the basic difficulty that in some sectors the state simply lacks capitalistic skills, it is also true that, to the extent that the public sector either subsidizes the earnings of private wealth *or* multiplies low productivity jobs, it abandons the greatest advantage of public ownership, that additional public profits may be a direct means of raising the level of aggregate saving. The exploitation of that advantage is crucial to the success of an industrialization strategy, given the difficulty of pursuing a strategy of rapid accumulation via agriculture when the instruments for returning any sizeable share in the additional agricultural incomes to the government are, for political and other reasons, so feeble. Yet in India this opportunity was in the 1960s passed-up. The poor financial performance of public enterprise was not simply the result of the post-1965 recession, though this naturally compounded their difficulties. It was evident to the Venkataraman Committee on the state electricity industry which reported in 1964, and the Committee on Transport Policy and Coordination which reported in January 1966.

Can the failure, noted earlier, to increase public authorities' capital formation even in money terms after 1965/66 be construed as a deliberate response to this poor performance? Did the government deliberately begin to erode the public sector's leading role in investment because the current returns were so poor, because they saw no prospect of being able to improve them and because they anticipated that the (taxable) returns on private sector investment would be better? This question can be answered with reasonable confidence in the negative. The government has remained optimistic that the financial performance of the public enterprises can be improved in the near future by reforms intended to promote a higher standard of management. In relation to the non-departmental enterprises, recent reforms of this sort have included the ending of secondment of Indian Administrative Service officials as enterprise managers, accounting write-offs of accumulated losses and experiments with the device of sectoral public holding companies. As one authority concludes, 'the public sector has come to stay in India ... [T]he recent hesitation in public sector investment is mainly due to budgetary problems and lack of a long-term investment programme, rather than to lack of faith in the sector.'[24]

24 Medhora (1973), p. 29.

5

Public expenditure and the industrial recession

The examination of general trends in public expenditure and other public finance variables in the previous chapter showed the strong contrast between the first and the second half of the decade. Broadly, the first five years might be characterized as years of growth, and the second five years as years of recession. The event which marks the boundary between these two sub-periods is the onset of severe drought in 1965.

It is natural to raise the question whether the drought of 1965–67 is to be regarded as an exogenous factor which directly caused the economic recession after 1965, to which levels of public expenditure were then adjusted, or whether public expenditure played a more active role in provoking the recession. The extent to which government policy was itself responsible for provoking the recession was debated publicly in India in the late 1960s. Positions on the question have more recently been taken by economists analysing the 1966 devaluation of the rupee.[1] The early debate was inconclusive because of the non-availability of relevant statistics (as will be argued at length in this chapter). The later foreign trade economists have also not gone very fully into the question, since to them it is of peripheral interest. With the later and more refined public expenditure statistics now available, it is opportune to re-open the debate. That is the aim of this chapter.

I THE POST-1965 RECESSION AND CAPITAL GOODS

The severe effect of the 1965 drought on agricultural output, and especially the output of foodgrains, is shown in Table 5.1.

[1] Bhagwati and Srinivasan (1975), pp. 116–18; Nayyar (1976), pp. 277–9.

TABLE 5.1 *Index numbers of agricultural 1960/61 to 1969/70 Output, (1949/50 = 100)*

	Weight	1960/61	1965/66	1969/70
I Foodgrains	(66.9)	137.1	121.3	168.6
II Non-foodgrain output	(33.1)	152.6	157.0	175.3
III Total agricultural output	(100.0)	142.2	133.1	170.8

Source: Ministry of Finance, Economic Survey, 1971/72, pp. 78–9, Table 1.4.

The fall in the industrial growth rate was also dramatic, from an average of 9 per cent a year (1960–65) to a mere 3 per cent (1965–70). Both industrial and the slower agricultural growth of the years since 1950 had demonstrated marked unevenness.[2] Even so, the crisis of both sectors in the mid sixties was of outstanding severity.

Over the previous fifteen years it had been usual to argue that bad harvests directly reduced industrial growth. The direct impact of harvest failure on industry could be traced through in a number of ways. Harvest failure restricted the supply and raised the prices of industry's wage-good, i.e. foodgrains, and of industry's agriculture-derived raw materials. The wage-good effect threatens a serious fall in real wages, which in turn may have one or several labour-reducing effects on industry – the physical performance of existing workers may be eroded, industrial unrest may escalate, and (in the absence of money illusion) recruitment will be discouraged. If, to avoid any of these consequences, industrialists raise money wages in the attempt to maintain constant real wages for their labour despite the rise in foodgrain prices, they increase their money costs of production without there being any compensating increase in the prices of the goods sold by the industry to final demand. This is equivalent to an upward shift in the industrialist's variable cost curve. Such an upward shift would induce a profit-maximizing producer to reduce his output from his existing plant and prune his investment plans.

If the government tries to prevent the initial supply reduction

2 Desai (1975), p. 16.

and price rise of foodgrains by using imports to augment the lowered domestic supply, industrial growth is slowed down by another brake mechanism. Assuming that the overall supply of foreign exchange is limited, the purchase of imported foodgrains will reduce the foreign exchange available for the import of spare parts and components (so-called 'maintenance imports') required by industry to keep up its present level of production. So, whether by loss of labour, by a rise in money costs relative to money revenues, or by restriction of the supply of maintenance imports, bad harvests lead to a slackening of industrial production.

Bad harvests had a further impact on the demand side. They reduced the demand for the final goods of industry, assuming their prices remain unchanged. This is because they divert income towards those who market agricultural output, the bigger landlords and richer peasants, whose marginal propensity to consume industrial goods is less than those in the non-agricultural sector from whom the income is diverted.

It seemed obvious that the post-1965 recession should also be attributed to these direct mechanisms. However, an examination of the composition of industrial production, as in Table 5.2, suggests that an explanation in terms of these direct causal mechanisms is inadequate.

Industrial output that is sold to final demand can, subject to two qualifications, be split up into manufactured consumer

TABLE 5.2 *Index numbers of industrial production 1961 to 1970 (1960 = 100)*

Industrial category	Weight	1961	1965	1970
I Mining and quarrying	(9.7)	105	132	149
II Manufacturing of which	(84.9)	109	154	175
a Consumer goods	(32.6)	107	124	154
b Intermediate goods	(35.9)	108	151	174
c Capital goods	(11.0)	117	237	197
III Electricity generated	(5.4)	116	191	334
IV All industries	*(100.0)*	*109*	*154*	*181*

Source: Ministry of Finance, *Economic Survey, 1971/72*, pp. 90–1, Table 1.11, from which index numbers have been derived.

goods and manufactured capital goods. The relevant index numbers are on rows II(a) and II(c) in Table 5.2. From these index numbers, comparative growth rates can be calculated, as in Table 5.3. Before going on to draw conclusions from these comparative growth rates, the qualifications that limit their usefulness must be clearly stated. Some proportion of the 15 per cent of industrial output arising from mining, quarrying and electricity generation is sold to final demand, but available information does not allow it to be estimated, nor its split between consumption and investment in each of the relevant years. In addition, the classification of manufacturing output by end use cannot be absolutely precise, since certain types of manufactures (e.g. tyres, desks, typewriters) are physically capable of being used interchangeably for intermediate, investment or consumption purposes. The growth rates in Table 5.3, therefore, give only a rough approximation to the growth rates of *all* capital and consumer goods.

As one might expect, manufactured intermediate goods output grew at the same rates as total manufacturing output. But manufactured output sold to consumption and investment final demand grew at dramatically different rates from each other. Manufactures for consumption grew at about 4½ per cent a year *both before and after 1965*: their growth rate was apparently quite unaffected by the post-1965 recession. In the starkest contrast, manufactures for investment under the Third Plan expanded at almost 20 per cent annually, but after 1965 actually contracted at a rate of 3 per cent a year. The plain inference to

TABLE 5.3 *Growth rates of industrial production, 1960 to 1970.*

		Growth rates (annual percentages compounding)		
		1960–1965	*1965–1970*	*1960–1970*
II a	Manufactured consumer goods	4.4	4.4	4.4
II c	Manufactured capital goods	18.8	(−)2.8	7.0
IV	All industries	9.0	3.1	6.1

Source: calculated from Table 5.2 above.

be made from the official figures is that the post-1965 recession is exclusively a phenomenon of the capital goods industry, plus those intermediate industries (such as iron and steel castings) on which it draws for its inputs. Any explanation of the recession must explain this spectacular crisis of the capital goods industry, if it is to be plausible.

This diagnosis is supported obliquely by an analysis of industrial growth with respect to inter-sectoral linkages. From Table 5.4, it is evident that industries with forward linkage to the transport sector exhibit the same kind of erratic growth path as has been seen to be characteristic of manufactures for investment. After leading with rapid growth rates, transport-related industries after 1965 become a lagging sector, showing an absolute decline in output in 1970 over 1965. Obviously, in spite of their similar weight in total industrial production, 'capital goods manufactures' and 'transport-related industries' are far from identical categories. Yet it is reasonable to suggest that their area of overlap – the railway equipment, lorry and bus industries – is responsible for the similar behaviour of their growth rates, rather than the coincidental flagging of the two sets of industries that fall into only one category.

The other significant point which emerges from a comparison of Table 5.3 with Table 5.4 is that the flagging growth of agriculture-based industries after 1965 is *not* reflected in the growth rate of manufactures for consumption. Thus the recession in the agriculture-based consumer industries such as tex-

TABLE 5.4 *Index numbers of industrial output by linkage categories, 1962–70 (1960 = 100)*

	Weights	1962	1965	1970
I Agriculture-based industries	(45.74)	108	120	135
II Transport-related industries	(10.89)	140	185	170
III Other industries	(42.28)	134	175	228
IV All industries	*(100.0)*	*120*	*154*	*181*

Source: Ministry of Finance, *Economic Survey, 1971/72*, from graph opposite p. 28.

tiles and food-processing (tea, sugar, vanspati, etc.), was offset by accelerated growth of modern light manufactures, such as radios, bicycles and motor scooters. At worst, the effect of harvest failures in restricting the supply of agricultural raw materials prevented an *acceleration* in the growth rate of manufactures for consumption.

II PUBLIC EXPENDITURE AND THE DEMAND FOR CAPITAL GOODS

The fact that, in the industrial sector, the recession was largely a crisis of the capital goods industries (and those industries with forward linkages to them) is highly significant to the subject of this study. It is significant because the supply capacity of the Indian capital goods industries, as it existed in the mid 1960s, had to a great extent been created by the expanding programme of public sector investment over the previous decade. The obvious question is whether, during the recession, the government was responsible for the starvation of its own progeny. Further, one might enquire whether, if indeed it was so responsible, this kind of economic infanticide could have been avoided. If it were to seem inevitable for any reason, one would have to conclude that the state accumulation policy is not feasible, even in principle. On the other hand, it might appear to be the result of an avoidable error in policy, in which case a clear definition of the type of error involved may be useful to other countries who wish to accumulate capital via the state.

Initially we must ask how far government expenditure policies were responsible for either precipitating or prolonging the industrial recession which India experienced in the late 1960s. In the public debate which took place in 1968, the chief protagonist, Medhora, argued that public expenditure had been 'tapering off' in the four years preceding 1967/68, and cited a variety of indicators to establish this.[3] He selected four types of time-series data as his evidence:

(i) central and state government expenditure on revenue account (deflated by the index of wholesale prices) which showed an absolute decline in 1964/65 over 1963/64;

3 Medhora (1968a).

(ii) central government exhaustive expenditure on commodities and services at current prices, showing an absolute fall in 1964/65 over 1963/64; and on wages and salaries at 1960/61 prices, showing a small rise in 1964/65 over 1963/64;

(iii) central government gross fixed capital formation at current prices, showing significant absolute increases in 1964/65 over 1963/64. It is stated that a 'tapering off of outlay on assets ... would also be true of state governments', although no figures were given;

(iv) railway expenditure 'at 1960/61 prices', showing a slight fall in 1964/65 compared with 1963/64.

S. Paul accepted these data as the relevant basic data but disputed Medhora's interpretation of it. 'To see what in fact has happened,' Paul wrote, 'the decline in government expenditure must be viewed against the decline in national income ... There is no evidence to show that a decline in the [government's] share set off recessionary tendencies if we accept 1966 as the year in which these tendencies became pronounced.'[4]

Although this exchange is helpful in setting out some of the basic issues, the position of neither participant is free from error. To make further progress towards settling the issue, it is necessary to spell out what these errors are. C.S.O. data on national income, which became available after Paul had written, make it clear that he is not correct in claiming that no decline in the government's share of national income took place before 1966. These figures, reproduced in Table 5.5 below, indicate a fall in this share from 12.4 to 11.7 per cent in 1964/65. This mistake arises from his uncritical acceptance of the adequacy of Medhora's data. Paul can also be criticized for not making it clear that a government share which does not decline only rules out a decline in absolute magnitudes of public expenditure as long as national income is constant or rising. Medhora, however, is doubly in error when he stated, in a rejoinder to Paul, that it 'is correct to say that the Government's share in the national income has not declined. But what industry is concerned with, is not the proportionate share of the Government in national income but the absolute amount of government

4 Paul (1968), p. 1341.

TABLE 5.5 *Changes in public sector product, 1961/62 to 1968/69*

	1960/61	1961/62	1962/63	1963/64	1964/65	1965/66	1966/67	1967/68	1968/69
1 Net domestic product at factor cost, 1960/61 prices (Rs. cr.)	13 366	13 859	14 155	14 958	16 061	15 173	15 392	16 842	17 233
Percentage change		+3.7	+2.1	+5.7	+7.4	−5.5	+1.4	+9.4	+2.3
2 Percentage share of public sector in 1, current prices	10.6	11.3	12.2	12.4	11.7	13.2	12.7	12.1	13.6
3 Of which									
a Government admin.	5.5	5.9	6.2	6.2	6.0	6.6	6.4	6.2	6.9
b Departmental enterprises	3.9	4.1	4.2	4.3	3.8	4.3	4.0	3.6	3.9
c Non-departmental enterprises	1.2	1.3	1.8	1.9	1.9	2.3	2.3	2.3	2.8

4 Estimated public sector product (Rs. cr., 1960/61 prices)	1419	1566	1727	1854	1879	2002	1955	2038	2344
5 Of which									
a Government admin.	735	818	878	927	964	1001	985	1044	1189
b Departmental enterprises.	522	568	595	643	610	652	616	606	672
c Non-departmental enterprises	162	180	255	284	305	349	354	387	483
6 Percentage change in estimated real public sector product (year-to-year)		+10.4	+10.3	+7.4	+1.4	+6.5	−2.3	+4.2	+15.0
a Government admin.		+11.3	+7.3	+5.6	+4.0	+3.8	−1.6	+6.0	+13.9
b Departmental enterprises		+8.8	+4.8	+8.1	−5.1	+6.9	−5.5	−1.6	+10.9
c Non-departmental enterprises		+11.1	+41.6	+11.4	+7.4	+14.4	+1.4	+9.3	+24.8

purchases from it [which], as my figures show, has declined.'[5]
As we have noted, there was some decline in the government
share in 1964/65: but, if there had not been, it would have
been impossible, at a time of economic growth, such as the
years before 1965/66 were, for the absolute level of government expenditure to have fallen.

		Change in 'Y'	
	Positive	*Zero*	*Negative*
Change in 'g'			
Positive	G rises	G rises	Indeterminate
Zero	G rises	G constant	G falls
Negative	Indeterminate	G falls	G falls

If the government's share is g, which equals $(^G/_Y) \times 100$, the
relationships between changes in g, Y and G over time can be
summarized in the simple matrix set out above. From this it is
clear that Medhora's case, of a constant g, and a fall in G, is
only possible when national income is actually declining –
although such a decline was no part of his case, and, empirically, the opposite of the truth. This reasoning tells us that
widespread absolute decreases in public expenditure are
unlikely to have occurred, although, given the new evidence
of a fall in g in 1964/65, not impossible in some areas in that
year.

The real weakness of Medhora's contribution lies in his basic
statistics, which Paul accepted at their face value. Three criticisms may be made. First, changes in bdugetary figures do not
automatically reflect changes in public demand on resources,
because they include accounting adjustments between different
pockets of the public purse. Only data of type (ii) and (iii) are
derived from an economic reclassification of expenditure. They
would not be subject to this criticism, but they refer to expenditure of the central government only, which is no more than
half of total expenditure. Second, the deflation of expenditure
seems to have been done on a highly arbitrary basis, some
series being deflated by the wholesale price index and some not,

5 Medhora (1968b).

without any apparent rhyme or reason. All series require deflation if the aim is to monitor changes in the volume of goods and services being absorbed by the government. Third, since the industrial crisis was predominantly a crisis of the capital goods industries, particular attention should be focussed on government capital expenditure: the absence of any data on the state governments or the non-departmental enterprises is a serious defect in the statistical basis of Medhora's case.

Table 5.5 focusses attention on the national accounts figures for the public sector between 1961/62 and 1968/69, rather than on budgetary figures which are, as they stand, misleading indicators of demand. Even these, however, do not resolve *directly* the question of the failure of public sector demand. The starting point is two sets of figures:

(a) Absolute figures of net domestic product at factor cost, valued *at 1960/61 prices:*
(b) The share of the public sector as a whole, and the three major sub-units of the public sector, in net domestic product at *current prices.*

The source of these figures is C.S.O. (1971), Table 5, line 15 for (a), and Table 7.1, line 5 for (b). It is unlikely that the share of the public sector in national income at constant prices is exactly the same as the share of the public sector in national income at current prices. There was probably some divergence between the size and timing of price rises for goods and services bought by the public sector and of price rises for goods and services bought by the private sector. There are no adequate studies of this divergence, but, in their absence, it does not seem unreasonable to make the assumption that it was not particularly large. Using this assumption, one can estimate with reasonable approximation the absolute size of the public sector's year-by-year contribution to net domestic product by applying the public sector's current price share to the total product at 1960/61 prices. The results of this procedure are shown in lines 4 to 5 of the table, while lines 6 and 7 express the percentage change each year compared with the previous year.

These results confirm the expectation that absolute decreases in public expenditure are the exception rather than the rule.

The trend in the years before the harvest failures is one of deceleration in public expenditure growth. In the three years 1962/
63 to 1964/65, the rate of growth of public spending was always
less than the previous year, though, taking public spending as
a whole, no absolute falls are evident. The same trend is evident
in spending by government administration as for total public
sector spending.

As has been argued previously, the industrial recession was a
problem pre-eminently of the capital goods sector, and particularly that part of the capital goods sector with forward
linkages into transport. In India, this means those industries
supplying equipment to the railways (a public sector monopoly
and a monopsony buyer) and the road transport industries,
in which large state transport enterprises operate alongside
private sector firms. Railways alone are the potential pur-
chaser of one third to one half of capital goods output and are
therefore an extremely important customer of the metal and
engineering industries. Changes in real total public expenditure is thus too highly aggregative a concept to be fully relevant
to an analysis of failing public demand for capital goods. It
would be more relevant to examine (i) the outlay of departmental enterprises – for this is what the public sector transport
industries are – and (ii) public sector expenditure on capital
goods – i.e. gross fixed capital formation in the public sector.
These categories overlap one another partially; and the area of
overlap (iii) the capital outlay of departmental enterprises is
the most relevant indicator of the three. The relevance of (i)
can be criticized on the grounds that public purchase of commodities for current consumption has only an indirect and
significantly lagged effect on the demand for capital goods. The
relevance of (ii) can be criticized on the ground that much of the
physical capital formation done by government administrative
departments consists of the construction of offices, houses and
other buildings, which creates industrial demand only on the
narrow front of cement, steel structurals and furniture. But
neither of these limitations applies to indicator (iii).

Indicator (i), the change in estimated real product of departmental enterprises is given in Table 5.5, line 6 (b). Prior to
1965/66, this does not exhibit a steady slowing down in growth;
instead year-to-year changes are erratic, but include an absolute

TABLE 5.6 Capital finance account of public authorities at current prices, 1960/61 to 1968/69

	1960/61	1961/62	1962/63	1963/64	1964/65	1965/66	1966/67	1967/68	1968/69
1 Gross fixed capital formation (Rs. cr.)	716	753	899	1042	1167	1257	1223	1210	1330
2 Annual increment		+37	+146	+143	+125	+90	−34	−13	+120
3 2 as a percentage		+5.2	+19.4	+15.9	+12.0	+7.7	−2.7	−1.1	+9.9
of which:									
4 G.F.C.F. of departmental enterprises	438	453	554	652	730	782	734	711	781
5 Annual increment		+15	+101	+98	+78	+52	−48	−23	+70
6 5 as a percentage		+3.4	+22.3	+17.7	+12.0	+7.1	−6.1	−3.1	+9.8
and									
7 G.F.C.F. of administrative departments	278	300	345	390	437	475	489	499	549
8 Annual increment		+22	+45	+45	+47	+38	+14	+10	+50
9 8 as a percentage		+7.9	+15.0	+13.0	+12.0	+8.7	+2.9	+2.0	+10.0

Source: C.S.O. (1971), Table 10, p. 20.

decrease in level in 1964/65 compared with the previous year. Indicators (ii) and (iii) are shown in Table 5.6, lines 3 and 6. Even using current price data, both clearly show a gradual deceleration in growth from 1962/63 to 1965/66. The deceleration in real terms was even more pronounced, as the rate of change in the general level of prices was increasing at this period. Evidence of the quickening pace of inflation is given by the all-India wholesale price index, as set out in Table 5.7.

Thus the case for a 'tapering off' in public sector demand some years before the serious harvest failures of 1965/66 and 1966/67 is established, both in terms of public expenditure in its widest sense and in the specially relevant area of departmental enterprises capital formation. But tapering off must be understood as a continuous decline in a positive rate of growth, rather than (as Medhora at times claims) falls below previously attained levels. This deceleration is consistent with (a) continuing economic growth and (b) a rising share of the public sector in national income (except for 1964/65). Between 1961/62 and 1964/65, the growth of the public sector was slowing down, while the growth of national income (both in real terms)

TABLE 5.7 *Index numbers of wholesale prices in India (new series), 1961/62 to 1970*

Year	Industrial raw materials	Machinery and transport equipment	Manu-factures	All commo-dities	Per-centage change
1961/62	100	100	100	100	
1962	98.1	103.5	102.4	104.2	+4.2
1963	98.6	107.2	104.2	108.0	+3.6
1964	111.7	110.8	107.5	119.3	+10.5
1965	127.7	116.1	115.3	129.1	+8.2
1966	151.8	124.1	125.5	144.5	+11.9
1967	161.1	131.1	130.9	166.2	+15.0
1968	152.7	132.3	132.7	165.3	−0.6
1969	175.4	134.7	140.9	168.8	+2.1
1970	193.7	145.2	151.7	179.2	+6.2

Source: *Statistical Abstract, India, 1970*, Table 162B, p. 464.

was speeding up, with the result that the public sector share in the economy shrank in 1964/65.

On the basis of these results, it would seem that a different evaluation of the government's fiscal policy from that offered by Professors Bhagwati and Srinivasan is called for. Bhagwati and Srinivasan conclude that 'both the deceleration in total [government] outlays and the compositional shift [away from capital expenditure] ... were to be traced to two causes: one exogenous and major and the other endogenous and *only minor*'. In their view, 'the exogenous and principal factor was... the agricultural drought'.[6] They deduce from economic policy statements that the government acted as it did because it 'was afraid that any sustenance of the trend expansion in outlays would accentuate the rise in food prices that followed from the drought'. However, because the issue is for them a subsidiary one in the analysis of the 1966 devaluation, these conclusions are reached from a brief inspection of figures on the overall budgetary deficit and the money supply with the public in 1965/66 and several subsequent years. However, an analysis of the relevant series of public expenditure for the years before 1965/66 as well as after 1965/66 shows that the demand generated by the public sector was slackening off for some years before the dramatic harvest failures of the mid sixties. The arrival of the drought, therefore, can only have persuaded the government to reinforce a government-induced deflation which had already by that time begun.

Thus, to the two direct mechanisms by which bad harvests undermine industrial growth, a third and indirect one must be added. It is the deflationary reaction of governments concerned about the rate of price rises. But the important point is that this deflationary reaction was superimposed on a drift into deflation which is discernible in government expenditure policies in the last few years of the Third Plan.

If the public expenditure figures showed that the government was merely reacting rationally to external circumstances beyond its control, confidence in its ability to pursue a policy of state accumulation would not be weakened. Most governments have, at one time or another, to postpone or modify their plans

6 Bhagwati and Srinivasan (1975), p. 117.

because of unforeseen natural adversity. But that interpretation seems, in the light of the foregoing analysis, excessively flattering to the capabilities of the government. That a government whose primary economic objective was the building up of a 'modern' industrial sector should allow its own capital goods purchasing programme to lose its growth momentum, and then to fall into absolute decline, demonstrates, at the least, a certain curious absent-mindedness.

Of course, during the Third Plan itself, certain adverse external circumstances occurred, which might be pleaded in mitigation. The timing of the Sino-Indian border war for the middle of the Third Plan was obviously fortuitous. The concomitant foreign exchange crisis was partly a consequence of the war, and partly a result of inadequate management by the government of the foreign exchange situation. However, having said that, one must note the failure to set or keep to year-by-year targets for the realisation of the total Plan targets. The phasing and sequence of expansion are of crucial significance for the achievement of balanced growth. Where, as in India, there are potential bottlenecks (like marketed food grains and foreign exchange) which could cripple economic growth, where the private sector is inefficient and unresponsive to certain kinds of profitable opportunity, and where public investment is the chosen engine of expansion, the timing of public outlays as between the earlier or later years of the Plan cannot be treated as a matter of indifference, as it was in the Indian Third Plan. The imbalances that arise do not act as signals and incentives to private entrepreneurship, à la Hirschman.[7] Instead, the economy simply loses the momentum of growth, and the task of recapturing that momentum is made harder.

Even after the drought had begun, the government acted hesitantly and with a poor sense of timing in its management of its own demands on the economy. Perhaps unavoidably, it could not cut its demand sufficiently at the onset of the crisis in 1965/66, so that its share in national income jumped to 13.2 per cent in that year compared with 11.7 per cent in the previous year. In 1966/67, a small rise in national income was accompanied by an absolute decline in public expenditure.

7 Hirschman (1958), p. 65–70

In 1957/68, a major recovery of 9 per cent in national income was matched by an increase of only 4 per cent in public expenditure. In 1968/69, the further small growth (by 2 per cent) of national income was matched by a very large (15 per cent) growth in public spending. Thus the share of the public authorities in these three years fluctuated from 12.7, to 12.1, to 13.6 per cent. The government was not able either to hold the public authorities' share constant or to expand it steadily. Part of the difficulty may have resulted from the financial calendar which is used. A financial year which runs from April to March is appropriate to agricultural economies under European climatic conditions, but not an agricultural economy, like India's, in which the short-run performance of agriculture is determined by the adequacy of the July–September monsoon. A Diwali budget for a financial year running from November to October might improve the chances of achieving particular objectives concerning the public sector share in national income.[8]

The overall conclusions to be derived from this chapter can be summed up as follows. The gradual slackening of public sector demand for some years before the dramatic harvest failures of the mid sixties indicates that the industrial recession was not merely a consequence of that particular act of God. Nor was the stagnation of public investment merely a reaction to the sudden, swift deterioration of the agricultural situation. This makes it easier to explain why the recession was not automatically succeeded by recovery once the better harvests of the late 1960s were realized. It is too sweeping to claim that 'the widespread belief that India can stimulate industrial growth by emphasizing the agricultural sector . . . represents a misunderstanding of the processes of Indian growth'.[9] But it is true that only about one third of industrial output is sold to the agricultural sector, and that high agricultural output can be achieved 'through the activities of a limited part of the Indian agricultural establishment'.[10] Thus short-run industrial recovery requires a government decision, at the appropriate time, to make a new start on the continuous expansion of its own

8 A.R.C. (1968a), p. 4; cf. Raj (1967), p. 583.
9 Hone (1968a), pp. 149–57.
10 Malenbaum (1971), p. 174.

demand for the output of those capital goods industries which its own past investments have created.

This logic did not escape the government, or at least some of its more thoughtful members and officials. In 1967, L. K. Jha, then head of the Prime Minister's secretariat, succeeded in persuading both the Prime Minister and the Finance Minister that it was desirable that the Railways Board should place additional orders for capital equipment. But the government's suggestion to this end was successfully resisted by the Railways Board. Its argument was that the existing rolling stock was not then fully utilized, and that additional investment which merely added to an existing surplus of equipment would not yield extra revenue and thus would contravene its obligation to act as a commercial undertaking.[11]

The conflict between macroeconomic objectives and the commercial autonomy of public enterprises is a familiar one in the annals of government attempts at economic management. The problem is that, to the extent that the state induces its public enterprises to behave indistinguishably from private enterprises (apart from the deposit of profit into public rather than private hands), it forgoes its potential ability to regulate the anarchy of accumulation. An effective state accumulation policy requires that this particular intra-public-sector conflict be settled in favour of the government, because it should be, as it was in this instance, taking both a less myopic and a more comprehensive view of accumulation. In fact, however, the government backed off, and a subordinate objective, the short-run profitability of a particular enterprise, was allowed to take priority over the requirements of state accumulation.

11 Private communication from L. K. Jha.

6

The degree of public expenditure centralization

I CHANGES IN PUBLIC EXPENDITURE CENTRALIZATION

As long as attention focusses on the Indian *national* economy, 'the government' tends to be thought of as a homogeneous institution with a single set of objectives and a single set of policy instruments for their realization. The assumption of a homogeneous government is a considerable simplification even for states, like the United Kingdom, where government is highly centralized. But for India, where a geographically fragmented civil society compelled the adoption of federal government as colonial rule was brought to an end, to imagine that government is homogeneous is wholly inappropriate. A study of India's state accumulation policy, therefore, which failed to come to terms with the different kinds of governments which operate in a federation would have rather little to recommend it.

This elementary proposition needs emphasis only because the majority of economists who have written about India have a marked preference both for the use of nationwide data and for the careful avoidance of any explicit consideration of politics.[1] Because of the numerous data problems involved in making a worthwhile state-level analysis, and because the subject of public expenditure falls in the curious no-man's-land between economics and politics as they are conventionally treated, public spending under a federal government is a subject where beaten paths are few, and not always very reliable. Perhaps the most thorough recent study of Indian states' finances has been described by its author himself as 'an exercise which

1 Franda (1970), pp. 206–7.

makes one familiar with all the landmarks ... but which is obviously inadequate for those keen to go into details'.[2]

It is indeed vital to go into details. If there is one theme which recurs in the more critical recent contributions to the debate on the 'determinants' of public expenditure, it is the need to disaggregate public spending data by level of government, as well as by economic category and function.[3] In what follows, the data have been disaggregated as far as this can be done. Data difficulties have been described, to allow the reader to make his own judgements of their reliability. Overall, the aim is to set out fully what seem to be the fiscal facts, and then to assess alternative interpretations of them.

It should be emphasized at the outset that we are *not* concerned here with public finance in the context of *regional economics*. In the first place that would require a prolonged discussion on the criteria for defining economic regions. When the Planning Commission attempted a regional division of India, based on topography, soils, climate, geological formations, land resources, irrigation and cropping patterns and availability of mineral resources, they produced a map quite different from the map of statewise political divisions. In only four instances (Assam, West Bengal, Gujarat and Punjab) did the Planning Commission's proposed economic regions coincide or nearly coincide, with state boundaries.[4] Of course, one might quarrel with the chosen criteria, arguing that greater weight should have been given to indicators of human, as opposed to indicators of physical, geography. But even so, it remains doubtful if a case could be made for regarding the states as economic regions. The present writer has argued for the weak proposition that statewise analysis is likely to be a better guide to regional differences than zonal analysis, that is, breakdown by groups of three or four states.[5] But this argument, though plausible, cannot be proved as a *general* proposition, since it is quite possible to construct imaginary cases which show the opposite. Whether it holds good in the specific case of India can only be known by actually comparing the coefficients of variation of key indicators for both statewise and regionwise data, and then for zonal and regionwise data. This would in-

2 Venkataraman (1968), p. 216.   3 E. g. Bird (1970), pp. 192–3.
4 Planning Commission (1964), Map 1.   5 Toye (1973), p. 262.

volve the use of district-by-district figures of the chosen indicators for the whole of India. Their absence is probably the reason why such an elaborate exercise never seems to have been done and why economists helplessly continue to identify 'statewise' and 'regional'.[6]

But, even if the states are rather arbitrarily accepted as surrogate regions, a second problem remains. To measure the statewise distribution of total public expenditure requires a measure of the statewise distribution of central government spending. In part this is possible: for example, it is clear that central Plan outlay on industry has been concentrated in Bihar, Orissa, Madhya Pradesh and West Bengal.[7] But to get much beyond this, it is necessary to make assumptions such as that central Plan outlay on agriculture and social services are shared by states according to population, and that non-Plan expenditure has no spatial dimension at all.[8] To assume that expenditure has no spatial dimension is the same as assuming that pure public goods are being purchased. But both the proponents and the critics of public goods theory agree on its very limited empirical significance.[9] Further, the production of even pure public goods, as opposed to their consumption, does have a spatial significance, through secondary effects on incomes in the area where production is located.

No fresh attempt has been made here to attack the twin problems of the definition of regions and the distribution by regions of central government spending, because they are not relevant to our central theme. That theme is the spending behaviour of the different governments that coexist in the Indian federal scheme, during the period 1960 to 1970. The related question of the impact of their combined spending operations on the different regions of the country is one which, for the reasons indicated, cannot be taken up at this point.

Once the discussion is limited in this way, there remain two different perspectives from which the role of state governments in a federation may be viewed. Firstly, they may be seen as a group of roughly similar units jointly engaged in some form

6 Lakdawala, Alagh and Sarma (1974), pp. 4, 65.
7 Nath (1970), pp. 247–59.
8 Gupta (1973), p. 247; cf. Zahir (1972), p. 148.
9 Head (1973), p. 21; Margolis (1954), p. 185.

of interaction with the federal (central) government. Secondly, individual states may be seen in relation to other individual states, so that the contrasts that exist within the framework of rough similarity are identified. These two different perspectives, when applied to the study of public expenditure, raise two quite distinct questions. The first is the question of the degree of expenditure centralization, that is, whether the spending of the central government has grown relative to that of the states as a group, or vice versa. The second is the question of differences between states in the level and growth of their expenditure. To the first of these two questions we now turn. The second is examined in the following chapter.

It is a common textbook proposition that economic growth is accompanied by an expenditure 'concentration process', which increases the central government's share in total public expenditure.[10] This is really a vulgarization of a theory developed by Peacock and Wiseman from an examination of long-run expenditure trends in the U.K. It supposes that improvements in transport and communication during economic growth operate both to create a potential demand for more uniform standards of public provision and to alter the supply conditions for the provision of collective goods by creating potential economies of scale. These potentials are not realized until 'catastrophes' like major wars or depressions change the political landscape so drastically that local pressures for autonomy can be overridden.[11]

However one may judge this theory as an explanation of expenditure centralization in the U.K., the question here is its relevance to India. Its fundamental assumption seems to be that the process of expenditure concentration arises from the transfer of responsibilities from the lower to the higher level of government. The theory is an elaboration of the mechanism whereby such transfers occur. Of course, one may also doubt the relevance of the details of this mechanism. Why is evidence of economies of scale in government activities so hard to find in today's poor countries?[12] Is the defence of local autonomy in the provision of public services really an important political

10 E. g. Burkehead and Miner (1971), p. 255.
11 Peacock and Wiseman (1967), pp. 29–30.
12 Gandhi (1970), p. 158.

TABLE 6.1 *Percentage of government spending by states (Reddy), 1938–68*

Year	1938	1948	1958	1968
States' share (%)	50.1	46.0	48.3	50.3

Source: calculated from Reddy (1972), pp. 180–1, Table A-4.

value for them? But the prior question, if the Peacock and Wiseman theory is to be accepted, is surely, 'do such upward transfers of responsibility actually take place?'

K. N. Reddy has recently attempted to explore the fruitfulness of the total Peacock and Wiseman approach to public expenditure in the Indian context. Alas, his treatment of the question of expenditure centralization is cavalier to a degree. He is content merely to assert that 'the change of responsibility of expenditures [sic] or what Peacock and Wiseman call "concentration process" has been taking place over the period [1872–1968]'.[13] Since in the period of his study, expenditure was almost entirely centralized before 1922, that is obviously not so. Even if one uses Reddy's own statistics for the period after 1937, when the present federal system was born, they show no concentration process at work. (The appropriate data are set out in Table 6.1.)

These figures would settle the whole issue if they could be trusted for the purpose of making expenditure centralization comparisons. But unfortunately, they will not do, for three reasons:

(i) it is unlikely that double-counting has been avoided, since central government expenditure includes grants to state governments, although the expenditure thereby made possible will already be included on state government account;[14]

(ii) expenditure by local authorities below state government level is omitted, so that changes in the extent of fiscal devolution to local authorities may offset the measured changes in expenditure centralization;[15]

13 Reddy (1972), p. 10.
14 Reddy (1972), pp. 181–2.
15 Reddy (1972), pp. 14–15.

TABLE 6.2 *All states' expenditure as a percentage of total public authorities' expenditure, 1960–70*

All states' share of total expenditure %	1960/61	1961/62	1962/63	1963/64	1964/65	1965/66	1966/67	1967/68	1968/69	1969/70
Annual basis	56	57	52	46	48	51	48	52	56	57
5-year average			51					53		

Source: C.S.O. unpublished data.

142

(iii) no explicit recognition is given to the problem of defining 'the states', although they have undergone a number of
reorganizations.

The data used here are such that the deficiencies mentioned
in the previous paragraph can be overcome. The C.S.O. public
expenditure reclassification permits the separate identification
of intergovernmental transfers and their elimination to avoid
double-counting. In addition, the data cover all kinds of non-
commercial public authorities, and not merely the central and
state governments. Thus the spending of municipal authorities and *panchayati raj* bodies can be aggregated with that of the
state governments, and Union Territories spending aggregated
with that of the central government. Finally, because the data
can be disaggregated by individual states, one can be absolutely
clear which states are included in any particular 'all-states'
totals, which is a pre-condition of handling the problems
raised by changing state boundaries. On the other hand, the use
of expenditure data organized according to national accounts
conventions for measuring expenditure centralization does
involve certain problems of interpretation. These problems
are discussed in Appendix B.

If one simply compares the measured centralization ratios
for the two five-year periods 1960–5 and 1965–70, it appears
that the decade witnessed a certain degree of expenditure
decentralization. The states' share rises from 51 per cent to 53
per cent (see Table 6.2). But the year-by-year figures show that
the five-year averages do not summarize a steady tendency towards decentralization. On the contrary, they show that at the
beginning and the end of the decade the centralization ratio was
about the same, while a temporary, but marked, shift toward
expenditure concentration occurred in the years around
1963–4.

Changes in expenditure concentration can arise because of
unbalanced expansion of spending as between the programmes
for which different levels of government are responsible. But
a major drawback with the C.S.O. data on which Table 6.2
is based is that it cannot supply a breakdown of expenditure
by function and programme. In order to appreciate the reasons

TABLE 6.3 *Central and state government expenditure by programmes, 1960/61 to 1969/70*

(Percentages to total expenditure)

	1960/61	1965/66	1969/70
I *Central government*	47.3	51.7	44.2
A Revenue account	31.4	36.0	34.8
a *Development**	9.5	5.0	5.3
of which:			
(i) Education and scientific depts	2.6	1.9	2.0
(ii) Medical and public health	0.6	0.3	0.4
(iii) Agriculture and allied services	1.8	0.3	0.4
b *Non-development*	21.9	30.9	29.3
(i) Collection of taxes, etc.	0.9	0.6	0.6
(ii) Administrative services	2.4	2.0	2.6
of which: (a) general	0.7	0.5	0.4
(b) police	0.5	0.7	1.3
(iii) Defence (net)	10.0	16.4	14.4
(iv) Debt services	3.1	8.0	8.4
(v) Other	5.5	3.9	3.2
B Capital account	15.9	15.7	9.7
a *Development*	10.5	11.5	8.0
(i) Railways	3.6	5.3	1.4
(ii) Post and telegraph	0.5	0.7	0.5
(iii) Industrial development	3.7	3.2	4.5
(iv) Irrigation and multipurpose schemes	0.1	0.4	0.2
(v) Civil works	1.6	1.5	0.8
(vi) Other	1.1	0.4	0.5
b *Non-development*	5.5	4.2	1.7
(i) Defence	1.3	2.6	2.0
(ii) Currency, mint, printing	0.3	1.7	0.1
(iii) State trading (net)	1.4	(−)1.8	(−)0.4
(iv) Other	2.5	1.7	0.0
II *State governments*	52.7	48.3	55.8
A Revenue account	39.8	40.6	48.2
Development	23.0	23.7	26.2
(i) Education	7.9	8.0	10.2
(ii) Medical and public health	3.3	3.2	4.1
(iii) Agriculture and allied services	2.7	3.3	3.1

TABLE 6.3 *(continued)*

(Percentages to total expenditure)

	1960/61	1965/66	1969/70
(iv) Rural and community development	2.1	1.8	1.1
(v) Civil works	2.7	2.9	2.8
(vi) Industries	0.9	0.6	0.5
(vii) Irrigation (non-commercial)	3.5	1.4	0.7
(viii) Other	0.0	2.2	3.7
b *Non-development*	*16.8*	*16.9*	*22.0*
(i) Collection of taxes, etc.	2.7	1.7	1.9
(ii) Civil administration	6.7	5.9	6.1
(iii) Debt services	3.4	5.8	8.2
(iv) Famine and food subsidy	0.9	0.4	2.6
(v) Other	3.2	3.2	3.1
B Capital account	*12.9*	*7.7*	*7.6*
a *Development*	*11.9*	*9.0*	*7.5*
(i) Multipurpose river valley schemes	1.9	1.5	1.4
(ii) Irrigation and navigation	3.3	3.2	2.4
(iii) Agricultural improvement	0.1	0.3	—
(iv) Electricity schemes	1.0	(−)0.2	0.6
(v) Road transport	0.2	0.1	0.1
(vi) Building, roads, water	4.6	2.7	1.9
(vii) Industrial development	0.6	1.0	1.0
(viii) Other	0.1	0.1	0.2
b *Non-development*	*1.0*	*(−)1.4*	*0.1*
(i) State trading	0.4	(−)1.5	0.0
(ii) Zamindari compensation	0.6	0.1	0.1

Notes: Excluding grants to state and Union Territory governments and excluding capital grants for development purposes.

Sources: Reserve Bank of India, *Report on Currency and Finance* for 1967/68 and 1970/71.

for the brief burst of expenditure centralization in the early 1960s, it is necessary to have recourse to data compiled by the Reserve Bank of India. It should be emphasized that there are many underlying conceptual differences between spending figures on a national accounts basis and on the basis used by the R.B.I. They are too numerous and technical even to summarize here. It may be mentioned, though, that the R.B.I. basis will understate the state governments' share in expenditure because it excludes the self-financed spending of local authorities which we have included as part of state government spending. As Table 6.3 shows, however, despite the conceptual differences, the R.B.I. data does confirm, in broad terms, the changes in expenditure centralization which have already been noted from Table 6.2. Thus some reliance can be placed on the changes in the R.B.I. data's functional categories.

The reasons for the shift towards expenditure concentration in the years around 1963/64 may thus be fairly readily inferred. The most important is the very rapid expansion of the central defence budget during and immediately after the Sino-Indian border war of 1962/63. While this happened, the central government maintained the momentum of its capital development programmes, in the sense of ensuring them a constant proportion of the growing total of public expenditure. In particular, the railways were permitted to go ahead with a large investment programme. Obviously, in this situation some restraint was required to prevent other programmes from growing as fast as total expenditure. The restraint was felt partly, but not entirely, by the state governments. The central government exercised an effective curb on the growth of its development spending on revenue account, but, apart from that, room to manoeuvre was created by restraining state expenditure on capital account. To the extent that capital spending was squeezed to allow a very rapid rise in defence spending without inflicting excessive damage on the centre's capital development programme, the ratio of expenditure centralization necessarily increased.

It may now be asked whether all this does not vindicate Peacock and Wiseman's account of the determination of the centralization ratio. After all, the period 1960–5 was a period of economic growth, defined as annual increases in output per head at constant prices.[16] Further, we have just shown that the centralization ratio did increase at this time, as the direct result of a 'catastrophe', the Sino-Indian border war. But this is not enough to establish that, for the situation with which we

16 C.S.O. (1971), Table 1, line 4.

are concerned, the Peacock and Wiseman explanation is the right one. At its roots lies, as has been noted, the idea that centralization occurs because of a persistent shifting of expenditure responsibilities from lower to higher levels of government in response to economic pressures. By contrast, what happened in India in the early 1960s was an increase in the centralization ratio arising from the (temporarily) more active prosecution of certain existing central government responsibilities (defence, infrastructural investment). There is no evidence that the economic growth experienced led to demands for more uniform provision of public services or made available economies of scale in their supply; and not much evidence, apart from a great deal of public rhetoric, that the catastrophe of war weakened the political defences of local autonomy. At the same time, however, it should be made clear that we are not claiming that the Peacock and Wiseman theory can be refuted with Indian data. It is a theory of the determination of centralization ratios in the long run. There is evidence, for some developed countries at any rate, that centralization ratios have different long-run and short-run determinants.[17] Since the existing Indian federal system dates from 1956, or 1937 at the earliest, the point is that long-run theories, like that of Peacock and Wiseman, are simply inappropriate for interpreting Indian experience. In future they might prove to have some validity, but the time to test them has not yet come.

Again, long-run theories which assume continuous economic growth are no guide in interpreting the short run, where discontinuities in economic growth loom large. Their implication is presumably that, in the absence of economic growth, the centralization ratio will remain constant. Yet it has already been shown that during the period of recession, 1965–70, when output per head at constant prices fluctuated about the level already attained, a process of expenditure decentralization set in, which reduced the centralization ratio, by 1969/70, to its value before the Sino-Indian border war. How is that to be explained? The discussion will proceed by examining the merits of two different lines of argument, the economic and the political.

17 Pryor (1968), pp. 72–3.

II POSSIBLE EXPLANATIONS CONSIDERED

The dominant economic features of the late 1960s were the twin harvest failures of 1965/66 and 1966/67. There are two major ways in which an economic emergency of this kind could be expected to affect public expenditure. In the first place, it is usual in a federation (and to this India is no exception) that, to the extent to which income distribution is pursued at all as a deliberate public policy, the responsibility for it lies more with the higher level than with the lower level of government. One might, arguably, attempt to justify this state of affairs by regarding relief of particular stricken areas as a form of public good with significant spill-over benefits.[18] Or one could simply explain it in terms of the residual nature of the central government's power and responsibilities, and its potential command of resources on a national scale. Government income redistribution through public expenditure is reflected in the economic category known as 'non-exhaustive current spending'.[19] As is clear from Table 6.4, which gives a broad breakdown of centre and states' spending by economic category, Indian current non-exhaustive spending is more highly centralized than either capital spending or current exhaustive spending. It might well be expected that, in an emergency such as the double harvest failure, the switch of expenditure towards income redistribution might lead to the greater centralization of public expenditure as a whole. Just such an effect seems to be visible in 1966/67.

But the 'income redistribution effect' on the overall expenditure centralization ratio was short-lived, and overwhelmed by another – the rapid decrease in the centralization ratio of capital expenditure, particularly after 1966/67. The second way in which a major economic emergency like the double harvest failure could be expected to affect public expenditure is by changing the balance desired by the governments between consumption and capital formation. For the economy as a whole, when consumption levels fall temporarily below the norm, it is rational to find future consumption (made possible by investment at the time of crisis) less attractive than it was previously

18 Cf. Head (1973), pp. 38–9.
19 Bator (1962), p. 17.

TABLE 6.4 *Centre and states' expenditure by economic category, 1960/61 to 1969/70*

(Percentages of total expenditure)

	1960/61	1961/62	1962/63	1963/64	1964/65	1965/66	1966/67	1967/68	1968/69	1969/70
I *Centre**	44.0	42.7	47.8	53.4	52.4	48.9	51.5	48.0	44.2	43.4
of which:										
a current exhaustive	19.8	20.0	22.6	29.1	27.0	26.8	26.3	26.0	27.7	25.8
b current non-exhaustive	8.6	8.7	9.1	7.8	7.7	8.9	14.3	12.1	10.3	10.1
c capital	15.6	14.0	16.1	16.5	17.7	13.2	10.9	9.9	6.2	7.5
II *States***	56.0	57.2	52.2	46.6	47.6	51.2	48.5	52.0	55.8	56.6
of which:										
a current exhaustive	31.7	31.6	28.1	25.5	26.6	28.3	28.0	29.1	32.2	32.9
b current non-exhaustive	6.7	7.4	6.4	5.9	5.8	6.4	6.8	7.2	8.2	8.8
c capital	17.6	18.2	17.7	15.2	15.2	16.5	13.7	15.7	15.4	14.9

Notes
* 'Centre' includes both central government and Union Territories.
** 'States' includes both state governments and sub-state-level local authorities.
Source: Unpublished C.S.O. data.

judged. In the private sector, slackening demand may be a sufficent deterrent to investment, but in the public sector some re-ordering of priorities away from investment will probably be required. The corollaries of this argument are (i) that, once consumption levels have been restored, the balance of advantage swings back again to favour investment and (ii) that, within the temporarily reduced volume of investments, it is desirable to discriminate in favour of quick-yielding forms and against forms with long gestation lags. There is no lack of evidence that, in the India of the late sixties, the government did find it increasingly difficult to resist the clamour for increased government employment and rises in cost of living bonuses (known in India as dearness allowance) for those already in government jobs.[20] But the point which should be made in the present context is that a temporary shift away from investment does not necessarily affect the degree of expenditure centralization – except on the assumptions that central capital projects are mainly slow-yielding, that states' capital projects are quick-yielding and that the governments concerned are in fact acting rationally.

But several aspects of Table 6.4 throw doubt on these assumptions. Although the central government began to cut back its capital programme in real terms in 1965/66, the big shift in the capital/consumption mix did not come until 1966/67. However, this shift was not the occasion for a dramatic change in the centralization of capital expenditure. A gradual decentralization of capital spending had begun in 1964/65, which continued through the period of acute crisis and its aftermath. Even if the states had had a near-monopoly of quick-yielding projects, the evidence does not really support the hypothesis of an emergency policy of discriminating rationally in their favour. The cutback in real public investment was in no way reversed in the years following the double monsoon failure which witnessed, as could have been predicted, an agricultural recovery culminating in the excellent harvest of 1969/70 and 1970/71. In 1968/69 and 1969/70, capital spending formed a lower proportion of total expenditure than at any other time in the 1960s. This, in itself, is an interesting insight on the official

20 Cf. Finance Commission (1969), pp. 14–16; Malenbaum (1971), p. 78, note 35.

resumption of planning in 1969/70. It is, moreover, in the post-harvest-failure years that capital spending continues to be further decentralized. The continuation of this process is the major influence causing the concentration ratio of total expenditure to return to the level at which it started the decade. For these reasons, it seems appropriate to reject the view that expenditure decentralization was a consequence of sensible short-term adjustments imposed by the double monsoon failure.

Of course, one can rehearse more general economic arguments to justify a policy of persisting in reduced capital investment once the immediate crisis was over. These are arguments about the growth-promoting tendencies of certain expenditures conventionally called 'consumption'; [21] or about the redistributive effect of certain public consumption expenditures which can compensate for a weak tax and transfer system. [22] The Planning Commission did endorse such arguments. [23] But such generalities do not necessarily provide a valid defence for the specific forms of additional consumption that actually occurred. Nor, even if accepted as such, would they justify or explain the fact that the cutback on capital spending fell almost exclusively on central government account, even allowing for the complementary capital used in state health and education programmes.

The timing of the move towards expenditure decentralization, coming as it did most markedly in 1968/69 and 1969/70, might be taken as an indication that we should be concerned more with the examination of political forces than with economic policy more narrowly conceived. It might be argued that the electoral defeat of Congress in eight states in February 1967 strengthened the states' political position as a group and weakened the political position of the centre. Thus at a time of overall limits on real expenditure growth, the states were able to maintain the growth momentum of their own spending programme and force the centre, against its will, to sacrifice the most expendable part of its programmes – the capital element.

21 Myrdal (1968), pp. 1533–51.   22 Margolis (1954), pp. 186–7.
23 Planning Commission (1970), p. 33.

The appealing simplicity of this viewpoint is, in fact, its major deficiency. The underlying premise is that anti-Congressism after 1967 provided the states with an increment to their political influence over the centre. Some observers have gone so far in their denial of this premise as to assert that the centre actually found it easier to have its way with the non-Congress state governments than with the Congress state governments of the time.[24] It is suggested that non-Congress states were on their best behaviour in relation to the centre, to avoid giving any opening for similar treatment to that meted out to the Communist government in Kerala in 1959; while the Congress states continued to manipulate the central government via influence in the Congress party hierarchy. But it is not necessary to turn the thesis on its head in order to rebut it. A less aggressively contrary rebuttal can also be advanced.

The elections in both centre and states held in February 1967 did show a continuation of the decline in Congress popularity which had started in 1957. For the first time (apart from the brief Kerala interlude at the end of the 1950s), Congress failed to form all the State Governments. In five States, Congress governments were replaced immediately, and subsequently, as a result of defections, Congress governments were swept away in three more States.[25] The Congress 'syndicate' leaders – Kamaraj, S. K. Patil and Atulya Ghosh – all suffered personal electoral defeats. The damage to Congress was done by regionally-based parties – the D.M.K. in Madras, Communists of varied affiliations in Kerala, Swatantra in Gujarat, Orissa and Rajasthan and Jan Sangh in Delhi. These results produced a groundswell of gloomy foreboding claiming that the forecasts of the centrifugal effects of the creation of linguistic states were now practically vindicated.[26]

The 1967 Elections did mark a stage in the development of Indian politics. There is some evidence to suggest that the 'vote-banks' of influential local men were less reliable than they had been in the past, and that the electorate voted somewhat more in response to its conception of political issues.

These issues centred around the performance of the Congress

24 Kothari (1970), p. 121.
25 Kothari (1970), p. 183.
26 Cf. Harrison (1960), p. 7; 336.

party in government, particularly the disappointing results of past economic and social policies. Inflation and food short-ages had crystallized a mood of discontent and disillusionment which spread from the results of defective planning to the concept of planning itself, and this mood was clearly articulated by the electors as well as by the candidates of all parties, in-cluding Congress.

However, there was nothing in the results to bear out two widely adopted conclusions – namely, that the dominance of the Congress was irretrievably broken or that a unique struc-tural shift had occurred in centre–state relations. The first point was seen almost immediately by the more acute Indian obser-vers. Congress losses in terms of popular votes were relatively small. The opposition parties had gained so many additional seats because of their improved skill in avoiding vote-splitting, by the tactic of careful electoral alliances among themselves. This tactic worked in Madras, where D.M.K. allied with Swatantra; in Gujarat, where Swatantra and Jan Sangh coope-rated; and in Kerala and West Bengal, where heterogeneous united front coalitions had been formed solely to promote anti-Congressism. It was aided by internal dissidence within Congress, particularly in Orissa and West Bengal.[27] The clear implication was that Congress could recover its position if (a) it could improve its own electoral tactics, (b) it could re-solve some of its internal rifts and (c) it could capitalize on the economic discontent which was the major issue underlying its 1967 loss of popularity. This implication was emphasized by the February 1969 mid-term poll in Punjab and West Bengal.

The prediction that anti-Congressism could develop a new, anti-centre coalition was unrealistic from the start. That each non-Congress government had a different and regionally limited political base militated against such a development. So did their high degree of fragility, which did not decrease even after clumsy Congress power-ploys to topple some of them. After merely a year, only the anti-Congress ministries in Kerala, Madras and Orissa survived in reasonably good shape. The anti-Congressism of the D.M.K. in Madras (Tamil Nadu) was itself, nevertheless, a very short-lived phenomenon. Des-

27 Desai (1967), pp. 475–6; Siddhartan (1967), p. 1088.

pite its history of demands for separation, its last show of
strength against the Congress Centre was a 'rebellion day' in
1968, pressing demands for a steel plant at Salem and the
expansion of Tuticorin harbour. By 1971, the D.M.K. was
ready to enter an electoral alliance with Mrs Gandhi's Congress.
More important than fragility was the fact that the line of
division between Congress and non-Congress States cut across
a number of other lines of division between the States which
continued to maintain their diffractive force. Thus both Congress and non-Congress States, as groups, remained internally
divided on food and language policy. On food policy, for
example, no cooperation was possible between foodgrain
deficit Kerala. One of the first acts of the new D.M.K. government was to enforce the prohibition on smuggling foodgrains
into Kerala where they could be sold at a premium. When the
so-called three language formula for education became an
issue, Madras and West Bengal allied in the anti-Hindi camp;
but among their opponents were the non-Congress Hindi
states of Uttar Pradesh and Bihar. When the future of economic planning was at issue in the National Development Council
in 1968, the non-Congress states were divided by ideology:
Kerala called for a more vigorous and socialistic approach
to planning, while Orissa advocated its complete abandon-
ment. The issues which united the non-Congress states were
(a) specific central proposals for state resource mobilization
and (b) parity between centre and states in the granting of
additional dearness allowance to government employees – but
these issues united all States, regardless of whether they had
Congress or non-Congress ministries. For all these reasons,
the anti-Congressism of post-1967 was not, despite much
opinion to the contrary, a watershed in centre–state relations,
whatever other political significance it may have had.

Post-1967 anti-Congressism probably had some impact
in persuading the centre to provide the bulk of its Plan financial
assistance to the states in a more flexible form. The amount of
central assistance for state plans was fixed for the entire period
of the Fourth Plan; the criteria for its distribution were ap-
proved by Chief Ministers and the central government through
the N.D.C. (National Development Council); the size of state
annual plans was thus made to depend solely (in theory) on the
resource-raising efforts of the state governments themselves;

the scope of 'centrally-sponsored schemes' and the Article 282 'plan grants' which financed them was drastically reduced. But this modification was also prompted in part by a style of economic policy which, after 1965, favoured some significant dismantling of the apparatus of detailed bureaucratic intervention in economic life.

The thesis of growing states' political power is only the most obvious political approach to the problem of expenditure decentralization. Alternatively, one could argue that the importance of the 1967 election was less for its impact on the states than on the centre itself. The first general election since Nehru's death was indecisive, in the sense that Congress performance was neither good enough, nor bad enough, to precipitate outright bids to alter the power balance of the central leadership group. It accordingly signalled a continuation of 'syndicate raj', the rule of the Congress bosses of the inter-regnum, unchallenged by a new Prime Minister who still bided her time. The energies of the central leadership became more consumed than ever with personal conflicts, intrigues, and faction-fighting. The 'leadership' could spare very little time even for putting together its occasional incoherent compromises on major policy disputes. This is the classic scenario for the collapse of planning, which, almost by definition, requires complete inter-departmental policy coordination at the highest level, and for the transfer of effective economic policy-making to a strong, 'orthodox' Finance Ministry.

Terming the Finance Ministry 'orthodox' is not intended as praise or dispraise, merely as a description. It means that the higher ranks held and expressed opinions consistent with safeguarding the economic and social system as it existed. It implies a bias towards conservatism and against planning as a method of inducing large-scale change in the economic and social structure. When a political leadership is fragmented and turns in upon itself in an attempt to resolve its own internal conflicts, orthodoxy emerges as an independent force. Personalities, which seem to loom so large, are in fact at a discount. That the Finance Ministry happened, as a result of post-election manoeuvring, to have fallen to Morarji Desai, the leading right-wing Congressman, served only as an incidental dramatization.

The orthodox economic view was dominated by a fear of the consequences of a declining net inflow of foreign resources, after growth had become critically dependent on such an inflow. The response to this fear was a new package of economic policies. Private foreign investment was encouraged as a potential substitute for declining government-to-government flows. Domestic private investment was relied upon to ease the recession in industry, presumably on the assumption that it would have the same demand effects as public investment, but a smaller balance of payments cost. An attempt was made to insure against future monsoon failures by directing complementary, high-technology inputs to already irrigated areas, despite the consequential narrowing in the geographical and social base of agricultural progress. Finally, and most important in the present context, it was preferred to accumulate foreign exchange reserves, rather than use them to resume the expansion of large centrally-financed development projects on the scale envisaged by the perspective planners at the time of the Third Plan. Formally, the 'plan holiday' which began in 1966 ended with the start of the Fourth Plan in 1969/70. Even though the Fourth Plan's investment targets were relatively modest by past standards, it was apparent that the flow of large development projects was much easier to stop than to re-start. Public investment was below target, even in money terms, for the first two years of the Plan, while circumstances were most favourable. Then the costs of the Bangladesh war in 1971/72, followed by the drought of 1972–74, ensured that no recovery could be made from the tardy start. Thus, despite the existence of the Fourth Plan, the general situation was that the 'plan holiday' after 1966 was not seriously interrupted.

Whether this set of economic policies, engendered by the 'orthodox' fear of foreign resource scarcity is defensible, in whole or part, is an all-embracing question. It would be senseless to imply that justice could be done to it in a digression here. Our concern is with establishing the following propositions. (1) Expenditure decentralization between 1965 and 1970 resulted from the central government's action of allowing its capital expenditure programme to decline in money, and, *a fortiori*, in real terms, while no similar degree of restraint was applied to, or observed in, the capital programmes of the states. (2) This action was taken deliberately as part of a wider set of central government economic policies adopted in response to a levelling off of net foreign aid flows, combined with poor resource mobilization domestically. (3) The political roots of this action were the political conditions which allowed the economic orthodoxy of the Finance Ministry to dominate policy making, rather than the events which allegedly strengthened the bargaining position of the states *vis-à-vis* the central government.

7

The growth of state governments' spending

I   INTER-STATE DIFFERENCES IN PUBLIC EXPENDITURE GROWTH

When the states are considered as a group, which is then contrasted with the centre, they have a broad similarity defined by their relationship to the centre. Each state is taken as having a geographically limited sub-jurisdiction, as receiving some central financial assistance, and as being charged with certain constitutional expenditure responsibilities and taxation powers. This is perfectly correct as far as it goes. But it obviously does not give a complete picture. State governments in a federation combine juridical similarity with pronounced economic and political dissimilarity.

India is a federation by disaggregation. Its federal scheme emerged by a process of devolution of central government powers on states (provinces), which was linked with the transition from a colonial to a post-colonial regime. Under the British, it is clear that a strong element of political calculation in the face of nationalist pressure prompted the twin moves towards quasi-democracy and federalism. But why, at independence, the federal provisions of British legislation were adopted so swiftly and with so little contest is not at all clear from the history of constitution-making.[1] There seems simply to have been general agreement that the size and diversity of India, and the fragmented nature of its civil polity, would have been incompatible with a unitary regime. In other words, economic and political dissimilarities between the units of the federation were the causes of the adoption of the federal form of government, given the prior decision in favour of a formal parliamentary democracy.

1 Austin (1966), pp. 188–94.

The dissimilarities between states which are normally held to justify a genuine decentralization of expenditure and taxation decisions are differences in income per head, population density and political preferences. [2] But, from a positive standpoint, the same three variables are frequently cited as the major influences on public expenditure. If the positive hypotheses are correct, therefore, one would expect that, in an economically rational federation, inter-state variations in levels and growth of public spending would be significantly different from zero.

In what follows, an attempt is made first to overcome the statistical problems of comparing states' expenditure levels and rates of growth. Secondly, the question is examined of how far these measured differences in levels and rates of expenditure growth can in fact be ascribed to differencces in the two classic economic 'determinants' of public expenditure, income per head and population density.

If expenditure by individual state governments is to be compared, the basic principle is that like must be compared with like. This requires, initially, that in preparing the expenditure figures at current prices, consistency of definition and classification between states is ensured. In fact, the budgetary conventions in use in different states differ, but a basic uniformity is achieved, in the data used here, by the re-classification of state budgetary documents according to national accounts conventions by the C.S.O. The C.S.O., however, while allocating local authority expenditure by states in 1965/66 and after, gives only a global figure for it between 1960/61 and 1964/65. For comparability, some method has to be adopted to distribute these global sums by states in the period 1960–5. The distribution was made by applying the 1965/66 distribution to all the earlier years. There is bound to be an arbitrary element in such an allocation since 'democratic decentralization' must have proceeded in different states at different speeds. The element of error was accepted as preferable to a thoroughgoing exclusion of all local authority spending, which would have involved the arbitrariness arising from the differing extents to which state governments devolved their functions on lower-level bodies. [3]

2 Head (1973), p. 25.   3 Maxwell (1969), pp. 2–3.

TABLE 7.1　*Three all-India price indices, 1960/61 to 1969/70.*

| | Wholesale prices, all commodities (1961/62 = 100) | Consumer prices | |
		Urban non-manual (1960 = 100)	Working class (1949 = 100)
1960/61	—	100	124
1961/62	100.0	104	—
1969/70	171.6	167	215

Source: Ministry of Finance, *Economic Survey, 1971/72.* Tables 5.1 and 5.3.

But the most important problem of ensuring comparability still remains. Too many writers on Indian public expenditure seem to have followed Miss Prism's advice in *The Importance of Being Ernest,* that one 'may neglect the chapter on the Fall of the Rupee – it is too sensational'. Too often the problem posed by the persistence of inflation has either been ignored, or else acknowledged only to be brushed aside.[4] It seems that, in the 1960s, the purchasing power of the rupee fell to between two thirds and one half of its initial value (Table 7.1). But if government spending doubles while the purchasing power of the currency falls by one half, the volume of goods and services absorbed by government will not change. If it is further assumed, as is conventional, that the volume of inputs absorbed by government is directly correlated with the volume of outputs produced by government, neither will the volume of government output change. Thus if one wants to eliminate the effects of a general inflation of prices, inputs absorbed by government must be valued at a single set of prices in all years, in the form of a time series 'at constant prices'. Theoretically, a further complication arises when, during a general inflation, the relative prices of labour and capital goods also change. This is ignored here, for reasons explained in Appendix C. Data limitations are serious enough for the task of producing a reliable constant prices series of government expenditure at the national level. For inter-state comparisons at constant prices, it is necessary to estimate the geographical differences

4 Gupta (1970), pp. 303–8; Venkataraman (1968), pp. 158–9.

TABLE 7.2   *Annual compound growth rates of government expenditure at 1960/61 prices by states, 1960–70.*

State	Expenditure at 1960/61 prices compound growth rates (% p.a.)
Andhra Pradesh	2.0
* Assam	6.6
Bihar	1.7
Gujarat	5.1
Jammu and Kashmir	7.8
Kerala	5.1
* Madhya Pradesh	2.0
Maharashtra	7.3
* Mysore	3.3
Orissa	4.0
Punjab and Haryana	1.2
* Rajasthan	4.7
Tamil Nadu	5.1
Uttar Pradesh	2.3
West Bengal	4.1

Note: the four asterisked states are not strictly comparable with the others, because of price index problems. See Appendix C.
Source: calculated from C.S.O. unpublished data.

in the rate of general inflation. Again, the precise methods used are discussed in Appendix C.

To arrive at the estimated growth rates of government expenditure at constant prices, set out in Table 7.2, involved the following steps:

(1) Allocation of a total figure for local authority spending by states between 1960/61 and 1964/65, according to the distribution which actually prevailed in 1965/66;

(2) Deflation of current price figures to figures at 1960/61 prices by the methods discussed in Appendix C;

(3) Calculation of a trend line for each constant price time series, by the method of ordinary least squares;

(4) Expression of the difference between the first-year and last-year trend values as an annual average rate of compound growth.

The growth rates in Table 7.2 are thus intended to show expenditure growth by states with the price change element removed.

But, apart from prices, there is another influence which contributes to expenditure growth rates, and for which due allowance must be made. When population is growing rapidly, an appreciable portion of the growth in the real volume of government spending is diverted to the 'widening' rather than the 'deepening' of collective provision. In other words, even when government spending is growing at constant prices, some part of that growth will be used to extend the existing standard of public facilities to an increasing population, rather than improving on that standard. The question is how to allow for the element of expenditure widening under the influence of population growth. Clearly there can be no well-founded presumption that expenditure widening is inevitably given priority over expenditure deepening: this is precisely the kind of distributional issue about which so little is known.[5] Nor is it always true that, if one per cent population growth is accompanied by one per cent real expenditure growth, existing standards of public facilities will remain unchanged. For example, population growth accompanied by a changing age structure of the population would upset such a neat assumption. However, although one can state quite clearly what some of its limitations might be, there is no better rule of thumb that can be adopted – given our ignorance of distribution and age structure – than to assume that every percentage point of population growth requires an extra percentage point of real expenditure just to preserve existing expenditure standards intact. To measure the rate of expenditure deepening, the rate of population growth is then simply deducted from the growth rate of real government expenditure, to give a figure that approximates closely the annual growth rate of real expenditure per head. The results of applying this rule of thumb are given in Table 7.3.

As is clear from the figures in column (2) of Table 7.3, even after allowance is made for differences between states in the rate of price inflation and in the rate of population growth, substantial underlying differences remain between them in

5 O'Connor (1969), p. 377.

TABLE 7.3   *Statewise growth rates of population and real government expenditure per head, 1960–70.*

State	(1) *Annual compound rate of population growth* (%)	(2) *Annual compound growth rate of real expenditure per head* (%)
Andhra Pradesh	1.88	0.1
Assam	3.00	3.6
Bihar	1.95	(−)0.3
Gujarat	2.60	2.5
Jammu and Kashmir	2.62	5.1
Kerala	2.34	2.8
Madhya Pradesh	2.55	(−)0.6
Maharashtra	2.42	4.9
Mysore	2.17	1.1
Orissa	2.26	1.7
Punjab and Haryana	2.34	(−)1.2
Rajasthan	2.48	2.2
Tamil Nadu	2.01	3.1
Uttar Pradesh	1.82	0.5
West Bengal	2.45	1.6

Sources: Col. (1): *Census of India, 1971: Paper I of 1971 – Supplement*, Statement I, from which growth rates are derived. Col. (2): Data in Table 6, *minus* figures in col. (1).

their rates of public expenditure growth. At one end of the scale, states like Punjab and Haryana, Madhya Pradesh, Bihar and Andhra Pradesh did not (for one reason or another – one must not prejudge the question of causes) manage to prevent an erosion of their average standard of collective provision for consumption and investment in the face of continued population pressure. At the other end of the scale, states like Jammu and Kashmir and Maharashtra not only prevented such erosion, but improved their average level of collective provision at around 5 per cent compound over the decade.

Wide variations in growth rates of real spending per head are, in logic, perfectly consistent with (a) small statewise variations in levels of expenditures per head and (b) a diminution in inter-state differences in expenditure levels, as these levels converge to a mean value. However, in fact, the statewise dif-

TABLE 7.4 *Government spending per head by state at 1960/61 prices.*

State	(1) 1960/61	(2) 1969/70
	Rupees at 1960/61 prices	
Andhra Pradesh	31.7	34.6
Assam	38.1	51.8
Bihar	20.2	21.7
Gujarat	38.8	46.2
Jammu and Kashmir	59.3	86.1
Kerala	30.4	36.4
Madhya Pradesh	23.9	23.3
Maharashtra	41.0	55.0
Mysore	36.6	45.4
Orissa	25.6	32.0
Punjab and Haryana	35.6	34.8
Rajasthan	31.3	43.8
Tamil Nadu	30.9	40.6
Uttar Pradesh	8.3*	19.7
West Bengal	32.3	36.9
All-India mean	*26.9*	*34.5*
Standard deviation	*12.1*	*16.9*
Coefficient of variation	*44.9*	*49.0*

Note: In 1960/61, Uttar Pradesh experienced unusually large receipts for netting off against capital expenditure, so that this figure very substantially underestimates the normal level of spending.
Source: calculated from C.S.O. unpublished data.

ferences in expenditure levels were large in 1960/61, and the differing expenditure growth rates reflect the process of their further enlargement. The relevant figures are set out in Table 7.4. The coefficient of variation, i.e. the standard deviation of the observations expressed as a percentage of their mean, was large in 1960/61 and even larger by 1969/70. The 1960/61 figure of 44.9 per cent is artificially high because of the inclusion of one extreme observation (for Uttar Pradesh): but on any reasonable calculation the true figure was at least 25 per cent, and the more the estimate of initial disparity is decreased, the more the estimate of the growth of inter-state disparity over the decade is thereby increased. Again, on any reasonable calculation, inclusion of a 'true' figure for Uttar Pradesh would not affect the ranking of the states in Table 7.4, column (1). If this ranking is compared with that of states' real expenditure growth rates per head (given in Table 7.3, column (2)), it is clear that they are correlated. The coefficient of rank correlation equals 0.575, which is significant at the 0.05 confidence level. Thus there is a significant tendency for states with high initial spending levels to show high growth rates of spending, and for states with initially low spending levels to have low growth rates. This means that the differences between spending levels must have grown over the period. Thus, while there is room for some doubt about the precise degree of initial differentiation, the evidence is that it was considerable, and that the direction of change in the 1960s was towards even greater differentiation.

II FACTORS RELATED TO PUBLIC SPENDING GROWTH IN THE STATES

There is nothing particularly surprising in such findings. They are what would be expected in a federation founded upon considerable economic and political dissimilarity between its units, if public expenditure is indeed importantly influenced by such variables as income per head and population density. Political dissimilarity between states is an important assumption for the following reason. To the extent that inter-state rivalry is overlaid by the development of a truly national outlook, it is possible for the centre to undertake more extensive income redistribution between states. If and when this happens, one would expect the classic economic determinants to weaken in their influence on public expenditure: they would need to be supplemented by consideration of the effect of central transfers. But it seems doubtful that this stage has yet been reached in India. Central transfers are, of course, a sizeable proportion of the finance for state expenditure. But in their distribution there is little bias in favour of the poorer states. Nor does it seem that the tax system is sufficiently progressive to cause very much redistribution in the process of raising the necessary central revenues.[6] If these arguments are correct, attention

6 Hicks (1968), pp. 227–8; Sundrum (1972), p. 1031.

may be directed, in the first instance, to examining the relationships between public expenditure and, on the one hand, state incomes and, on the other, state population density.

A cross-section comparison for 1960/61 shows a statistically significant association between average public spending and average income. The rank correlation coefficient, r', defined in the note to Table 8.11 on page 202, is 0.63. This tells us only that, in most states, the size of the state government sector hovers around the all-India mean of 9–10 per cent of state income. The main exception is Jammu and Kashmir, a poor state enjoying a level of state government spending per head out of all proportion to its own resources because of the centre's strategic concern for its political loyalty.[7] However, what must be asked is whether the growth of real public spending per head in the 1960s was associated with growth in real income per head.

This question confronts us squarely with one of the greatest impediments to economic analysis at the level of the state. As far as one can ascertain, comparable time series of state incomes at constant prices do not exist for 1960–70. The only comparable published time series data for states incomes, prepared by the C.S.O., covers only the years 1960/61 to 1964/65 and are at current prices.[8] The states themselves prepare estimates of state income, which are at constant prices and which (with a few trivial exceptions) cover all of the relevant years. But one must remain sceptical of their comparability even when they are apparently following a standard methodology – which four states in any case have not adopted. This must make any conclusions derived from their use highly tentative, and subject to revision – perhaps radical revision – as soon as better data become available.

If one calculates growth rates of average real income from the states' own estimates and then compares them with the growth rates of average real expenditure (Table 7.3, column 2), a curious state of affairs is revealed. For twelve of the fifteen states, i.e. all except Maharashtra, Mysore and Punjab–Haryana, a very close association exists between the two sets of

7 Anon (1968), pp. 832–3.
8 Finance Commission (1969), pp. 127–8, Tables 4 and 5.

growth rates ($r' = 0.78$, significant at the 0.01 confidence level). But when the three excluded states are included, the correlation coefficient falls to 0.22, which is statistically insignificant. The behaviour of the government sector in the three maverick states appears to stand in dramatic contrast to the general rule. On the one hand, Maharashtra achieved substantial expenditure deepening despite constant average real income, while on the other hand Punjab and Haryana, and to a lesser extent Mysore, achieved no expenditure deepening despite having the fastest rates of average real income growth in India.

Naturally, it would be convenient if some special explanations could be offered for this maverick behaviour. In the case of Punjab and Haryana such an explanation might not be too difficult to construct. The splitting of the state in 1966 obviously caused some dislocation of expenditure programmes in the years immediately before and after the split. Further, vigorous agricultural entrepreneurship, combined with the irrigation infrastructure resulting from large-scale government investment in previous decades, created the conditions for rapid agricultural growth in the late 1960s, despite the sluggish growth of public expenditure at the state level. For Maharashtra, it might be suggested that public spending has been heavily concentrated on the provision of high-quality urban services for metropolitan Bombay, and that 'metropolitan parasitism' accounts for the observed lack of relation between public expenditure growth and statewide income growth. It is not clear, however, that an explanation in terms of special circumstances could be constructed equally well for Mysore.

One wonders whether the situation would be further illuminated by breaking down state income or public expenditure into their components, to see whether these would reveal what it is that made the exceptional states exceptional. It would not seem that a breakdown of state income would be very revealing. Broadly speaking, states which experienced economic growth in the period grew, or failed to grow, in all major categories of production – foodgrains, cash crops and industrial activities.[9] As for a breakdown of public expenditure, although

9 Mitra (1970), p. 21–26.

detailed economic-cum-functional classifications have been prepared for six states (see Appendix A), such information is not available to any of the three exceptional states. There is no way of establishing statistically whether they deviate in some way from the 'normal' distribution of outlays.

It may be that the answer to the problem is simply that the state income data are unreliable. But assuming the contrary, as one must until better data are available, the question arises whether an explanation is to be found by considering the other classic determinant of public expenditure, the degree of urbanization.

Before trying to answer that question, it is necessary to re-mind ourselves that urbanization as a process has been given a number of distinctly different meanings by sociologists, geographers and economists. The concept of an urbanization process is 'a balloon into which each social scientist blows his own meaning'.[10] Not surprisingly, therefore, there is also some difference in approach between one country and another in the official measures used of the number of people living in 'urban places'. The Indian Census of 1971 implicitly adopted the conceptual approach of Louis Wirth, who argued that 'on the basis of the three variables, number, density of settlement, and degree of heterogeneity of the . . . population, it appears possible to explain the characteristics of urban life and to account for the differences between cities of various sizes and types'.[11] The 1961 and 1971 Census definition of 'urban', on which we rely in what follows, covers all places with a Municipality, Corporation, Cantonment or notified town area, plus all other places with a minimum population of 5000, a population density of 1000 per square mile and 75 per cent of the male working population in non-agricultural occupations. Using these criteria, just over a half of the 1971 urban population lived in cities of 100 000 or more people, and one third in towns of between 5000 and 50 000 people.[12]

It is frequently asserted, rather loosely, that urbanization accompanies rising income levels, both being envisaged as twin, but indivisible, aspects of economic development.[13] If

10 McGee (1971), p. 10.   11 Quoted by McGee (1971), p. 39.
12 Census of India (1971), p. 3; 6–7.
13 E.g. Thorn (1967), p. 24; Burkehead and Miner (1971), p. 5.

TABLE 7.5 *Growth of real government spending per head, and of urban population in the more urban states, 1960–70.*

	Percentage of urbanization 1960/61	Growth of real govt spending per head 1960–70	Rank by col. (2)	Growth of urban population 1961–71	Rank by col. (4)
	(1)	(2)	(3)	(4)	(5)
1 Andhra Pradesh	17.44	0.1	7	+33.81	6
2 Gujarat	25.77	2.5	4	+41.20	2
3 J. and Kashmir	16.66	5.1	1	+42.04	1
4 Maharashtra	28.22	4.9	2	+40.68	3
5 Mysore	22.33	1.1	6	+35.09	5
6 Punjab and H.	28.53	(−)1.2	8	+28.53	7
7 Tamil Nadu	26.69	3.1	3	+38.44	4
8 West Bengal	24.45	1.6	5	+27.95	8

Source: Cols. (1) and (4): *Census of India, 1971: Paper 1 of 1971 – Supplement,* Table A, p. 49, Columns 6 and 10 respectively.

this were strictly true, it would evidently be gratuitous to see urbanization as an alternative influence to income growth determining public expenditure growth. But in the India of the 1960s it was not true by any means: among the most rapidly urbanizing states were Orissa, Madhya Pradesh and Bihar, where average real income was virtually constant. However, when states are ranked both by rate of change of urbanization and by growth of real expenditure per head, the correlation is only weakly positive, and not statistically significant. Once again, the experience of three states (Bihar, Madhya Prades and Orissa) strongly contradicted the generalization which was satisfactory for the other twelve. Thus the urbanization hypothesis does not, any more than does the state income hypothesis, provide on its own a complete explanation of statewise public expenditure growth.[14] But at the same time both appear to be partially sound. Is there then some way of combining them, so that their merits are complementary and their defects eliminated?

14 But cf. Lewis (1978), pp. 39–43.

It is possible to propose a solution along the following lines. The states may be separated into two groups, the more urbanized and the less urbanized, according to the degree of urbanization which prevailed in 1960/61. The urbanization hypothesis can then be tested against expenditure data for the more urban states, and the average real income hypothesis can be tested against data for the less urban states. The relevant figures are set out in Tables 7.5 and 7.6.

What are the results of separating the states into two groups according to their initial level of urbanization? In the more urban states, the growth of real government spending per head was closely associated with the growth rate of the urban population. The coefficient of rank correlation equals 0.78, which is significant at the 0.05 confidence level. In the less urban states, the association between expenditure growth and growth of average real income was not quite so close. In this case the rank correlation coefficient was 0.72, which is significant only at the 0.10 confidence level. The interpretation of this result is particularly difficult because no less than three of the seven less urban states were using non-standard methodologies in

TABLE 7.6   *Growth of real government spending per head, and of average real income in the less urban states, 1960–70.*

	Percentage of urbanization 1960/61	Growth of real govt spending per head 1960–70	Rank by col. (2)	Growth rate of real income per head 1960–70	Rank by col. (4)
	(1)	(2)	(3)	(4)	(5)
1 Assam	7.37	3.6	1	1.31	1
2 Bihar	8.43	(−)0.3	6	(−)0.38	6
3 Kerala	15.11	2.8	2	1.08	3
4 Madhya Pradesh	14.29	(−)0.6	7	(−)0.30	5
5 Orissa	6.32	1.7	4	(−)0.75	7
6 Rajasthan	16.28	2.2	3	1.25	2
7 Uttar Pradesh	12.85	0.5	5	0.02	4

Sources: Col. (1): as for Table 6.5, column (1); Col. (4): unpublished estimates by State Statistical Bureaux.

preparing their state income estimates (Assam, Madhya Pradesh and Rajasthan). Whether truly comparable state income data would improve the closeness of the association, or worsen it, can only be a matter for conjecture at this stage.

Before proceeding any further with the argument, it is appropriate to point out the limitations of empirical associations of the kind we have been trying to identify. To be reasonably sure that no relevant variable has been ignored would require a very elaborate factor analysis of a kind which has not been attempted here. Further, even when covariation between public expenditure growth and all the other major relevant variables has been established, the direction of the causal links remains a matter of judgement, and often of dispute. Even when the direction of the causal links seems to be clear, the question arises of how the independent variables operate on the dependent variable. This requires an attempt to separate out influences on the demand side from those on the supply side, and the different influences that can operate in opposing directions either on demand, or on supply.

Nevertheless it might be useful, as a contribution to debate, to speculate what economic mechanisms might be at work, on the assumption that the foregoing results have some statistical validity. Taking urbanization first, is it a consequence or cause of public expenditure growth? In India, the pattern of migration in the 1950s was for migrants to move to states that were in the process of rapid urbanization, rather than to states which were already highly urbanized.[15] This suggests that the growth of urban population in the more urban states is not a consequence of their attraction – because of higher average levels of public expenditure – for migrants from other states. There is still the very real possibility that internal migration is in response to the higher levels of collective provision in the urban areas, however, or that the pattern of inter-state migration altered in the 1960s. If urbanization is also a cause of public expenditure growth, by what channels does it exert its influence? Urbanization is normally assumed to reduce the unit costs of public services: but for urbanization to stimulate public spending there must obviously be other influences as

15 Greenwood (1971).

well. Urbanization will increase the demand for public services in a number of ways. It will increase the number of people who can be organized at low cost to press mass claims to better health, education and welfare services. If income distribution is highly unequal, it will increase demand for government services, such as police, para-military and fire services, whose task is the protection of property. In addition, urbanization operates on the supply side by relaxing the taxable capacity constraint on public expenditure. This is partly a reflection of the fact that urbanization increases the product of indirect taxes by promoting monetization: and partly a reflection of the chronic inability to tax agricultural incomes directly in India. The correlation between state tax revenues (as a percentage of state income) and the level of urbanization in India has been established with cross-section data.[16] We are speculating here that this relationship also holds good for the more urban states over time.

The relationship between public expenditure and state income is probably even more complicated. It must surely be one of mutual interaction, in the manner of Myrdal's 'circles of cumulative causation'. The richer states can afford better public provision, which promotes economic growth; which, in turn, leads to demands for further improvements that (because of growth) can now be supplied; and so on. Meanwhile the poorer states cannot afford the public expenditure they would need to break out of their existing position. Of course, if taken literally, the excessive determinism of such an argument renders it absurd. The scope for growth-promoting government activity is not infinite, and long before the theoretical limits are approached, the practical difficulties of project choice may well prove overwhelming. Similarly, it is doubtful that any cumulative circles are so vicious that under no historical circumstances could they be broken. Yet, applied to a medium-term situation, when the social and institutional framework is stable, the cumulative causation argument has some merit. There is evidence that the faster growth states devote a larger proportion of their budgets to economic expenditures, rather than to gen-

16 Nambiar and Govinda Rao (1972), p. 1037, Table 1.

eral or social services, which could be taken as an indication of the existence of 'virtuous' and 'vicious' circles. As for the manner in which economic growth influences public expenditure, it may be conjectured that the effect is strong on the side of supply and weak on the side of demand. At very low levels of income, demand would presumably be little changed by a marginal increment to income: the income increase would raise public spending by relaxing the taxable capacity constraints.

To combine these two sets of arguments in a manner consistent with our empirical results, it is necessary to postulate an asymmetry in the effects of income growth and urbanization according to the level of urbanization. In less urban states, urbanization cannot have the demand and supply increasing effects on public spending which have been mentioned, while, in the more urban states, further urbanization rather than further income growth must be assumed to be the key to the creation of additional fiscal capacity. It is difficult to suggest from *a priori* reasoning why this should be so. One would need to have much more information about the nature of the urbanization process in the two groups of states. Was it, for the less urban states, a distress phenomenon – the flight to the towns of impoverished agricultural workers when starvation was imminent? Was it, for the more urban states, by contrast, a process more attributable to natural increase of the urban population plus the inflow from the rural hinterland of a more enterprising and prosperous type of migrant? For the moment, these questions must remain unanswered.

Attempts to construct an explanation must, however, take account of one important negative point. The grouping of the states into more and less urban does not produce a division which is the same as that given by two other dichotomies familiar in the literature on the Indian states – the more and the less developed states; and the 'heartland' and the 'rimland' states. It is true that on any of the three criteria – level of urbanization, degree of development, or geographical position – Gujarat, Maharashtra, West Bengal, Tamil Nadu and Punjab will always stand in contrast to Uttar Pradesh, Madhya Pradesh, Rajasthan and Bihar. But the way in which the other six states are assimilated to this fundamental cleavage does differ significantly according to which criterion is being discussed. The degree of urbanization is not synonymous with the degree of general economic development, as is clear by contrasting Kerala with Jammu and Kashmir. Even less is it synonymous with location on the 'rimland', as is clear by contrasting Andhra Pradesh and Mysore with Assam, Kerala and Orissa. It follows that the equation between rimland location and economic development is far from perfect also.[17] In other words, the search for an explanation of the empirical associations noted above will probably be more rewarding if directed towards further research into inter-state differences in urbanization, rather than towards approaches which regard urbanization as a proxy for some allegedly more 'basic' geo-political distinction.

Returning, in conclusion, to the question of political influences on state government expenditure, one must remain agnostic as to whether preferences regarding public expenditure differ markedly between states. The direct evidence for such preferences is lacking and the indirect evidence, in terms of actual expenditure patterns, is too fragmentary for sound inference. Where 'deviant' spending patterns can be noted (e.g. the preference for technical education in Orissa) they reflect the personal influence of a local, and inevitably passing, political leader. Political influences on spending have tended to be of two major types. First, strong inter-state rivalry exists, based on a mutual suspicion that chronically inhibits cooperation even when the gains would be large for all parties. Consequently, the centre can do little that is visible to redistribute income between states. Expenditure in most states remains firmly linked to its own resource base. Only when very obvious defence interests are involved (e.g. Jammu and Kashmir, Nagaland) can the centre do otherwise. It will be recalled that, in defining the idea of mimetic nationalism in Chapter 2, its coexistence with a low level of national integration was noted. The inability to re-distribute purchasing power regionally except to a few areas under constant military threat is a concrete expression of that characteristic.

The second type of political influence arises from the relative

17 Rudolph and Rudolph (1969), Table 4, p. 1043.

ease with which urban business and urban labour can be politically organized, and their relative proximity, both physical and psychological, to the state's civil and military employees. This relative ease of organization and proximity to those who decide how public funds are spent is the chief political reason why, within the boundaries of any one state, the growth of urban population stimulates state government spending.[18]

18 Lipton (1977).

8

Public investment, public saving and the state governments

Overall trends in public investment and public saving during the period 1960–70 were surveyed in Chapter 4. It became clear that, at least from the end of the Third Five-Year Plan, public sector investment fell both as a percentage of net domestic product, and of total gross fixed capital formation. At the same time, public saving showed an absolute decline, despite quickening inflation, and therefore (until 1969/70) served as a dwindling source of finance for a public sector investment programme that was virtually stagnant. The purpose of this chapter is to probe behind the aggregate trends, in order to see how the activities of the different types of governmental spending agency contributed to them. The approach follows that adopted in Chapter 5 in relation to total public expenditure. That is, we begin by examining changes in the degree of centralization of public investment and saving, treating the state governments as a unified group that can be contrasted with the central government. Thereafter an attempt is made to give estimates of inter-state differences in the rate of growth of their investment and saving, and to find statistical regularities that might point towards an explanation of these differences.

I PUBLIC INVESTMENT CENTRALIZATION

The total gross capital formation done by the public sector can be disaggregated to show the shares of the central government, the state governments, local authorities (together defined as the 'public authorities') and the share of the non-departmental enterprises (i.e. government companies and statutory corporations). This breakdown is given in Table 8.1.

In Table 8.1, we have to operate with data on gross capital

formation, because there is no available breakdown of public sector fixed capital consumption by spending authority. In any case, it may be doubted how realistic the aggregate figure of fixed capital consumption is, since it is probably determined by the depreciation policies of the various public enterprises, which themselves may well be arbitrary. Gross capital formation is the sum of new fixed capital formation, the difference between purchases and sales of existing physical assets and the difference between the inflow to and outflow from owned stocks of physical goods. Because stock changes are usually more volatile than changes in fixed capital formation, and because they are likely to respond to different economic pressures, they have been separately identified.

The story told by the figures in Table 8.1 manifestly falls into two chapters, the period of the Third Plan and the succeeding five years. During the Third Plan public sector gross capital formation was growing rapidly in money terms, and somewhat less rapidly in real terms. While this growth took place, central government increased slightly its relative contribution, while the state governments somewhat decreased theirs. The slight drift in the relative contributions of central and state governments is visible regardless of whether 'state governments' are defined narrowly (i.e. to exclude local authorities) or broadly (i.e. to include them).

This result is interesting because it shows that, under the Third Plan, the growing centralization of total expenditure, which was noted in Chapter 5, was accompanied by a growing centralization of gross capital formation. One might be tempted to think that this is additional evidence that the centre substantially maintained its development effort despite its increased defence commitments as a result of the Sino-Indian border war. That inference would be incorrect, because, as explained in Appendix A, the Indian definition of capital formation includes expenditure on physical construction and machinery and equipment undertaken for defence purposes. Since it is impossible separately to identify defence and non-defence capital formation, the capital formation data cannot be used to add anything to the previous discussions of the extent to which defence and development accumulation competed for the central government resources.

TABLE 8.1 *Public sector gross capital formation by spending authority, 1960/61 to 1969/70.*

	1960/61	1961/62	1962/63	1963/64	1964/65	1965/66	1966/67	1967/68	(Percentage shares) 1968/69	1969/70
A Public authorities										
a Central govt	28	27	31	33	33	23	22	19	12	18
1 New G.F.C.F.	26	28	29	32	30	27	25	20	22	20
2 Change in stocks	2	(−)1	2	2	3	(−)4	(−)3	(−)1	(−)9	(−)2
b State govts										
1 New G.F.C.F.	31	30	25	24	24	24	26	24	29	30
2 Change in stocks	(−)1	(−)1	1	(−)1	(−)1	3	(−)3	3	2	30
c Local authorities	6	7	7	7	7	8	7	8	8	8
1 New G.F.C.F.	6	7	7	7	7	7	7	8	8	8
2 Change in stocks						1				
d Net purchase of physical assets by public authorities	(−)6					(−)2				

B Non-departmental enterprises	*41*	*38*	*36*	*38*	*37*	*44*	*48*	*46*	*49*	*45*
1 New G.F.C.F.	30	30	28	31	34	36	39	35	40	40
2 Change in stocks	5	6	6	7	4	8	10	12	10	5
3 Net purchase of physical assets	6	2	1		(−)1	1	(−)1	(−)1	(−)1	
C *Total gross capital formation by public sector* (Rs. cr., current prices)	1137	1169	1464	1671	1920	2184	2114	2311	2146	2234
(percentage)	*100*	*100*	*100*	*100*	*100*	*100*	*100*	*100*	*100*	*100*

Note: Totals do not necessarily add exactly because of rounding.
Source: C.S.O. (1976a), calculated from data in Table 22.

The capital formation data do, however, serve to confirm previous observations about the decentralization of capital spending in the five years after the Third Plan. In these five years, public sector capital formation was stagnant in money terms, and, as a result of accelerating inflation, progressively declining in real terms. Yet, using data in money terms (since spending authorities' price indices are not strictly comparable), the gross capital formation of state governments, local authorities and non-departmental enterprises each increased, while that of the central government drastically declined. This absolute and relative decline of central government capital formation effort is not affected if we choose to take account of the large stock decumulation by the centre and stock accumulation by the state governments and non-departmental enterprises; or if we choose the alternative of ignoring all stock changes. The stock changes only reinforce the trends in relative shares which are evident in the figures for new fixed capital formation.

We have already argued that the drastic decentralization of expenditure for capital formation was the principal influence leading to decentralization of total expenditure in the second half of the 1960s. The motivation of the central government in cutting back its own capital formation while permitting increases in other parts of the public sector was discussed in the context of total expenditure centralization, and that discussion need not be recapitulated here.

II CENTRALIZATION OF PUBLIC SAVING

What changes took place simultaneously in the degree of centralization of public saving? Unfortunately, in order to answer this question, much murkier conceptual and statistical waters have to be navigated. Since the saving of non-departmental enterprises has been extremely small, the problem is essentially that of determining the correct method of allocating the saving of the public authorities between the central government, the state governments and the local authorities.

The saving of public authorities is the difference between current revenues and current expenditure. To give a more precise definition, assume a three-sector world, where the subscripts 1, 2 and 3 refer to the public authorities, the remainder of the domestic economy and the rest of the world, and a threefold division of the public authorities, where the subscripts a, b and c refer to the central government, the state governments and the local authorities. Public authorities' saving is defined as

$$S \equiv R - (C + Z + Q'_{2,3}) \tag{1}$$

when
$$R \equiv T + Y + P + (I_2 - I'_2) \tag{2}$$

Also
$$S \equiv S_a + S_b + S_c \tag{3}$$

In these definitions, R is current revenue, the sum of taxes (T), income from fees, rent, etc. (Y), the operating surpluses of the departmental enterprises (P), and net interest earned from loan transactions with sector 2, $(I_2 - I'_2)$. C indicates current consumption of goods and services by the public authorities, Z the payment of subsidies and $Q'_{2,3}$ current transfers paid to the rest of the domestic economy and abroad. Although S is simply the sum of the saving of each spending agency, it does not follow that the definition of saving, for each spending agency, must be identity (1) re-written with appropriate letter subscripts. It does not follow because, of course, current transfers and interest-generating loan transactions take place between the three spending agencies in sector 1.

If we wish to take account of these intra-public-authorities transactions, the definitions of saving for each spending agency will be as follows:

$$S_a \equiv (R_a + I_{1a} + Q_{1a}) - (C_a + Z_a + Q'_{(2,3)a} + I'_{1a} + Q'_{1a}) \tag{4}$$
$$S_b \equiv (R_b + I_{1b} + Q_{1b}) - (C_b + Z_b + Q'_{2b} + I'_{1b} + Q'_{1b}) \tag{5}$$
$$S_c \equiv (R_c + I_{1c} + Q_{1c}) - (C_c + Z_c + Q'_{2c} + I'_{1c} + Q'_{1c}) \tag{6}$$

In these definitions I_1 and Q_1 indicate receipts of interest and transfers from other agencies in sector 1, and I'_1 and Q'_1 indicate payments of interest and transfers to other agencies in sector 1. Since, as a mere matter of accounting,

$$I_{1a} + I_{1b} + I_{1c} \equiv I'_{1a} + I'_{1b} + I'_{1c} \tag{7}$$

and,
$$Q_{1a} + Q_{1b} + Q_{1c} \equiv Q'_{1a} + Q'_{1b} + Q'_{1c} \tag{8}$$

it can readily be seen that definitions (4)–(6) are consistent with definitions (1) and (3).

Now if, for each separate spending agency, its payments of interest and transfers to other public authorities equalled its receipts of this kind from them, it would make no difference to the amount of its saving whether it were estimated with definitions like (4)–(6) or with a simpler definition of the form

$$S_x \equiv R_x - (C_x + Z_x + Q'_{(2,3)x})\qquad(1a)$$

But the whole purpose of intra-public authority loans and transfers, both in federations, like India, and in more centralized forms of government, is to shift resources to lower levels of government, which tend to have expenditure responsibilities markedly in excess of their revenue-raising capabilities. That purpose would be defeated if each spending agency received back in transfers and loan interest from the others exactly what it paid out to them. Instead, one would expect fiscal devolution to work roughly as follows:

$$I'_{1a} = I_{1c} = 0\qquad(9)$$

$$Q_{1a} = Q'_{1c} = 0\qquad(10)$$

$$I_{1a} = I'_{1b} > I_{1b} = I'_{1c} > 0\qquad(11)$$

$$Q'_{1a} = Q_{1b} > Q'_{1b} = Q_{1c} > 0\qquad(12)$$

$$Q_{1b} > I'_{1b}\qquad(13)$$

$$Q_{1c} > I'_{1c}\qquad(14)$$

With these weak behavioural assumptions, it could easily be shown that the use of definitions (4)–(6) will give higher values for the saving of state governments and local authorities than the use of definition (1a).

We are now in a position to consider the concept of saving by type of government spending agency that is used by the Indian Central Statistical Organization. When the first estimates of saving by spending agency for the period 1960/61 to 1969/70 were published in November 1973, the concept used was that of definitions (4)–(6) – or what can be called, for brevity, the post-devolution concept of saving. This can be stated with confidence not because the concept is explained in the relevant notes, but because the published estimates can

be reconciled with estimates made from C.S.O. detailed working sheets, on the basis of equations (4)–(6).

The post-devolution concept of saving yields the spending
agency breakdown set out in Table 8.2, with absolute amounts
in current prices given in crores of rupees. The percentage
shares of each spending agency are given in Table 8.3. The
picture presented there shows (i) that local authorities contributed about one quarter of public authority saving, apart
from two exceptional years, and (ii) that, of the remaining
three quarters, the central government contributed most during the Third Plan, while the state governments contributed
most in the last five years of the decade. Thus, in the second
five years, not only did the central government allow public
authorities' capital formation to become increasingly decentralized, it allowed public authorities' saving (after allowing for
fiscal devolution) to become more decentralized also.

However, there is a further complication which must be
noted. When the C.S.O. reissued figures for savings by public
authorities in January 1975, it originally simply re-printed the
figures given in Table 8.2 above. But, before the document was
published, a new and completely different breakdown was
pasted in over the top, without any explanatory note on why
the change had been made or on the basis on which the new
breakdown had been arrived at. This new breakdown was
subsequently incorporated in the document *National Account
Statistics, 1960/61–1973/74* issued in February 1976 and in
National Accounts Statistics, 1960/61 to 1974/75 issued in October
1976, again without a single word of explanation about the
reason for the change or its conceptual basis. Evidently there
had been some internal dispute, probably between the C.S.O.
and the Reserve Bank of India, about the conceptual issues
involved, and the C.S.O. has been forced to alter its practice.
But no indication of what these issues are has been permitted to
reach the public – even the scholarly public.

The 'new breakdown' of public saving (including for the
first time the saving of the non-departmental enterprises) is
reproduced in Table 8.4, and the percentage shares derived
therefrom are given in Table 8.5. A comparison of these figures
with those previously given suggests certain conclusions about
the nature of the new breakdown. First, the saving of the non-

TABLE 8.2   *Public authorities' saving (post-devolution concept) at current prices, 1960/61 to 1969/70.*

(Rs. crores)

	1960/61	1961/62	1962/63	1963/64	1964/65	1965/66	1966/67	1967/68	1968/69	1969/70
Public authorities' total saving of which,	298	366	408	513	598	542	408	360	543	625
a by central government	89	211	170	207	271	297	49	(−)65	92	190
b by state governments	134	60	131	195	191	136	249	310	322	325
c by local authorities	75	95	107	111	136	109	110	115	129	111

Source: C.S.O., (1973) *Estimates of National Product, Saving and Capital Formation, 1960/61 – 1971/72*, Table 9, p. 10.

TABLE 8.3 *Percentage contributions to public authorities' saving (post-devolution concept), 1960/61 to 1969/70.*

(Percentages)

	1960/61	1961/62	1962/63	1963/64	1964/65	1965/66	1966/67	1967/68	1968/69	1969/70
Share of public authorities' saving done by										
a central government	30	58	42	40	45	55	12	(—)18	17	30
b state governments	45	16	32	38	32	25	61	86	59	52
c local authorities	25	26	26	22	23	20	27	32	24	18

Source: calculated from Table 8.2 above.

TABLE 8.4 *Net saving of public sector ('new breakdown') at current prices, 1960/61 to 1969/70.*

(Rs. crores)

	1960/61	1961/62	1962/63	1963/64	1964/65	1965/66	1966/67	1967/68	1968/69	1969/70
Net saving of										
A Public authorities	298	366	408	513	598	542	408	360	543	626
of which										
i central government	113	236	202	242	312	376	148	59	196	338
ii state governments	121	49	117	177	175	97	190	217	251	221
iii local authorities	64	81	89	94	111	69	70	84	96	67
B Non-departmental enterprises	11	(−)3	—	26	13	50	(−)1	(−)5	(−)21	19
Total	309	363	408	539	611	592	407	355	522	645

Source: C.S.O., (1976a) *National Accounts Statistics, 1960/61–1973/74,* Table 22, p. 50.

TABLE 8.5 *Percentage contributions to net public sector saving ('new breakdown'), 1960/61 to 1969/70.*

(Percentages)

	1960/61	1961/62	1962/63	1963/64	1964/65	1965/66	1966/67	1967/68	1968/69	1969/70
Share of public sector saving										
a central government	37	65	50	45	51	64	36	17	38	52
b state governments	39	13	29	33	29	16	47	61	48	34
c local authorities	21	22	22	17	18	12	17	24	18	10
d non-departmental enterprises	4	(—)1	—	5	2	8	—	(—)1	(—)4	3

Note: Columns do not necessarily sum to 100 due to rounding.
Source: calculated from Table 8.4 above.

departmental enterprises can be effectively disregarded, since in the whole decade it amounted to only 89 crores of rupees. Second, since the saving totals for public authorities remain virtually unchanged in the new breakdown, it is clear that the basic data have not been revised: they have merely been re-classified with a new definition of 'saving' for each spending agency. Third, if the basic data remain those which appear on the original C.S.O. working sheets, we can be sure that the new definition is not that of equation (1a), i.e. with intra-public-authority interest and transfer payments and receipts totally excluded. It must be a compromise definition, with the saving of each spending agency being calculated after certain methods of fiscal devolution are taken into account, but before certain other methods of devolution are allowed for. But it does not seem possible to infer directly from the original working sheets precisely which intra-public-authority trans-actions are included and which excluded. Fourth, the effect of the new definition is easy to see. Whereas in the Third Plan period it raises the central government's share of public autho-rity saving by about 8 percentage points, taken roughly equally from the shares of the state governments and the local authori-ties, in the following five years it raises the centre's share by between 15 and 34 percentage points, taking approximately twice as much from the state governments' as from the local authorities' share. In other words, the excluded type (or types) of transactions become quantitatively more significant as the decade proceeds, and their exclusion has the effect of re-attributing a relatively larger segment of saving to the central government. Finally, because we are unable to infer precisely what the definition behind the 'new breakdown' is, it is im-possible to discuss properly its conceptual validity. It cannot be assumed that the change is a cosmetic one, designed to give the centre more credit for saving than is its due; but nor can it be assumed that it represents a definite conceptual improve-ment. When we come later to a disaggregated study of state government saving, the post-devolution definition of saving is used. It may or may not be the most appropriate definition; but at least one can be quite sure what the figures actually mean.

However, when looking at state government saving in aggregate, it is interesting to note that, even if the 'new breakdown' is taken to be the most appropriate one, it does not overturn all the conclusions derived from the post-devolution definition of saving. It remains true that, comparing the Third Plan period with the following five years, the centre's contribution to public authority saving fell – from 50.6 to 45.0 per cent, while the share either of state governments alone or state governments and local authorities taken together rose. The process of gradual centralization of saving within the Third Plan period, followed by gradual decentralization thereafter, does disappear if the 'new breakdown' figures are accepted. The year-to-year changes becomes larger and more erratic.

It is now possible to go on to explore how the different changes in the centralization of public capital formation and public saving combined to affect the ability of each type of spending agency to finance its own capital formation by its own saving. Given below are alternative presentations. Variant A, in Table 8.6, uses the post-devolution definition of saving, while variant B, in Table 8.7, uses the 'new breakdown' saving data.

It is evident in these figures that, whichever definition of saving is used, the ability of local authorities to save was being progressively outstripped by their capital programme. But the choice of definition is crucial for assessing the success of both central and state governments in matching saving with capital formation. For in variant A, the central government's achievement in this respect is shown (with the exception of 1967/68) to be roughly constant through the decade, while the state governments' performance is shown as improving. By contrast, variant B shows the state governments' achievement as roughly constant, and that of the central government (again excepting 1967/68) to be improving. Without knowing the precise meaning of the Variant B figures, it is impossible to draw firm conclusions about comparative saving efforts of the central and state governments.

However, one conclusion is possible on the basis of the Variant A figures taken by themselves. We know from the Reserve Bank's analyses of state government budgets that, between 1965/66 and 1969/70, the methods of fiscal devolu-

TABLE 8.6 *Shares of gross capital formation financed by own saving (Variant A), 1960/61 to 1969/70.*

(Percentages)

	1960/61	1961/62	1962/63	1963/64	1964/65	1965/66	1966/67	1967/68	1968/69	1969/70
a Central government	28	66	37	38	42	60	11	0	36	48
b State governments	38	18	34	51	43	23	50	50	50	48
c Local authorities	100*	100*	100*	100*	100*	65	76	60	73	62
d Non-departmental enterprises	2	0	0	4	2	5	0	0	0	2
e Public sector	27	31	28	32	32	27	19	15	24	29

Note: * During the Third Plan, saving of local authorities exceeded their gross capital formation by annual amounts of 8, 18, 6, 2 and 10 crores of rupees at current prices.

Source: calculated from data in C.S.O., (1976a) *National Accounts Statistics, 1960/61–1973/74*, Table 22, pp. 50–1 and Table 8.2 above.

TABLE 8.7 *Shares of gross capital formation financed by own saving (Variant B), 1960/61 to 1969/70.*

(Percentages)

	1960/61	1961/62	1962/63	1963/64	1964/65	1965/66	1966/67	1967/68	1968/69	1969/70
a Central government	35	74	44	44	49	75	32	13	76	85
b State governments	34	15	30	46	39	16	38	35	38	33
c Local authorities	96	100*	88	86	88	41	49	44	54	38
d Non-departmental enterprises	2	0	0	4	2	5	0	0	0	2
e Public sector	27	31	28	32	32	27	19	15	24	29

Note: In 1961–62, saving of local authorities exceeded their gross capital formation by 4 crores of rupees at current prices.
Source: calculated from data in C.S.O., (1976a) *National Accounts Statistics, 1960/61–1973/74*, Table 22, pp. 50–1.

tion were changing in relative importance. In particular, the various arrangements for sharing the proceeds of centrally-levied taxes were providing a growing proportion of central government assistance to the states, while the importance of central loans (net of repayments of past loans) was declining.[1] This change in method of devolution swells the saving of state government, on Variant A definitions, because it involves a substitution of current for capital transfers. It may simply be this change that produced the state government's improved ability to finance its own capital formation apparent in the Variant A figures. It may also be that the secret of the 'new breakdown' of public authority savings lies in a re-allocation of some elements of the transferred taxes, perhaps those central excises whose assignment in part to the states is at the centre's discretion. Instead of counting as tax revenues of the state governments, they may be counted as tax revenues of the centre, with a consistent adjustment for taxes levied by state governments and distributed to local authorities. If this guess is correct, then it is clear that we have entered very thorny ground. In deciding which level of government should be credited with the revenue of transferred taxes, legal and constitutional arguments can come into conflict with practical arguments in particular cases. For example, the proceeds of the Central Sales Tax belong, under Article 269 of the Constitution, to the states, and yet the tax is actually levied, for reasons of sound administration, by the central government, which thus determines how much revenue the tax shall yield.[2] Thus to follow the pragmatic rule, that the authority whose policy controls the tax yield should be credited with revenue, does create an allocation which makes no sense from a legal point of view.[3] At the same time, it seems the only sensible rule as long as the objective is to arrange statistics in such a way that they are relevant to the assessment of policy. If the 'new breakdown' is indeed an attempt to follow this rule more closely, then it follows that Variant B figures are superior, and the central government can be commended for not allowing its contribu-

1 Toye (1973), p. 265.
2 Chatterji (1971), pp. 62–3.
3 Toye (1973), p. 274.

tion to public saving to fall as drastically as its contribution to public capital formation. We must rest with this hypothetical judgement until the Central Statistical Organization makes public the conventions underlying the 'new breakdown'.

If enquiry is made into the reasons why public authorities saved what they did, it is not really possible to advance explanations such as have been offered previously for the rapid cutback on central government capital formation. This is because it is highly doubtful that public saving is seen by any level of government as a policy target, even indirectly, in the way that a concern to start up (and, less powerfully, to complete) big projects makes capital formation a policy target. It was shown at the start of this study that, at the time the Fourth Plan was being prepared, the officially articulated view of the policy of state accumulation (including the role therein of public saving) veered towards confusion and vagueness. It is reasonable to suggest that official practice was even more confused, and that public saving was a residual, not merely in terms of formal categories but in terms of the motivations of those who shaped fiscal policies.

The information that would be needed to make a given level of public saving a policy target was available for the central government only; but, even for the centre, it is stretching the imagination to believe that it was seriously attended to at budget-making discussions. Sectoral sources of finance must have been a minor concern compared with the overall budgetary deficit (misleadingly taken as an indicator of government-induced inflation) and even the size of the overall deficit was not always attended to very strictly in setting the combination of expenditures and instruments of finance. The increase of public saving never became the focus of year-to-year budgeting; it always remained the last resort of planners squaring the circle for the next unfeasible plan. As for the allocation between spending agencies of what public saving emerged, that was determined ultimately by the allocation of tax bases and spending functions and the poorly coordinated and inflexible system of fiscal devolution, as well as by the parsimony and tax effort of the different levels of government.

III INTER-STATE DIFFERENCES IN GROWTH OF PUBLIC CAPITAL FORMATION

Throughout the decade the gross capital formation of the state governments and local authorities taken together grew in money and in real terms. There were two setbacks, in 1961–2 and 1966–7, but, viewed overall, it was a decade of reasonably steady growth. However, as has been shown in the previous chapter, total public expenditure, adjusted for price changes and population growth, grew at significantly different rates in different states (again adding together the spending of the state government proper and the local authorities within its boundary). The inter-state differences in total expenditure growth create a presumption that states (in the extended use of the term) contributed to the overall growth of capital formation in the state and local authority sectors in different degrees. The task, then, is to explore whether the statistical data bear out this presumption, and, if so, to test plausible explanations of inter-state differences in the growth of public capital formation.

Hypotheses about the growth of public capital formation in the current literature are very sketchy, and suffer from two weaknesses that lessen their usefulness in the present context. They are framed to give an account of developments in the very long run, rather than changes occurring within a mere decade. In addition, they are not free from European bias, because they assume that certain European political norms will in fact be adhered to. The underlying idea is that public capital formation will constitute a relatively larger part of (a) the government budget, (b) total capital formation and (c) gross national expenditure in the 'early stages' of economic development, will decline relatively in the 'middle stages' and may increase again relatively (depending on specific technical, institutional and productivity influences) in the 'later stages'.[4]

This hypothesis does not appear to have been tested rigorously, even for advanced capitalist countries for which long-period historical data are available.[5] Perhaps the most exhaus-

---

4 Musgrave (1969), pp. 75–8; Bird (1970), p. 142; Burkehead and Miner (1971), pp. 305–6.
5 Musgrave (1969), pp. 91–124.

tive econometric investigation of expenditure determinants of recent times focusses exclusively on public consumption expenditure.[6] For India, the most exhaustive recent analysis of public expenditures lumps capital outlay in with that amorphous category, social and developmental expenditure, and relies on the conventional Indian definition of capital outlay, rather than capital formation in the national accounting sense.[7] But, although the hypothesis cannot be said to have survived after rigorous testing, it retains a certain intuitive appeal as the most plausible of possible explanations of changes in public capital formation. If this hypothesis were true, one would expect that the rate of growth of public capital formation would always be less than the growth rate of state income, state government expenditure and total capital formation. This is consistent with the idea that public capital formation acts as a catalyst for economic growth, which is fuelled increasingly by private investment. Since, as explained at the beginning of Chapter 6, the distribution of central government capital formation by state is not known, it is only possible to test the hypothesis with data for public capital formation at the state level only.

An alternative hypothesis which migh also be tested is that the economic composition of state government budgets (as between capital formation and other items) tends to remain constant, because of bureaucratic inertia, or conservative expenditure control practices such as incremental budgeting.

Before either of these theories can be confronted with evidence, it is necessary to establish precisely what growth rates of state public capital formation are to be used. The basic data source is again the C.S.O. working sheets used in the compilation of the public authorities' elements in the national accounts. As in the previous statewise analysis of total public expenditure, the operations of local authorities within each state boundary are not distinguished from the operations of the state government itself, for the reason already given. In order to club the two sorts of operations together in this way, a slightly arbitrary allocation procedure had to be used to dis-

6 Pryor (1968).   7 Reddy (1972), pp. 114–16, 216–19.

tribute total local authorities' gross fixed capital formation between the states for the years 1960/61 to 1964/65. The capital formation for which we give statewise growth rates is indeed gross fixed capital formation. It is the sum of the gross fixed capital formation of the administrative departments of state governments and local authorities plus the capital outlay and the renewals and replacement expenditure of their departmental enterprises. Our figures thus take no account of the accumulation or decumulation of stocks of raw materials and finished products, nor the purchase and sale of secondhand assets, nor capital grants given to other sectors of the economy for the purpose of capital formation. The reason for ignoring stock changes is their considerable year-to-year variation in response to short-run circumstances. Net purchase of assets is irrelevant because it reflects shifts in ownership of assets already in existence. Capital transfers for capital formation are ignored because they are negligible in size.

Since the rate of price inflation during the decade was different in different states, an inter-state comparison of growth rates of capital formation requires that due allowance first be made for geographically differentiated inflation. Unfortunately, there is no very sophisticated way to make this allowance. Ideally, capital formation should be disaggregated by broad type of asset (e.g. construction, machinery and equipment) and a separate and appropriate price deflator applied to each element. But while such indices exist for all-India, they are certainly not publicly available in a state-by-state breakdown, and probably are based on too few points of observation for it to be possible in principle to extract from them a sound statewise breakdown. It is therefore necessary to fall back on the much less satisfactory procedure of adjusting the gross fixed capital formation figures by the price deflators that are implicit in the estimates of state income. The weakness of this procedure (apart from the inherent unreliability of some of the state income estimates themselves) is obvious. We know that the inter-sectoral terms of trade shifted in the relevant period in favour of agriculture. Therefore the use of general deflators (reflecting changes in both industrial and agricultural prices) will 'over-deflate' gross fixed capital formation figures at current prices, so that the estimated growth

TABLE 8.8 *Share of agriculture in state domestic product, by state, 1964/65.*

State	Total net domestic product	Agriculture and animal husbandry sectors	(2) as percentage of (1) %	Degree of 'over-deflation' rank
		(Rs. crores at current prices)		
	(1)	(2)	(3)	(4)
Uttar Pradesh	2985	1899	63.6	1
Punjab and Haryana	1141	715	62.7	2
Rajasthan	795	486	61.1	3
Assam	580	341	58.7	4
Andhra Pradesh	1690	975	57.7	5
Madhya Pradesh	1320	752	57.0	6
Orissa	658	367	55.8	7
Mysore	1075	569	52.9	8
Jammu and Kashmir	127	66	52.0	9
Bihar	1505	781	51.9	10
Kerala	725	358	49.4	11
Gujarat	1189	568	47.8	12
Tamil Nadu	1552	638	41.1	13
West Bengal	1916	700	36.5	14
Maharashtra	2277	829	36.4	15
Total	19535	10044	51.4	

Note: To derive the degree of 'over-deflation' directly from the share of agriculture in state domestic product relies on the assumption that the movement of the inter-sectoral terms of trade was uniform throughout India. This assumption may not be strictly correct.
Source: *Report of the Finance Commission, 1969*, Table 4, p. 127.

rates will be too low for all states. In addition, given that the relative importance of the agricultural sector varies between states, the 'over-deflation' will be worse for states with a large agricultural sector, thus distorting the inter-state comparison of growth rates. In this case, it is at least possible to state the direction of the bias. The states are ranked by degree of 'over-deflation' in the final column of Table 8.8. The existence of this bias simply has to be borne in mind when interpreting the meaning of the growth rates estimated with a general deflator. It will not be possible to do better than this until the states compile, on a uniform methodology, price indices for each major sectoral component of state domestic product, as has

TABLE 8.9   *Deflated growth rates of gross fixed capital formation
by state, 1960/61 to 1969/70.*

State	Annual compound growth rate of deflated G.F.C.F. (percentages)	Rank
1 Andhra Pradesh	(−)0.3	8
2 Assam	4.9	2
3 Bihar	(−)1.4	13
4 Gujarat	4.4	3
5 Jammu and Kashmir	2.3	4
6 Kerala	(−)0.1	7
7 Madhya Pradesh	(−)2.1	14
8 Maharashtra	6.6	1
9 Mysore	(−)0.7	10
10 Orissa	(−)0.6	9
11 Punjab and Haryana	(−)4.8	15
12 Rajasthan	(−)1.4	12
13 Tamil Nadu	0.7	6
14 Uttar Pradesh	(−)1.2	11
15 West Bengal	1.2	5

Source: Calculated from unpublished C.S.O. working sheets.

been recently recommended.[8] Even the adoption of this improvement will leave the researcher without the statewise and
asset-type price indices which, ideally, is the information he
needs.

Having deflated the annual figures for gross fixed capital
formation by states (albeit in a biassed way), a time trend was
fitted to the data by the method of ordinary least squares, and
an annual compound growth rate estimated from the initial
and final trend values. The growth rate of gross fixed capital
formation for each state, deflated in the manner described,
is set out in Table 8.9. These figures must be read with care,
because of the weakness of the deflation procedure. All are
likely to be somewhat too low, so that the large number of

8 C.S.O., *First Report of the Committee on Regional Accounts* (1974), pp. 31, 49, 67.

states shown to have negative growth rates is misleading. Kerala, Andhra, Orissa and Mysore ought possibly to be shown with some positive, but small, growth; while the rate of contraction for Punjab and Harayana, Madhya Pradesh, Uttar Pradesh and Rajasthan ought to be significantly reduced. But, even after having made these kinds of mental adjustments, one could suggest that the areas where public capital formation at the state level grew fastest were the more developed industrial areas – Maharashtra, Gujarat and West Bengal and – to a lesser extent – Tamil Nadu and relatively underdeveloped border areas of strategic significance such as Assam and Jammu and Kashmir.

Before testing the two hypotheses on the growth of public capital formation with which this discussion began, it must be decided whether the ranking of growth rates given in Table 8.9 is to be allowed to stand, or whether, given the different degrees of 'over-deflation' embodied in that ranking, it would be preferable to re-order some of the states. The problem here is the lack of an objective criterion according to which a revised ranking might be carried out. Since we do not know the quantitative effect of over-deflation on the estimated growth rates, only one procedure is justifiable, namely that, where two states have clearly similar growth rates, but widely differing degrees of over-deflation (as indicated in Table 8.8), the more over-deflated should be ranked above the less over-deflated. As a comparison between Tables 8.9 and 8.8 shows, this situation does not in fact arise. Where two states have very similar growth rates, their respective degrees of over-deflation do not differ very much either. Thus, although the ranking of states by growth rates may not be reliable, there is no reliable way of making them more so. Thus, logically, they must be allowed to stand as they are.

We can now proceed to test, as far as this is possible, the two competing hypotheses on influences on public capital formation, beginning with the favoured theory that it declines in relative importance as development takes place. It is a handicap here that indicators of relative development over time of the different states are not available, with the result that the tests must be done in two stages.

Some data are available on comparative levels of overall

development of the states in 1961. They are derived from the 1961 Census, and make use of 35 separate indicators for each district combined to form an unweighted development index. The states are then ranked by the percentage of their 1961 population living in districts which, according to the constructed index, are above the average level of development. Obviously there must be deficiencies in such an index arising from poor quality of some of the initial districtwise data, quite apart from the arbitrariness of giving each of 35 indicators equal weight in the combined index.[9] However, since this is the most thorough exercise available, it must be pressed into service. It is then possible to compare levels of development in 1961 with (a) the share of public capital formation in total public expenditure for 1960/61 and (b) the share of public capital formation in state domestic product for 1960/61. The relevant figures are given in Table 8.10, and the coefficients of rank correlation are given in Table 8.11.

The correlation coefficients show that there is a tendency for less developed states in 1960/61 to devote a higher percentage of both their total domestic product and total public expenditure to public capital formation. However, the coefficients are not significant at the 0.05 confidence level, and thus, if this confidence level is accepted as our decision rule, the hypothesis must be rejected because we cannot be sufficiently sure that the observed association is not a result of chance influences. These negative findings do not, of course, exclude the possibility that in less developed states a significantly higher proportion of total capital formation is done by public authorities. This variation of the hypothesis cannot be put to the test as long as statewise breakdowns of total capital formation remain to be undertaken.[10] As sometimes happens, the most intuitively appealing variant of the hypothesis is the hardest one to test. It remains a promising line for future enquiry.

The hypothesis that public capital formation declines in relative importance as development occurs is clearly a hypothesis about a process. Thus, while cross-section tests such as the foregoing may be useful as indirect auxiliary evidence, what is essentially required is a test with time-series data. Only such

9 Rudolph and Rudolph (1969), p. 1043.
10 C.S.O., First Report of the Committee on Regional Accounts (1974), p. 13.

TABLE 8.10 *Statewise share of public capital formation in domestic product and total public expenditure, 1960/61.*

State	(A) Development rank*	(B) 1960/61 Public G.F.C.F. as % of state domestic product	(C) 1960/61 Public G.F.C.F. as % of public exp.	(D) 1960–70 average public G.F.C.F. as % of public exp.
1 Andhra Pradesh	7	4.04	40.06	33.5
2 Assam	8	3.2	28.97	26.0
3 Bihar	3	2.8	29.93	28.5
4 Gujarat	13	4.1	39.86	32.7
5 Jammu and Kashmir	2	11.2	50	38.2
6 Kerala	14	2.52	23	20.5
7 Madhya Pradesh	4	2.48	28	22.9
8 Maharashtra	11	2.9	29.98	29.7
9 Mysore	10	6.0	48	38.8
10 Orissa	1	4.8	42.79	37.3
11 Punjab and Haryana	12	3.97	41.5	29.4
12 Rajasthan	6	4.98	43.1	31.3
13 Tamil Nadu	15	2.3	25	22.5
14 Uttar Pradesh	5	2.0	31	26.6
15 West Bengal	9	2.25	27	23.3

Note: * 'Development rank' is derived as explained in the text, but the ranking sequence runs from least to most developed.
Sources: Col. (A), from Rudolph and Rudolph (1969), p. 1043. Cols. (B)–(D), from C.S.O. unpublished data.

a test can directly address the question whether a rapid rate of development is, in general, associated with a relatively rapid decline in the two ratios on which we have evidence – namely, the ratio of public capital formation to state domestic product, and of public capital formation to total state public expenditure.

Since rates of development, measured even with the degree of sophistication embodied in the estimates of 1961 levels of development which we have already used, are unobtainable, it is necessary to use, as a proxy for them, rates of growth of

TABLE 8.11　*Rank correlation coefficients for variables in Table 8.10.*

Variables	Rank correlation coefficient (r')*
1 (A) with (B)	+0.24
2 (A) with (C)	+0.42
3 (A) with (D)	+0.37

Note: *The rank correlation coefficient is given by the formula

$$r' = 1 - \frac{b\left(\Sigma d_i^2\right)}{n(n^2 - 1)},$$ where d is the difference in rank for each observation, and n is the number of observations. The significance test at the 0.05 confidence level is given by

$$r' \gtreqless \pm \frac{1.96}{(n-1)^{1/2}},$$ which with 15 observations means

$$r' \gtreqless \pm 0.52,$$

state domestic product at constant prices. It is not a very satisfactory proxy, and furthermore, the figures themselves are unreliable in important ways previously mentioned. Their use is only justified on familiar *faute de mieux* grounds. To measure the change in the ratio of public capital formation to state domestic product (G.F.C.F./S.D.P.) and of public capital formation to total state public expenditure (G.F.C.F./S.P.E.), the difference is taken between the G.F.C.F. growth rate and the S.D.P. growth rate for the former, and between the G.F.C.F. growth rate and the S.P.E. growth rate for the latter. The reasoning here is that if G.F.C.F. grows more slowly than S.D.P., or S.P.E., the G.F.C.F./S.D.P. or G.F.C.F./S.P.E. ratios will be declining, and the larger the difference between the two growth rates, the larger will the decline in the ratios be. The growth rate differences are given in Table 8.12, columns (F) and (G), and these can then be correlated with the rate of development proxy variables given in column (E). The rank correlation coefficients are given in Table 8.13.

　The positive sign of the coefficients indicates that the relationship is of the kind which the hypothesis predicts: that is to say, it is indeed the case that a faster rate of development (as measured by the proxy) is accompanied by a greater shrink-

TABLE 8.12   *Indicators of income growth and changes in G.F.C.F./S.D.P. and G.F.C.F./public expenditure ratios by state, 1960–70.*

		(E) Growth rate of real S.D.P. per head, 1960–70 (Rank)	(F) G.F.C.F. growth rate minus real S.D.P. growth rates (Percentages)	(G) G.F.C.F. growth rate minus real public spending growth rate (Percentages)
1	Andhra Pradesh	12	−1.98 (8)	−2.3 (12)
2	Assam	3	+0.59 (13)	−1.5 (13)
3	Bihar	14	+0.17 (12)	−3.1 (10)
4	Gujarat	9	+1.60 (14)	−0.7 (14)
5	Jammu and Kashmir	7	−0.99 (10)	−5.5 (3)
6	Kerala	6	−3.32 (4)	−5.2 (4)
7	Madhya Pradesh	13	+0.15 (11)	−4.1 (7)
8	Maharashtra	10	+4.08 (15)	−0.7 (15)
9	Mysore	1	−5.50 (2)	−4.0 (8)
10	Orissa	15	−2.11 (7)	−4.6 (5)
11	Punjab and Haryana	2	−9.33 (1)	−6.0 (2)
12	Rajasthan	4	−5.13 (3)	−6.1 (1)
13	Tamil Nadu	5	−2.51 (6)	−4.4 (6)
14	Uttar Pradesh	11	−3.04 (5)	−3.5 (9)
15	West Bengal	8	−1.75 (9)	−2.9 (11)

Sources: Growth rates of state domestic product, and S.D.P. per head, at 1960/61 prices were calculated from data provided by State Statistical Bureaux and collated by the C.S.O. in a mimeo, dated December 1971.

Growth rates of gross fixed capital formation are those that appear above in Table 8.9. Growth rates of state public expenditure at 1960/61 prices are those that appear in Table 6.2.

The bracketed figures are statewise rankings.

TABLE 8.13   *Rank correlation coefficients for variables in Table 8.12.*

Variables	*r'*
1 (E) with (F)	+0.48
2 (E) with (G)	+0.30

age in the relative importance of public capital formation as measured by the G.F.C.F./S.D.P. and G.F.C.F./S.P.E. ratios. However, neither coefficient is significant at the 0.05 confidence level, although result 1 comes very close to being statistically significant.

From inspection of our calculated growth rates of capital formation, it appears that the main thrust of public capital formation at the state level occurred in two distinct contexts, support to private capital and the building up of infrastructure in militarily sensitive border areas. The hypothesis under test is logically related to the former context. One would expect that the test results could be improved by excluding the observations for those two states (Assam, and Jammu and Kashmir) where a quite different motive for public capital formation is thought to operate. If those two states are excluded, both correlation coefficients do improve, but not to the same extent. The coefficient for the association between development rate and fall in the G.F.C.F./S.D.P. ratio rises to + 0.66. This is significant at the 0.05 confidence level, which, with thirteen observations, equals + 0.565. On the other hand, the coefficient relating development to the fall in the G.F.C.F./S.P.E. ratio rises only to + 0.38, which remains insignificant.

The conclusions to be drawn from this exercise are:

(a) that, provided the militarily sensitive border areas are omitted from consideration, the hypothesis that, with development, a declining share of state domestic product is channelled to public capital formation is not refuted;
(b) that the theory that, with development, the share of public capital formation in total state public expenditure also falls has to be rejected at the chosen confidence level. This means that, as yet, we have no satisfactory explanation of the composition of state public expenditure between capital and current elements;
(c) that a variant of the hypothesis that might seek to relate the share of public to total capital formation and the progress of development cannot be tested until a statewise breakdown of total capital formation becomes available.

Following on from (b) above, it may be asked whether the

question of economic budget composition can be resolved by using the second major hypothesis that was put forward earlier. That hypothesis suggested that the economic composition of public spending remained constant as spending grew, because of bureaucratic inertia. Intuitively, this is a rather far-fetched hypothesis, since it seems to require the use of some historical capital–current balance as a rule of thumb in budget-making. The point has already been sufficiently laboured that there is still in India at the state level inadequate knowledge of the economic classification of public spending. Further, from a factual point of view, it is evident from inspection of column (G) in Table 8.12, that the capital–current balance did not remain constant in the period 1960–70. On the contrary, without a single exception, the share of capital formation in state's spending declined. The size of the share was also different in different states, ranging from 20 per cent in Kerala to 39 per cent in Mysore, on the basis of ten-year average figures, and a hypothesis framed in terms of conventional historic norms effectively side-steps the problem of explaining these differences in the level of the capital–current balance.

In order to come to grips with these difficulties, it is necessary to open up a new line of theorizing. It begins from the notion of 'the degree of government activity'. To this rather vague notion, some initial clarity may be given by indicating what it does not imply. It does not necessarily imply a preference for government activity among legislators or voters, since that preference may be strongest, and most strongly expressed by elections and legislative votes, precisely in those states where the degree of government activity is relatively low. It does not necessarily imply sound or effective government, since a relatively inactive government may be able to operate more rationally and purposefully precisely because the scope of its ambition is more narrowly limited. The degree of government activity is a concept of how much a government tries to do, whether willed by its citizens or not, and regardless of how well or badly it actually does what it attempts.

Capital formation is never the first priority of a government. Its priority functions, justice, police, revenue and arms, make their financial demands on current expenditure, and the capital services they require can, at a pinch, be provided by the

TABLE 8.14   *Indicators of government activity and the share of capital formation in government spending by state, 1960/61 and 1969/70.*

State	(H) S.P.E./S.D.P. 1960/61 (per cent)	(J) G.F.C.F./S.P.E. 1960/61 (per cent)	(K) S.P.E./S.D.P. 1969/70 (per cent)	(L) G.F.C.F./SPE 1969/70 (per cent)
1 Andhra Pradesh	10.1	40.1	12.0	25.9
2 Assam	10.9	29.0	15.0	27
3 Bihar	9.3	29.9	10.6	21
4 Gujarat	10.2	39.9	14.8	34
5 Jammu and Kashmir	22.5	50	30.9	33
6 Kerala	10.9	23	14.7	17.3
7 Madhya Pradesh	8.7	28	7.8	17.4
8 Maharashtra	9.8	30.0	13.1	26.2
9 Mysore	12.5	48	13.9	32
10 Orissa	11.2	42.8	16.7	22
11 Punjab and Haryana	9.6	41.5	7.1	25.5
12 Rajasthan	11.6	43.1	18.3	23
13 Tamil Nadu	9.0	25	10.1	20
14 Uttar Pradesh	6.4	31	6.8	25
15 West Bengal	8.4	27	11.7	19

Sources: Figures for total state public expenditure (S.P.E.) and gross fixed capital formation by public authorities (G.F.C.F.), both at current prices, are taken from C.S.O., unpublished data. Figures for state domestic product (S.D.P.) for 1960/61 are taken from Finance Commission (1969), Table 4, p. 127. Figures for S.D.P. in 1969/70 are those calculated by State Statistical Bureaux and reproduced in a C.S.O. mimeo, dated December 1971.

existing stock of building and equipment in government ownership. It follows from this that one would expect the capital–current balance in public expenditure to be an increasing function of the degree of government activity. The exact shape of the function is of no consequence, provided that it is upward-sloping in the relevant range. The major problem in making this theory operational is the absence of a unit by which the degree of government activity can be measured.

In order to put this theory to the test, it is proposed to take, as a proxy for the degree of government activity, the ratio of state public expenditure to state domestic product. As is well known, this ratio is something of a bastard statistic, since public expenditure includes transfer payments while domestic product excludes them. It therefore gives only an imperfect measure of the size of the public sector. Even so, for comparative purposes, it seems reasonable to suggest that more active governments will have a higher SPE/SDP ratio than less active governments, and that is the only assumption which needs to be valid in this context.

Results 1 and 2 in Table 8.15 seem to be consistent with the hypothesized relationship. But only result 1, for 1960/61, is significant at the 0.05 confidence level. How much weight can be placed on the apparently satisfactory result for 1960/61? It might be objected that the two variables under consideration are not independent of each other, since the ratios S.P.E./S.D.P. and G.F.C.F./S.P.E. both contain the common element, S.P.E. To this objection it can be conceded that the observed correlation may not result from co-variation of mutually distinct behavioural variables, as should be the case

TABLE 8.15 *Rank correlation coefficients for variables in Table 8.14.*

Variables	r'
1 (H) with (J)	+ 0.63
2 (K) with (L)	+ 0.40
3 (H) with (K)	+ 0.88
4 (J) with (L)	+ 0.66

when regression analysis is used to test for functional dependence. However, the presence of a common element in both ratios does not imply that either the hypothesis is tautological, or that the observed correlation of the ratios is spurious and a statistical artifact. Variations in S.P.E. can arise either from the G.F.C.F. element or from the element of state spending which does not result in capital formation. It is possible that the marginal growth of S.P.E. comes mainly from the non-G.F.C.F. element. If this were indeed the case, it would produce an inverse relationship between the S.P.E./S.D.P. ratio and the G.F.C.F./S.P.E. ratio. A positive r', as in results 1 and 2, shows that, while logically possible, this case was not the Indian experience. Whilst these results are perhaps not very surprising, they are neither meaningless nor contrived. That the positive correlation became weaker between 1960/61 and 1969/70 indicates that restraint on the growth of capital formation after the Third Plan operated rather arbitrarily. Some states (Assam, Gujarat) were affected hardly at all, while others (Orissa, Rajasthan) were seriously affected, and the severity of restraint had no evident connection with the existing extent of state governmental activity. Results 3 and 4 above show that the weakening of the correlation owes much more to changes in G.F.C.F./S.P.E. ratios, than to changes in S.P.E./S.D.P. ratios.

The main conclusions of the foregoing examination of capital formation by state governments may now be summed up. The Indian experience is broadly consistent with the theory that the share of an economy's resources devoted to public capital formation declines as development takes place. Having said that, one would want to go on to criticize the rather abstract and positivistic formulation of the proposition. In particular, it should be made clear that development, in this context, refers to the irregular and unbalanced growth which tends to occur as capitalism penetrates underdeveloped mixed economies. The evidence presented should not be taken as a reinforcement of an abstract universal proposition, perhaps even with normative overtones. On the contrary, it merely isolates one characteristic of a specific historical and institutional complex, with no normative implications at all. The historical and institutional concreteness is underlined by the fact that the proposition needs to be qualified to give special recognition to the role of public capital formation in underdeveloped, but militarily sensitive, areas of the country. This serves as a reminder of the ambiguous response to capitalist penetration – a synthesis of reception and resistance – which 'developing' mixed economies display.

Since the level of development is not significantly correlated with the economic composition of the state government budget, and nor is economic composition of the budget a conventional constant, alternative explanations were sought. On a cross-section basis, it could be shown that budget composition was related to the degree of government activity in the state economy, lending support to the notion of capital formation as a 'superior good' in state government budget-making. Absence of data, however, make it impossible at the moment to follow the desirable procedure of conducting a further test on a time-series basis. Obviously such a test is required. The weakening of the cross-section relationship, between 1960/61 and 1969/70 suggests that different cross-section and time-series determinants may be at work. On the other hand, it may merely indicate the hasty and ill-planned nature of restraints on public investments in the late 1960s.

IV STATEWISE COMPARISON OF PUBLIC CAPITAL FORMATION
AND PUBLIC SAVING

Finally, it may be instructive to enquire whether, at the state level, the availability of public saving acts as a constraint on the amount of capital formation that is undertaken. At the all-India level, total domestic capital formation cannot exceed the sum of total domestic saving plus net capital inflow, but public saving can, and indeed did, fall as a proportion of public capital formation. This happened as a static rate of capital formation was combined in the late 1960s with increasing diversion of the saving of other sectors to public sector use. In the state government segment of the public sector, state governments as a group did not falter in the share of their capital formation financed by their own saving, and may (depending on the definition of 'saving' to be used) even have raised that share. This contrast between the state government

segment and the public sector as a whole suggests that the
state governments may have particularly restricted opportuni-
ties for diverting non-public sector saving to their use, and
that they are therefore particularly constrained to finance formation of capital by their own saving (including therein either
all or some of the transfers received from other segments of the
public sector).

The notion of a public saving constraint on state government
capital formation is inconsistent, in theory, with the determinants which have fitted our data best up to this point. If the
growth of state government spending is related to variables
like growth of income per head and urbanization, and if the
division of state government spending between capital and
current items is related to its relative importance in the state
economy, or the 'degree of government activity', changes in
the level of capital spending are thereby determined. The
introduction of an exogenous financial constraint, stemming
from state revenue effort and the intricacies of transfers
between public authorities, would leave the original simple
model over-determined. Thus, one would be inclined to expect
no relationship between the growth of capital formation and
public saving at the level of the individual state government.

How well-founded is this expectation? As the lengthy discussion of alternative estimates of public saving in a previous
section will have indicated, the answer to this question cannot
be entirely straightforward. Without knowing which definition of public saving has, since 1975, been used in official
publications, saving estimates using 'new breakdown' definitions cannot be made for individual state governments. However, from the pre-1975 working sheets which form the empirical basis of this work, the saving of individual state governments (and local authorities within state boundaries) are known
on the 'post-devolution' basis, i.e. including all intra-public-
sector transfer payments as own expenditure, and similar
receipts as revenue, before calculating saving by subtraction.
These figures of 'post-devolution' saving have then been
deflated for each state, using the same implicit deflators as were
used for the statewise capital formation series. Inspection of
the deflated saving figures showed that they exhibited much
greater year-to-year volatility (including 13 out of 150 negative

values). When observations do not cluster around a trend line, the calculation of such a line by the method of least squares can be heavily influenced by a few extremely eccentric values. The growth rates of deflated 'post-devolution' savings over the years 1960/61 to 1969/70, as shown in Table 8.16, cannot therefore be regarded as very reliable.

We can now compare the saving growth rates shown in Table 8.16 with the deflated G.F.C.F. growth rates previously set out in Table 8.9. Even allowing that the former contain relatively large margins of error, it does not seem unreasonable to assert that there is no relationship between the two variables. Orissa, Mysore, Madhya Pradesh and Punjab and Haryana show high rates of saving growth with low rates of capital formation growth. Maharashtra, Assam and West Bengal had

TABLE 8.16   *Growth rates of deflated 'post-devolution' saving by state governments, 1960/61 to 1969/70.*

State	Annual average growth rate (%)
1 Andhra Pradesh	− 4.2
2 Assam	− 6.8
3 Bihar	− 3.5
4 Gujarat	+ 5.5
5 Jammu and Kashmir	+ 12.9 *
6 Kerala	+ 1.5
7 Madhya Pradesh	+ 13.5
8 Maharashtra	− 0.7
9 Mysore	+ 13.9
10 Orissa	+ 8.8
11 Punjab and Haryana	+ 10.7
12 Rajasthan	**
13 Tamil Nadu	+ 4.6
14 Uttar Pradesh	+ 5.2
15 West Bengal	− 6.3

Notes: * refers to period 1961/62 to 1968/69 to avoid extreme values.
          ** growth rate cannot be calculated because of some negative values.
Source: calculated from unpublished C.S.O. data.

low saving growth and high capital formation growth. The remaining eight of the fifteen states exhibit a closer correspondence of the two rates of growth. But even at its closest, this correspondence leaves a gap of one percentage point between the two rates (Gujarat). On the whole, then, the statistical evidence points to a random association between saving and capital formation. Thus growth of the former seems to be neither a necessary, nor a sufficient, condition for growth of the latter. This result is consistent with the previous results noted in this work on the determinants of public spending and capital formation at the level of the states.

Part Three
Conclusions

9

The Indian state accumulation policy in retrospect

The empirical core of this work has been a detailed examination of the development of public spending at the all-India and at the state level. What remains to be done is to connect some of the empirical findings with the broader themes of mimetic nationalism and state accumulation which were explored in the two opening chapters.

It is proposed to examine the connections in three stages of argument. The first considers the constraints which mimetic nationalism imposed on the process of state accumulation, and suggests what additional conditions would have to be satisfied before a state accumulation policy could operate successfully within those constraints. The second considers the desiderata, purely within the sphere of the public finances, of a successful state accumulation policy against the background of the actual state of the Indian public finances. The third examines briefly the prospects for improved control over public expenditure in the present state of Indian federalism.

I MIMETIC NATIONALISM AND STATE ACCUMULATION

There is no necessary connection between mimetic nationalism and state accumulation. The former is quite compatible with private accumulation, and the latter policy could be operated in advanced capitalist nations on whom the pressures that produce mimetic nationalism do not bear. Thus the only link between mimetic nationalism and state accumulation is one of historical contingency.

The state accumulation policy was discussed in Chapter 1 in the abstract. Any general rule of accumulation, such as maximizing reinvestible surplus in the hands of the state subject to unspecified feasibility contraints, is, again, a purely abstract norm. All concrete realizations of the policy, however, will have their own historic contexts which must involve departures, in one direction or another, from the clarity and simplicity of its abstract form.

In India, in the last thirty years, the historical context which has shaped, or distorted, the attempt to realize the policy of state accumulation has been that of mimetic nationalism. As the late Harry Johnson wrote, in a passage from which we have already quoted briefly,

the promotion of economic development by deliberate economic policy has throughout modern history been associated with the political objective of building a nation-state ... The nationalist objective, with its overtones of possible military conflict, provides the motivation for bearing the costs of establishing a 'modern' national economy and polity ... On the other hand, nationalist motivations in evitably lead to economic policies that waste economic resources and inhibit the economic development they aim to stimulate.[1]

Mimetic nationalism sets as the overriding policy goal the acquisition of desirable types of 'modern' property, such as heavy armaments, industrial factories, public utility systems similar to those of advanced nations and so on. Johnson suggested that such a goal was set as a result of an intellectual mistake or misconception of the true nature of development, which involves the raising of income rather than the accumulation of property. Other liberal economists join him when they point out that 'there is rather seldom any very good reason for making (relative or complete) self-sufficiency in particular goods a policy objective'.[2] This is surely true within the logic of utilitarianism. Whether it is equally true in the context of the statecraft forced on an ex-colony by the actual international environment of the present day is a much wider, and more debatable, question. However, the aim here is not to assay the rationality of the objective: it is merely to trace through the consequences of its pursuit by successive Indian governments.

The desire to minimize the period before which India acquired a comprehensive 'modern' structure of production led the government to modify the state accumulation policy in two

1 Johnson (1967), p. 67.
2 Little and Mirrlees (1968), p. 47.

major ways that are not characteristic of the policy in its abstract form. The first modification was a pro-industry bias in the allocation of investment. The second was the adoption of a foreign trade regime which encouraged indiscriminate import substitution. It is worth stressing that neither of these modifications is inherent in the state accumulation policy as such. Maximizing the reinvestible surplus subject to feasibility constraints is an accumulation rule which disregards entirely the sectoral location of an investment project. It attends only to the project's production of reinvestible funds. Similarly, it is possible, in principle, to use international prices extensively in the appraisal of state investment projects which produce tradable goods, with a view to investing only in producing output that would be exportable in the international market. But the Indian government, motivated by mimetic nationalism, in fact followed neither of these courses.

It is a truism of development planning that one of the most common constraints on the overall rate of economic growth is the agricultural growth rate, which it is very difficult to raise above a long-run trend of about 3 per cent a year. With such a constraint, development can only be balanced if the overall growth rate is somewhere in the range of $4\frac{1}{2} - 4\frac{3}{4}$ per cent. The Indian Second Plan, with its 5 year target of 25% growth, and the Third Plan with its target of 30% – and both without any careful annual phasing of investment – were attempts to make the economy grow faster than the agricultural constraint would permit without imbalances. The consequent imbalances were price inflation of wage goods, which typically originate in the institutionally backward agricultural sector (e.g. food), falling real wages in the organized sector, an increasingly unequal income distribution, internal terms of trade which increasingly favoured agriculture, and a stimulus to the consumption and production of non-essential consumer goods.[3] In the Indian economy of the 1960s, each one of these imbalances can be observed.

(1) The wholesale price of food articles doubled in the decade.[4]
(2) By 1969/70, real wages in the organized sector show a slight

3 Lewis (1966), pp. 43–4; Kalecki (1972), pp. 150–4.
4 Simha (1974), p. 367, Table 20, Column (B).

TABLE 9.1 *Price indices implicit in national income estimates, 1960/61 to 1969/70*

Year	Price index N. D. P. at factor cost (1)	Price index agricultural output (2)	Price index manufacturing output (3)	Col. (3) ÷ col. (2) (4)
1960/61	100	100	100	100
1961/62	102	102	100	98
1962/63	106	107	102	95
1963/64	115	121	109	90
1964/65	126	136	112	82
1965/66	137	154	119	77
1966/67	157	188	127	67
1967/68	170	202	133	65
1968/69	167	193	135	69
1969/70	173	197	144	73

Source: Derived from C.S.O. (1971), *Estimates of National Product 1960/61–1969/70*, Table 3.1.

decline.[5] Thereafter the decline became more substantial – partly owing to the price rise of imported oil, but not wholly so.

(3) Several major studies attest the worsening income distribution.[6]

(4) The purchasing power over agricultural commodities of sellers of manufactures fell by more than a quarter, as can be seen from Table 9.1.

(5) The exceptionally rapid growth of consumer goods for high-income classes has also been established.[7]

The combination of all these different types of evidence certainly makes it plausible to suggest that the growth of India's industrial and services sector was 'too fast' in relation to the realized growth of agriculture. (This statement does not, of course, imply that actual growth has been too fast in relation

5 Ministry of Labour and Rehabilitation (1972), p. 61, Table 4.8.
6 E. g. Swamy (1967); Dandekar and Rath (1971), p. 26 and passim; Mukherjee and Chatterjee (1967), pp. 1259–68.
7 Malenbaum (1971), pp. 129–30.

to other criteria, such as need, or the unrealized growth potential of agriculture.)

For the state accumulation policy, the agricultural constraint
poses a long-term problem. It should be clear that such a policy
cannot be operated with 'excessive' industrial growth inde-
finitely. Even if a government succeeds in keeping its own demand for industrial goods at a high and increasing level, sooner
or later one of the three direct braking mechanisms from the
supply side will take effect, as discussed in Chapter 5. If balanced
growth is not planned *ex ante*, it will tend to be realized *ex post*,
either by supply constraints on industrial growth or by the
inducement of growth-promoting private or public investment
in agricultural projects. Balanced growth reached by the first
route will be slow and wasteful of resources. This was, in a nut-
shell, the history of Indian growth in the 1960s. Balanced
growth reached by the second route would have been faster and
would have led to a generalized scarcity of resources. The
Kaleckian analytical framework emphasizes that agriculture is
not the exclusive constraint on the success of a policy of state
accumulation. State accumulation can take place in its presence
if the problem of public saving is solved, although the rate of
accumulation will necessarily be slow. If the constraint is lifted,
state accumulation can still be frustrated if the problem of public saving is never solved.

The second major modification which was made in India,
under the pressure of mimetic nationalism, to the abstract
characterization of a state accumulation policy was the use of
indiscriminate import substitution as the forcing house for the
excessive industrial growth. High and extensive tariff walls
mean that, in the long run, industrial demand is limited by the
size of the domestic market with the prevailing distribution of
income. However, there seems no reason to dissent from the
Indian planners' view that 'the argument that India has reached
the limit with regard to import substituting industrialization,
does not appear to be valid'.[8] As late as 1966, as much as two
thirds of India's capital goods requirements were still being
imported.[9] The capital goods crisis of the late 1960s cannot,
then, be regarded as the nemesis of 'inward-looking' indus-

8 Planning Commission (1974), p. 17.
9 Medhora (1972), p. 1326.

trialization in the ordinary sense. In the short run, however, indiscriminate import substitution, short-sightedly designed to maximize direct savings of foreign exchange, introduced an additional rigidity into the environment in which the state accumulation policy had to be operated. Protection sufficient to prohibit imports was granted to any product previously imported for which domestic production capability could be demonstrated, with the result that new domestic industries suffered from costs high enough to exclude them from international markets.[10]

Consequently, if, long before the long-term demand constraint begins to bite, domestic investment demand for any reason flags, the excess supply of capital goods cannot be switched to foreign outlets. Levels of capacity utilization instead fall, and with them the industrial growth rate. Indiscriminate import substitution eliminates the potential export proceeds of the capital goods sector, which, had they existed, could finance extra consumer goods imports. Thus a shift in domestic expenditure towards consumption cannot leave the previously planned pattern of domestic output undisturbed.[11] This rigidity was originally claimed as a virtue of the chosen complex of economic policies. The phrase attributed to Mahalanobis that 'people cannot eat steel' implies no wish to use foreign trade transformation to enable them to do so.

The only way to relax this rigidity is for the government to offer incentives to capital goods exporters. But it is very difficult to create incentives that work in a form which does not involve either additional public expenditure or the forgoing of tax revenue, and thus a reduction in the level of public saving.

A 'pure' or unmodified state accumulation policy is by no stretch of the imagination an easy policy to initiate and persist with. But the state accumulation policy moulded by the pressures of mimetic nationalism was not so much difficult as impossible in the Indian political economy of the 1950s and 1960s. What it amounted to was the pursuit by the unhappy Indian planners not only of a policy of state accumulation, but of one that would generate a predetermined structure of pro-

---

10 Bhagwati and Desai (1970), p. 326; Nayyar (1976), pp. 347–50.
11 Ezekial (1971), p. 1183.

duction, i.e. a comprehensive 'modern' structure, while effectively ruling out foreign trade as a method of reconciling domestic production with domestic consumption and investment. To succeed in that task, and, at the same time, to avoid creating gross imbalances between the goods supplied and the goods demanded in the domestic economy, it is necessary, as a mere matter of logic, that domestic demand be so controlled that the planned volume and pattern of production, and not any other, is in fact always purchased. However much social democrats and Fabians would like to believe otherwise, the Indian government was simply not in a position to exercise the required degree of control over the level and composition of demand, because it was not able to control the volume or structure of money incomes generated by the state industrialization drive. [12]

It has been said that the owl of Minerva flies at night, and, in India, several nights after that. The validity of what is argued above received belated official recognition in the following passage:

> If the development process is not to generate disproportionalities of various sorts, the needed changes in the structure of demand and production must harmonize. If . . . the pattern of output capacity is changed in favour of investment goods but there is no corresponding change in the structure of gross national expenditure in favour of investment outlays, the economy could experience underutilization of capacity in the industries producing investment goods and strong inflationary pressure in respect of consumer goods sectors. It was this disproportionality that lay at the root of the phenomenon of so-called stagflation – stagnation in some sectors and inflation in others – that characterized the greater part of the period of Plan holiday in the mid-sixties. [13]

Official recognition of this not very esoteric point remains, however, inadequate. The suggestion that the disproportionality correctly identified did not appear before the plan holiday, and ended with it, is not, as has been shown, consistent with the facts. The further identification of the appropriate remedy as 'selective and effective curbs on *private* consumption' seems to overlook entirely the role of public consumption in produc-

12 Bagchi (1971), p. 1673.
13 Planning Commission (1974), pp. 11–12.

ing the disproportionality.[14] Nonetheless, in its limited way, this is a significant admission that the instruments normally relied on to curb private sector consumption, and guide it into appropriate channels (namely taxes and subsidies), do not prove effective, for a variety of political and administrative reasons. This ineffectiveness would continue to frustrate a state accumulation policy, even given balanced agriculture–industry growth, as long as domestic industry remains internationally uncompetitive. In these circumstances, state accumulation still could not be self-sustaining; it would produce only an episode of growth, as did Colbertism in seventeenth-century France.

But, as has just been suggested, inability to control private consumption is by no means the whole story of the government's failure to manage demand. Formally, at least, the balance of supply and demand in the capital goods sector is much more within the government's area of control than it is in the consumer goods sector. In 1965, the public sector was probably producing at least one third of the output of the capital goods industries (bearing in mind how difficult the public/private comparisons are when public output is administratively under-priced); while the public sector share in their paid-up capital almost certainly exceeded 50 per cent.[15] On the demand side, 'the bulk of development outlay in those sectors which are substantial users of investment goods comes out of government expenditure'.[16] Yet it has been shown that it was in the capital goods sector that the industrial recession was most pronounced. It was severest in those industries, such as railway equipment, where, for all practical purposes, the government is a monopsonist. Thus, in assessing the causes of India's poor economic performance in the second half of the 1960s, the temptation to exaggerate the catastrophic effects of the mid 1960s harvest failures should be avoided. The industrial recession of the late 1960s onwards was primarily a crisis of the capital goods industries, the bulk of which were of very recent origin. They had been largely established by the state in the initial phase of the industrialization strategy and their profitability largely depended on the maintenance of a

14 Ibid. (1974), p. 12, emphasis added.
15 Sitaramaswami (1968), pp. 12–14; Shirokov (1973), pp. 144–5.
16 Chaudhuri (1971), p. 83.

high level of demand by the public sector itself. Yet, public sector demand in total, and the most relevant components of that demand, can be shown to have been decelerating during the Third Plan period, that is, well before the harvest failures struck.

II STATE ACCUMULATION AND PUBLIC EXPENDITURE

Although it is probably true that failures in public finance policy have been overshadowed by larger macroeconomic inhibitions to rapid economic growth in India, it remains important to document them for two reasons. On the one hand, it is important to be clear why the modest potential for successful state accumulation was far from fully realized. On the other hand, it is necessary to establish which existing trends in public finance would have to be reversed if rapid economic growth in the near future were to become a real possibility, and if it were desired to try and avoid the usual social and economic consequences of a burgeoning private capitalism.

The elements of the problem of financing a state accumulation policy are simple enough. The government can expect to have difficulty raising the marginal saving rate in the private sector, so that rapid expansion of public (and so total) investment depends on finding ways of filling a rapidly increasing saving gap. In India, household savings as a share of G.N.P. are estimated to have risen from $6\frac{1}{2}/7\frac{1}{2}$ per cent to only 9 per cent over the fifteen years up to 1965.[17] Private corporate saving still makes a very small contribution to the total, despite recent growth. The saving gap can be filled by domestic public saving, net capital inflows from abroad on government account or large scale deficit finance (i.e. money creation not covered either by revenues or borrowings from the private sector).[18]

But we have seen that the programme of domestic public saving has, for a whole variety of different reasons, fallen markedly below what is required for any sensible and consistent plan, official or unofficial.[19] This failure was less important during the period 1958–64 when net foreign capital inflows

17 Raj (1970), p. 294.
18 Cutt (1969), pp. 41, 383.
19 E.g. Planning Commission (1976), p. 42; cf. Swamy (1971), pp. 118–19.

on government account increased very considerably. Alas, that increase itself was necessarily a transient phenomenon, given that the bulk of the inflows were in the form of loans. To maintain an increasing inflow of net loan 'aid', even if it could have been secured from the various consortia, would have forced a request for debt cancellation much sooner than the eventual date of December 1973.[20]

It could be argued that a financial constraint on a state accumulation policy need never operate, since whatever the shortfall of public saving and net foreign capital inflows, it can always be filled by means of deficit finance. Price stability – at least for essential commodities – is normally assumed, or recommended, to be one of the objectives of fiscal policy for development.[21] Deficit finance, in an economy where specific bottlenecks produce 'structural inflation' of the type that has been described, does not have a simple, calculable impact on the general level of prices.[22] But, on the other hand, this in no way implies that limitless deficit finance can be undertaken without producing some severe inflationary consequences. In India, some of the normal reasons for avoiding these consequences are irrelevant: international economic competitiveness was not an official objective, and the balance of payments is subject to extensive quantitative controls. The potentially damaging consequences of severe inflation were domestic – the political effects of a rapid redistribution of real income, away from landless labourers, poor farmers, the urban underemployed and those in the modern sectors whose money wages and salaries are sticky upwards. It is true that the Indian government had since the Second Plan undertaken markedly more in the way of inflationary deficit finance than both the planners and their critics considered prudent. However, one cannot infer from this that the government would have been indefferent, in the then existing political framework, to the much greater deviation from prudence that would have been required to continue a state accumulation policy with both public saving and net foreign capital inflows levelling off. It may well be that he most affected groups would have been precisely those on

20 Bauer (1974), pp. 49–50.
21 E. g. Kalecki (1972), p. 145; Cutt (1969), pp. 66–73.
22 Myrdal (1968), pp. 1923–32.

whom Congress relied marginally more than other parties for support. In addition, the whole drive for a domestic consensus would have been threatened by a widespread and drastic change of this sort.

Of course it is always possible for the public sector to dis-save, and finance part of its current expenditure with part of the saving of the domestic household and enterprise sectors. This leaves a financing problem. Additional taxation will have to be raised to service a greater volume of debt at higher interest rates than those currently prevailing. Further, the very solution of this financing problem will worsen the income distribution, since it requires transfers, presumably found by additional commodity taxation, to those with the capacity to save, who are the relatively well-off. Thus this is not a path which could be recommended, although it may be the one which India actually follows.

Thus, if the state accumulation policy were to be revived, some solution to India's budgetary problems would have to be found. It seems very doubtful that those weaknesses that have to be highlighted on the revenue side (in agricultural taxation and public enterprise surplus) can be remedied by the sort of measures that the government is prepared to execute. Nor can it be assumed that the staple revenue producers of the past, the various types of commodity taxation, will be as productive of additional revenue in the future. The coverage of excises in the last ten years has been greatly extended, and the most recently taxed items have been the poorest revenue producers. The rates, although extremely diverse, are in many cases quite high on an *ad valorem* basis. Increasing the revenue from sales taxation requires the active cooperation of the state governments, as would any proposal to replace sales taxes with a value added tax.

A major part of the solution to her current budgetary impasse must be restraint in the growth of current government expenditure.[23] It must be recognized, however, that the design of a sensible policy of government current expenditure control is far from being the straightforward matter it is often represented to be. It is perfectly true, for example, that the public authori-

23 Edwards (1969), p. 16.

TABLE 9.2 *Employment in the public and organized private sectors, 1961–71*

(millions)

	1961*	1966*	1971*
1 *Public sector*	7.1	9.4	10.7
a Central government	2.1	2.6	2.8
b State government	3.0	3.7	4.2
c Local bodies	1.2	1.7	1.9
Sub-total	6.3	8.0	8.9
d Other public sector	0.8	1.3	1.9
2 *Private organized sector†*	5.0	6.8	6.7

Notes: * Figures relate to the position at the end of March in each year.
†These figures exaggerate the increase in private organized sector employment, because from 1966 coverage was widened to include establishments employing 10-24 workers, whereas in previous years the cut-off point was 25 workers.
Source: Ministry of Finance, *Economic Survey, 1971/72*, pp. 105–6.

ties expanded the number on their payroll very much faster than did the organized part of the private sector in the 1960s, as is shown in Table 9.2. But it will not do to characterize this as 'the reckless expansion of the bureaucracy' and to define all public authorities' employees as 'unproductive workers'.[24] This is no doubt an important element in the growth of current expenditure. But to mistake it for the only element is to imply that a drastic curb on all forms of public authority employment is a sufficient remedy. On the contrary, the essence of the problem is selection. The need is to attack those types of current expenditure which do not raise the productivity of labour in the commodity production sector, either in the present or in the future. After all, government employees include a not negligible proportion of teachers and doctors. The purchase of their services can, in part, be regarded correctly as 'productive' consumption. They create a flow of future benefits, and, in greater measure, contribute to the present productivity of labour in the commodity producing sector.

There is little indication that the Indian government is

24 Cf. Jha (1973).

tackling seriously the task of planning and, much more vitally, controlling public expenditure. The planners continue to provide detailed estimates of centre and states non-Plan revenue expenditure for the five years ahead which are arithmetically consistent with the total required Plan outlay and its anticipated sources of finance. But the method used to arrive at the estimates is not disclosed, except to note that the public expenditure variables are given exogenously and not endogenously by the planning model. Because there is no year-by-year breakdown, the estimated growth rate cannot be compared with the experience of the immediate past. The separation of non-Plan and Plan revenue expenditure, the latter being given no sectoral breakdown, compounds the difficulty of making such a comparison. This makes it almost impossible to test the feasibility, as distinct from the consistency, of the estimates. Previous plans have regularly turned out to be not feasible.

As is rightly noted in the *Approach to the Fifth Plan, 1974/79*, 'in the past, major efforts at resource mobilization were often largely neutralised by unanticipated increases in non-developmental outlays' and, in the future, 'the order of public saving envisaged calls for . . . a high degree of fiscal discipline'.[25] It is necessary, therefore, to ask what new political and administrative machinery has been devised to ensure this fiscal discipline, and the 'rigorous restraints on inessential . . . public consumption' which are called for. One may search in vain the planners' discussions of 'plan implementation' for any mention of this as a task of implementation, despite the stern warning that 'any complacency can lead to a serious inflationary situation'. Yet some system of coordinated administrative control over expenditure is obviously needed. The need arises to ensure that the plan estimates of non-Plan revenue expenditure are not exceeded in aggregate, if all the other targets and assumptions of the Plan are being fulfilled. But since that condition is most unlikely to be met, given the incorrigible over-optimism of the planners and the shocks that unexpected events can give even to the most realistic plan, the need also arises to ensure that, if overall growth is slower, new and lower estimates of non-Plan revenue expenditure can be decided upon and adhered to.

25 Planning Commission (1973), p. 27.

India simply does not seem to possess, or be willing or able to devise, any political and administrative machinery which would make possible the coordinated and flexible management of public expenditure. One high official in the Expenditure Department of the Ministry of Finance indicated that expenditure decisions in India were reached by achieving 'understandings at the highest possible level'. In other words, where public expenditure decisions are concerned, India has experienced not government by Cabinet, but government by courtiers. She has suffered from the age-old vices of courtly control of financial decisions – short-sightedness, incoherence and amateurism.

Sadly, one must emphasize that there is no simple professional expenditure control technique whose adoption will quickly set matters right. Such techniques are, of course, well known in India, and their transposition from the developed countries where they originate, with the minimum delay, is one feature of the modernism characteristic of mimetic nationalism. In Chapter 3 the diffusion of the technique of economic/functional classification of public spending has been analysed in detail. In that case it was impossible not to remark on the gulf which existed between the formal adoption of the technique and its integration with the process by which expenditure decisions actually get taken.

Another germane example is the technique of programme and performance budgeting. In 1968, the Administrative Reforms Commission advised, and the government accepted, the immediate introduction of this budgeting technique for departments at central and state level responsible for development projects. By 1970, a rash of the required documents had issued forth. As far as one can tell, the rationality of the budget process has improved, as a result, hardly at all.[26] In any case, such a measure does nothing to prevent the the swelling of non-development spending.

Since disillusion with programme and performance budgeting has grown in advanced countries so quickly after its formal adoption in India, no doubt the disillusion will soon be imported too.[27] Let us hope that, if it is, the experience of disillusion

26 Cf. U.N. (1975), p. 16 and Toye (1981).
27 Cf. Caiden and Wildavsky (1974), pp. 159–65 and Premchand (1969), pp. 26–8.

will be a constructive one. No expenditure control technique 'works' in the sense that, if wound up and opened, a musical box works by playing a pretty tune. It is too mechanistic even to compare spending control methods with tools. They are less tools than rules that are invented and imposed in the course of some specific historical conflict, such as the conflict between civilian politicians and bureaucrats on one side, and the chiefs of the armed forces on the other, for control over U.S. and U.K. military decision making in the 1950s and early 1960s.

The conflicts within the Congress Party leadership at the end of the 1960s did produce attempts to concentrate and centralize political control. These steps expanded the size, and tightened the line of command, of federal police and paramilitary forces. They reflect, alas, the decay rather than the growth of institutions of governmental decision making.

Even the further upheavals in India in the mid 1970s were not of a character to strengthen control over public spending – rather the reverse.[28] On the other hand, the Emergency years of 1975/77 marked the culmination of a government campaign to break the power of organized labour, particularly in the public sector. Draconian anti-labour measures did have a marked effect on the economic performance of the public sector enterprises during those two years of authoritarian rule. Their output and level of capacity utilization increased sharply, and so did their financial surpluses and the rate of return on their assets.[29] The fact that the Congress Party, at the twilight of its uninterrupted rule in India, attacked the obstacles to state accumulation by repressing the public sector labour force, rather than by improving its own public expenditure control or its taxation performance seems to confirm Petras' view that,

> while squeezing out imperial capital, the state capitalists share with imperial capital an interest in maximizing exploitation of the labour force: the slogans and goals include maintaining production, labour discipline and popular demobilization ... The initial poly-class euphoria and mass appeals which accompany the initial period during which the state capitalists come to power and foreclose the imperial option is ... followed by repressive measures against the trade unions and autonomous working class mobilization.[30]

28 Toye (1977), p. 312.   29 Toye (1977), p. 310.
30 Petras (1977), pp. 13, 14.

III PUBLIC EXPENDITURE CONTROL AND THE STATES

The fiscal problem of the Indian state governments is normally understood to be one of excessive and increasing 'dependency' on the central government for financial assistance, as a result of inadequate tax bases and a crushing burden of debt. Such an understanding may have had some relevance to changes which took place in the 1950s. But for the period between 1960 and 1970 it is completely misleading. All the major adjustments of federal fiscal relations made the financial position of state governments more comfortable and independent.

The percentage of the state governments' total revenue plus net capital receipts contributed in various forms by the central government rose from 41 to 42 per cent between 1960/61 and 1969/70. The composition of central assistance shifted away from the more onerous form (repayable loans) to less onerous forms, such as transferred taxes and grants-in-aid.[31] Successive Finance Commissions have raised the states' share of central income tax from 50 to 75 per cent, and increased the absolute size of the divisible pool of excise revenues by bringing more and more excises into the distributable pool.[32] At the end of the decade, the use of Article 282 grants by the central government to promote the adoption by state governments of centrally-sponsored plan schemes was restricted, and the bulk of central grant-aid was fixed for an entire five-year plan period in relation to population (60 per cent of the total), income per head (10 per cent), tax effort (10 per cent) and large project commitments (10 per cent).[33]

In the 1960s, the fiscal problem of the state governments centred on the increasing independence of state governments from the central control over public expenditure. When, after the National Development Council meetings of July and September 1968, it was agreed to limit severely the use of Article 282 grants to promote specific plan projects in the states, the central government's sole instrument (apart from ineffective moral suasion) for influencing the composition of state plans was blunted. The size of the state plans henceforth depended on their block grants plus their own ability to mobi-

---

31 Toye (1973), pp. 264–5.   32 Eapen (1970), p. 541.
33 Chatterji (1971), pp. 97–8; Frankel (1978), pp. 310–13.

lize resources. The composition of state plans now depended entirely on the state government, which could pay as much or as little heed to the advice and wishes of the central government as it cared to.

It should further be borne in mind that, while there are lengthy centre–state consultations on the contents of state plans, there are hardly any centre–state consultations on the state governments' annual estimates, which are the operational documents for the sanctioning of much (but not all) plan expenditure by the states. Further, there is no machinery at the national level for the scrutiny of, and joint centre–state deliberations on, non-Plan expenditure by the state governments.[34] Thus, from the viewpoint of the central planners, through the 1960s the public expenditure of the state governments became increasingly like a Juggernaut's car.

It was easy for state governments to depart from the level and pattern of outlay in their state plans. Until 1968, it was very difficult for the central government to reconcile the figures that appeared in the state budgets with those that appeared in its own budget, because the development heads in the two budgets were quite different.[35] Even when these departures from plan could be traced by the central government and the plan grant withdrawn, its loss could be made good by a miscellaneous development loan, or, until 1972, by an unauthorized overdraft at the Reserve Bank of India.[36] Nothing in the long process of centre–state consultation, negotiation and bargaining gave the centre control over the outcome of state plans.

If one compares public expenditure control in a federation with that in a centralized state, one would expect central influence over lower-level authorities' expenditure to be both absolutely weaker in the former, and of a kind less suited to bringing about changes in the short run. Therefore, the burden of adjustment, to what the central government considers to be the public expenditure requirements of the economic conjuncture, would tend to fall much more heavily in a federation on the expenditure of the central government itself. This seems to be true of India's experience in the 1960s. State government spending was less flexible in terms of its rate of growth and

34 Eapen (1970), p. 555.   35 A.R.C. (1968b), pp. 28–9.
36 Hanson (1968), p. 27; Griffiths (1969).

pattern of composition than that of the central government. The greater flexibility of central spending was what produced the short-term changes in the centralization ratio noted in Chapter 6 for public expenditure as a whole, and in Chapter 8 for capital formation.

One is brought up against the possibility that, if the central government cannot control state government spending, and if it is forced frequently enough to treat its own capital budget as the residual in macroeconomic adjustment, the consequence will be a ratchet-like decentralization of public authorities' capital formation, and perhaps even of public expenditure. There are many in India who would consider that possibility as something to hope for, either out of respect for a Constitution which, strangely, makes no provision for planning; or from powerful regional loyalties; or from the backwoodsman's sentiment that the only good government is hardly any government at all. Two inconvenient little facts should be brought to their attention. One is that between 1960 and 1970 the share of state government expenditure devoted to developmental uses declined from 62 to 59 per cent. The second is that, in the same period, expenditure priorities switched away from agricultural and industrial infrastructure and towards health and education spending.[37] Both of these tendencies are detrimental to a policy of state accumulation of industrial property and skills (except where education spending is for relevant technical education).

The Resolution establishing the Indian Planning Commission noted that 'the States will give the fullest measure of help to the Commission so as to secure the maximum coordination of policy and unity of effort'. It quickly became clear that this was merely a pious hope. Any federal system is a politically conservative system, because 'the sharing of responsibility and authority for governmental programmes is inherently ponderous'.[38] In highly particularistic societies, even a well-contrived federal regime might, as Shils put it, 'be recalcitrant to the idea of a strong state, such as is thought necessary for an energetic programme of modernization'.[39] The political and admini-

37 Toye (1973), pp. 267–9.
38 Burkehead and Miner (1971), p. 259.
39 Shils (1965), p. 33.

strative assumption underlying the state accumulation policy was voiced by Nehru when he told the National Development Council in 1954 that 'planning was cent per cent centralization and nothing else'.[40] But, the reality was different. As one of Nehru's Finance Ministers acknowledged, 'political arrangements are such as to make central ministers very much dependent on the goodwill of local party leaders [so that] many decisions are not taken [so much] on their merit as on the insistence of strong local leaders'. [41]

Just as, for the economy as a whole, the state accumulation policy broke down because, in the end, the government could not control the level and pattern of consumption in the private sector, so, for the government sector itself, the policy broke down because state government expenditure increasingly departed from the level and pattern that would be consistent with rapid, self-reliant and government-promoted industrialization. While central fiscal devolution continued to fill the expenditure gap in the states' budgets, the one potential instrument of central influence on state government expenditure (Article 282 Plan grants) was virtually dismantled. The state accumulation policy was free to fade gently into revered desuetude.

40 Nayar (1972), p.60, n.81. (N.b. 'Cent per cent' means 'one hundred per cent' in India).
41 Deshmukh (1972), p. 76.

10
Summary of conclusions

Public expenditure is discussed by economists in a variety of different abstract frameworks. Wagner's 'law of expanding state activity', expressed as the functional dependence of the ratio of government spending to national income on per capita national income, correctly characterizes a feature of modern economic growth, but does little to explain that feature. As a theory of the long run, it is not susceptible to testing with medium-term empirical evidence. Peacock and Wiseman's public spending 'displacement effect' is not, *pace* K.N. Reddy, visible in Indian expenditure data, which is unsurpising since it is an abstraction from the U.K.'s social and economic history. Apart from these theories of the long run, economists view public spending from two other perspectives, one derived from microeconomics and the other from macroeconomics. The microeconomic perspective, explored in the literature on 'public goods', is a branch of welfare economics, so that attempts to use it for description or explanation are misconceived. The macroeconomic perspective leads to the building of macroeconomic models incorporating a disaggregated government sector. These models are intended to simulate the consequences of changes in fiscal policy. But the fiscal changes are themselves exogenous to the model, and thus inexplicable, apart from the fact that their consequences are worked out in a drastically simplified environment. Dissatisfaction with all these types of theorizing led in the 1960s to a proliferation of ultra-empirical public expenditure studies, hoping to produce inductive generalizations from the covariances detected by regression analysis. Among the several weaknesses of these studies were the false inference of diachronic changes from cross-section differences and the uncritical use of the simple regression technique.

The basic value premise of this work is a desire for rapid improvement in living conditions for the Indian masses. This implies a concern with active, dirigistic development and the attempt to mould an entire economy into a rationally pre-selected form. Our interest in public expenditure in this book is solely in relation to this attempt. In India, the concrete manifestation of this attempt was a policy of state accumulation. Our perspective, therefore, is to consider public expenditure as one of the major policy variables that regulate the rate of state accumulation. In the absence of foreign 'aid', inter-sector borrowing and lending and saving forced by the printing of extra money, the rate of government sector accumulation is inversely related to the level of government expenditure on current account. The rate of public sector capital formation can also be raised by either increasing government revenues, or by increasing the surpluses of non-departmental public enterprises.

The question of whether the state accumulation policy, and the planning and control of public expenditure which it implies, is a 'progressive' policy is often not confronted directly. Potentially, the state is a superior agent of accumulation to the private sector. It is better able to mobilize the existing surplus for productive investment and to enlarge the actual surplus. In countries with a weak fiscal system, these potential advantages cannot be secured merely by state direction of investment; public ownership of productive assets is necessary. It is possible to operate a state accumulation policy in a way that improves income distribution as well as increasing public capital; and also in a way that moderates the anarchy of private accumulation. However, whether a state accumulation policy is a progressive policy depends on the social structure of the regime which attempts it. It is doubtful that an economy where a powerful private sector is retained will realize the potential advantages of state accumulation. But those who criticize the naivety of social democratic advocacy of state accumulation themselves fall into self-contradiction. For they, too, regard the state accumulation policy as progressive, after overturning all the bases on which such a belief could rest.

The forces which influenced state action in India must be delineated to place the Indian state accumulation policy in its proper historical context. No single social class dominates Indian society; social dominance is shared uneasily by a number of different classes and groups. The state's partial independence of this uneasy coalition of classes and groups is increased because of the relative "over-development" of the post-colonial state *vis-à-vis* all indigenous classes. But the overdeveloped state faces the pressures generated by the outwards penetration of the capitalist model of production from its European places of origin. Its response to these pressures is double-sided, a combination of resistance to European social and political hegemony and an absorption of the technoeconomic basis of that hegemony. This historical materialist view of Indian nationalism must be distinguished both from liberal accounts of economic nationalism and teleological theories of a 'modernization imperative'. Mimetic nationalism has three characteristic attributes; first, it coexists with a low level national integration; second, its style of politics is populist and its political institutions centre on a 'united front' which is heterogenous in terms of class; third, despite an initial radical anti-imperialism, it begins to accept foreign resources in the hope of accelerating the transition to economic independence.

The early history of the state accumulation policy in India shows that it was never urged on a *laissez-faire* colonial government by a progressive nationalist movement. Its first feeble manifestations came under the aegis of the British government of India. Meanwhile, Indian nationalist opinion favoured indirect state promotion of private industry by means of tariffs, procurement and banking regulation. Nehru's socialistic ideas were timid and confused, and always subordinated to his desire to preserve the nationalist united front. Even on the verge of the transfer of state power, it is impossible to ascribe a coherent policy on state accumulation to Congress's National Planning Committee. In the nationalist camp much greater agreement existed on the need for rapid industrialization (whether private or public) as the means to encourage national economic independence and self-dependence. This near-consensus was faithfully reflected in the economic strategy that was adopted after independence. From the mid 1950s onwards, industrialization took place with substantial public and private investment, after 1958 with heavy quota and tariff protection. Thus the environment of the Indian state accumulation policy was an industialization drive in a heavily protected economy.

The overall performance of the public sector in the period 1960/61 to 1969/70 parallels the change from the confidence in the public sector voiced in the Third Plan to the confusion about its role in the abortive Fourth Plan. Over the whole decade, the share of the public authorities in total national expenditure increased, as did the level of real public expenditure per head. But both of these increases reached a peak in 1964/65, after which they were partially reversed. The 'Wagnerian' tendencies visible in the Third Plan public expenditure statistics merely indicate the government's efforts to operate a state accumulation policy. A functional breakdown of public authority spending shows that, even during the Third Plan, non-development spending was growing faster than development spending, to which the doubling of the defence budget in real terms was a major contribution. (One cannot, however, conclude that the increment to defence spending was a direct subtraction from the public development outlay that would otherwise have taken place.) In the second half of the 1960s, public spending grew very little in real terms, while a marked change in programme priorities took place. Non-development spending continued to increase its share of the total, but not because of defence spending. In this sub-period, the expanding programmes were famine relief, food subsidies and expenditure on police forces. Plan development spending shrank in real terms, particularly irrigation and flood control, small-scale industries, transport and communications, education and scientific research and health and family planning. Non-Plan development expenditure grew. This probably reflects the shift in responsibility for many development projects from the national planners to the state governments; except in the case of transport and communications, which suffered severe cuts in real terms. The economic composition of government spending was mostly stable during the Third Plan, but changed markedly in the 1965–70 period, as gross fixed capital formation was cut back.

The 'Plan holiday' cutback in public authority and public sector investment led to a decline in both public authorities' and public sector capital formation as a share of G.N.P. and of total fixed capital formation. Despite these falls in the level of public investment, a diminishing proportion of public investment was financed by public sector saving. The drastic decline of public sector saving stemmed from the inability to exploit the two revenue sources which constitute the crucial advantages of the state as agent of capital accumulation – taxation of the subsistence sector, and the surpluses of public enterprises. While the excessive fragmentation of Indian land holdings may mean that large revenues cannot be raised equitably from the former source, the removal of existing inequities would produce a non-negligible increment to tax revenue. The reasons why the public enterprises never produced the anticipated surpluses are various. The departmental enterprises of state governments, such as electricity and irrigation, concentrated too heavily on grandiose schemes, were managed badly and continuously under-priced their products. The departmental enterprises of the central government are dominated by the railways where the small size of surpluses is attributable to excessive labour costs and irrational tariff-making. Among the non-departmental public enterprises, the losses incurred by the public steel units were usually sufficient to offset any profits made by smaller and better-run public enterprises. However, the public sector investment famine of the late 1960s cannot be construed as a deliberate policy switch decided on in the light of the failures of public entrepreneurship.

The mid-decade switch from economic growth to recession is normally attributed to the double harvest failure which started in 1965/66. But it has also been suggested that government policies themselves provoked and/or prolonged the recession. Analysis of production statistics indicates that the post-1965 recession in the organized sector was largely confined to capital goods industries, and especially transport equipment. The debate over the role of government in reducing the demand for the products of capital goods industries has suffered from some conceptual confusion and empirical weakness. A more searching examination of public expenditure statistics indicates a deceleration of the rate of growth of public spending in the three financial years before the harvest failures of 1965/66. The growth rate of the departmental enterprises' gross fixed capital formation also decelerated between 1962/63 and 1965/66 both in money and in real terms. The government's deflationary reaction to the onset of drought was thus superimposed on a drift towards deflation which is discernible from the middle of the Third Plan. Once the immediate crisis of agricultural supply was over, the government did not move to raise again its own demand for the capital goods whose production capacity its past investments had created.

Since India has federal government, the role of public expenditure in a state accumulation policy must be studied for both levels of government, the central and the state (including in the latter all local authorities). For various reasons, however, it is not possible to measure the regional impact of Indian public expenditure. Instead, the initial concern is with changes in the centralization of public spending. The attempt to apply Peacock and Wiseman's theory of the expenditure concentration process to India is basically misguided. A proper measure of the centralization ratio indicates nearly the same figure at the end of the decade as at the beginning, but with a lurch towards centralization at the time of the Sino-Indian border war and its aftermath. To accommodate the extra spending caused by that war while maintaining central development outlay on its growth path, state government capital spending was held in check, thereby increasing the expenditure centralization ratio.

The double harvest failures of 1965/66 and 1966/67 caused an initial small shift towards further centralization, as central responsibilities for income redistribution through transfer payments were acted on. However, this shift was more than cancelled out by another shift in the opposite direction caused by a cutback on capital spending that bit much deeper into the centre's capital budget than into those of the states. Such a cutback is difficult to justify in terms of normal economic logic. If explanations are sought in the realm of politics, it might be suggested that the Congress losses in the 1967 general Election weakened the political power of the

centre *vis-à-vis* the state governments. But the political record
does not support this argument. Post-1967 state-level opposition to the Congress Party was localized, uncoordinated and
unstable. Its main achievement seems to have been the dismantling of the apparatus by which central planners exercised
detailed control over the bulk of state-level plan schemes –
but this was as much the achievement of the Congress as of
the non-Congress states.

A more convincing political explanation for the post-1967
decentralization of capital, and thus total expenditure, starts
from the proposition that the 1967 Election was indecisive,
and prevented any change in leadership from 'syndicate raj'
presided over by a new and hesitant Prime Minister. Internal
Congress intrigues and faction fights preempted the time and
energy required for economic decision making and, in the
policy vacuum, the Finance Ministry became dominant. The
Finance Ministry hoped to stave off the effects of a sharp
decline in the net inflow of foreign resources by increasing private foreign and domestic investment, concentrating
agricultural investment on a 'green revolution', and building up the foreign exchange reserves. The other element in
the orthodox policy package was a severe cutback in public
investment in the organized sector, which was achieved largely
on central government account.

One would not expect that states with different levels and
growth rates of income and population density, as well perhaps
as differences in political preferences, would exhibit the same
levels or growth rates of public expenditure. To test this expectation it is first necessary to deflate the money expenditure
figures of the state governments to allow for inflation at different rates in different parts of the country. If the issue is
improvement in the standards of public provision, allowance
must also be made for simple population growth. After these
allowances are made, it is clear that substantial inter-state
differences remain in the growth rate of real public spending
per head. Thus, during the 1960s, the disparities in the standards of public provision by the state governments and local
authorities increased. Using rank correlation analysis, the
variables associated with real public expenditure growth per
head were sought. The results obtained were not very clear-cut.

It appeared that the states which were least urbanized in 1960 had public expenditure growth rates significantly associated with state income growth rates. At the same time, the states which were most urbanized in 1960 had public expenditure growth rates significantly associated with the progress of urbanization. It is difficult to explain this apparent causal assymetry without further research into the process of migration and urbanization during the 1960s.

Just as total expenditure became more centralized during the Third Plan, so did the gross capital formation of the Indian public authorities. However, the definition of capital formation includes machinery and equipment used for defence purposes, so the developmental implications of more centralized capital formation are obscure. In the 1965–70 sub-period, the central government's money expenditures on capital formation declined, while those of all other public authorities increased, thereby more than offsetting the centralization that had occurred during the Third Plan.

The attempt to examine changes in the centralization of public saving is hindered because of a change in the Central Statistical Organization's practice in attributing public saving to different spending authorities. This change relates to the treatment of transfers between one spending authority and another. If one looks at the breakdown of public saving after all intra-authority transfers have been made, the state government's contribution to total public saving shows an absolute and a relative increase. If the new breakdown of public saving is taken to be more appropriate, the central government's average share during the Third Plan was 51 per cent and in the 1965–70 sub-period fell to an average of 45 per cent.

The effect of the public capital formation and public saving changes taken together also depends on whether the post-devolution or the 'new breakdown' concept of saving is used. If the former concept is used, the central government's ability to finance its capital formation by its own saving remained roughly constant, while that of the state governments improved. If the latter concept is used, this conclusion is reversed, i.e. the state governments' ability to finance their capital formation by their own saving remained constant,

while that of the central government improved. Choice between
these alternative concepts of saving would still be difficult
even if the definitions employed in the 'new breakdown' were
known. Under the revenue-sharing provisions of the Indian
Constitution, revenue can legally 'belong' to one spending
authority, while the policy and practice of levying it is
entirely the responsibility of another spending authority.
There is no reason to believe that levels of public saving were
ever policy targets of any type of spending authority, so that
the outcomes registered in national accounts statistics cannot
even be regarded as plans that failed.

It is often argued that, as economic development takes place,
the share of public capital formation in (a) the government
budget, (b) total capital formation and (c) gross national
expenditure gradually declines. There is some correlation
between level of development in 1960/61 and the share of
state government expenditure devoted to public capital formation, and between the rate of development and the shrinkage
in the share of public capital formation in state income and
state government expenditure. Neither of these correlations
is statistically significant, however. If one excludes military
sensitive border states, there is a significant correlation
between the rate of development and the shrinkage of the
share of public capital formation in state income. Explaining
the economic composition of state government budgets
remains a problem. The supposition of constant economic
composition, because of bureaucratic inertia or conservative
budgeting procedures is clearly against the empirical evidence.
Budget composition seems to be related to the degree of
government activity, with those states where the public sector
is largest being those in which the share of the state devoted
to capital formation is the largest. Evidence for this view,
however, comes only from cross-section analysis, and a time-
series test may refute it. Any suggestion that state governments'
capital formation is constrained by the volume of resources
which they save has no empirical backing.

A retrospective survey of the Indian state accumulation
policy indicates that, although in the abstract there is no
necessary connection between state accumulation and mimetic nationalism, the latter did in fact provide the historical

context within which the policy of state accumulation was attempted in India. The policy of state accumulation was thereby affected in two ways. The first was a pro-heavy-industry bias in the allocation of investment which caused growth to be unbalanced in the sense of Lewis and Kalecki. The second was to use indiscriminate import substitution to force unbalanced growth, and the proliferation of domestic industries with unit costs so high that they were unable to export. Thus the Indian state accumulation policy was set the task of producing a pre-determined structure of output without the possibility of using foreign trade to reconcile domestic production with domestic consumption and investment. The planned structure of domestic production had to match the structure of domestic demand. But, in fact, with its small public sector and weak fiscal system, the Indian state was quite unable to shape the structure of domestic demand to the form which its domestic production plans required. Even in the public sector itself, where the government had most control over supply and demand, a match between them was not achieved.

Although these macroeconomic mismanagements dominated the evolution of the Indian economy in the 1960s, so that even sound public finance policies could only have produced a slow rate of state accumulation, it is still interesting to ask what changes ought to be made in the public finances if macroeconomic circumstances were to alter. Since borrowing abroad and at home, and printing money, are financial devices which have been used to, and indeed beyond, the limits of prudence, the revival of the state accumulation policy in India would then rest on the solution to budgetary problems, particularly on the expenditure side of the budget.

The problem of expenditure control is not one to be solved by insisting on across-the-board reductions on a radical scale. It is a problem of intelligent selection based on detailed information about the economic effects of existing and potential items of public expenditure. There is little indication that this is understood by government circles in India. The planners do not reveal how they arrive at the public expenditure figures which appear in the plans, and there is not the slightest indication that the administrative and political institutions which would be needed to operate the choice process for public expenditure are being built up. The formal adoption of the administrative technique of programme and performance budgeting is no substitute for the creation of a series of official and political Cabinet committees whose remit is to decide priorities over the entire field of public expenditure. Even setting up such committees will achieve little unless they become the arena for conflicts between centralizing and decentralizing political forces. Such conflicts were not evident in India in the 1960s, not even up to and including the 'Emergency' of 1975/77. If anything, the 1960s saw a drift towards decentralization of control over public finance as the methods used for fiscal devolution became increasingly favourable to the independence of the states. While this was happening the state governments were switching their own spending priorities away from agricultural and industrial infrastructure and towards health and education programmes, and away from developmental to non-developmental outlay. The way in which the central government used its own capital budget as the balancing factor in macroeconomic adjustment suggests that the continuing decentralization of public expenditure is a real possibility. The operation of a state accumulation policy is hard enough in an inherently conservative political framework such as federalism. If public expenditure does continue to become more decentralized, now that the old Article 282 planning grants have been drastically reduced, the state accumulation policy in India will only continue to wither away.

APPENDIX A

Checklist of state-produced economic reclassifications

(*Note*: This list covers all those economic reclassifications of state government budgets that (a) were produced by state statistical bureaux and (b) were known to the author at the time of writing this work. It therefore excludes (i) economic reclassifications of state government budgets that were produced by other bodies than the state governments themselves (e.g. by the C.S.O., the N.C.A.E.R., etc.) and (ii) economic reclassifications of other budgets than state budgets (e.g. the Central Finance Ministry's reclassification of central government budgets). Also, it is not claimed that the list is exhaustive for the period 1960–70. Other examples are believed to exist, but it was not possible to inspect them for one reason or another. The list is arranged alphabetically by state, and then chronologically by date of publication.)

ANDHRA PRADESH

1. Bureau of Economics and Statistics, Hyderabad, 'An Economic Classification of Public Revenue and Expenditure of the Government of Andhra Pradesh for 1964/65, 1965/66, 1966/67 and 1967/68', no date.
2. Ibid., 'An Economic and Functional Classification of Budgetary Transactions of the Government of Andhra Pradesh for the years 1966/67 (Accounts), 1967/68 (Revised Estimates), 1967/68 (Budget Estimates)', no date.
3. Ibid., 'An Economic and Functional Classification of Budgetary Transactions of the Government of Andhra Pradesh for the years 1967/68 (Accounts), 1968/69 (Revised Estimates), 1969/70 (Budget Estimates)', no date.

ASSAM

4. Department of Economics and Statistics, Government of Assam, 'An Economic Classification of the State Government Budget, 1962/63', 1962.

5. Ibid., 'An Economic Classification of Assam Government Budget, 1969/70', 1969.

6. The *Bulletin of Economics and Statistics*, Vol. IX, No. 2 gives a re-classification of state budgets for 1966/67 (Accounts), 1967/68 (Revised Estimates) and 1968/69 (Budget Estimates).
7. Bureau of Economics and Statistics, Government of Gujarat, Ahmedabad, 'An Economic and Functional Classification of the Gujarat Government Budget, 1967/68 to 1969/70', 1971.

8. Economic and Statistical Adviser to the Government of Haryana, 'An Economic Classification of the Haryana Government Budget, 1967/68', 1968.
9. Ibid., 'An Economic Classification of the Haryana Government Budget, 1968/69', 1969.
10. Ibid., 'An Economic Classification of the Haryana Government Budget, 1969/70', 1970.
11. Ibid., 'An Economic Classification of the Haryana Government Budget, 1970/71', 1970.
12. Ibid., 'An Economic Classification of the Haryana Government Budget, 1971/72', 1971.

13. Directorate of Economics and Statistics, Jammu and Kashmir Government, Srinagar, 'An Economic-cum-Functional Classification of the Jammu and Kashmir State Government Budget, 1966/67 (Accounts)', no date, probably 1971.

14. Bureau of Economics and Statistics, Trivandrum, 'An Economic Classification of the Kerala Government Budgets, 1962/63 to 1964/65', 1965.
15. Ibid., 'An Economic and Functional Classification of the Kerala Government Budget 1963/64 to 1967/68', 1967.

16. Directorate of Economics and Statistics, Madhya Pradesh, 'An

Economic. Classification of the State Government Budget, 1965/66', 1966.

17. Ibid., 'An Economic Classification of the State Government Budget, 1966/67', 1968.
18. Ibid., 'Economic and Functional Classification of State Government Budget, 1968/69', 1970.

MAHARASHTRA

19. *Maharashtra Quarterly Bulletin of Economics and Statistics*, Vol. IX, No. 2, July–September, 1968, 'An Economic Classification of the Maharashtra Government Budget 1961/62 to 1966/67'.
20. Bureau of Economics and Statistics, Bombay, 'Economic Classification of Maharashtra State Government Budgets, 1965/66 Accounts), 1966/67 (Accounts) and 1967/68 (Accounts)', 1971.

MYSORE

21. Finance Department (Research Section), Government of Mysore, 'An Economic Classification of the Mysore Budget (1966/67 Accounts)', 1968.

ORISSA

22. Bureau of Statistics and Economics, Orissa, Cuttack, 'An Economic Classification of the Orissa Government Budget 1970/71', no date.
23. Bureau of Statistics and Economics, Orissa, Bhubaneswar, 'An Economic-cum-Functional Classification of the Orissa Government Budget 1971/72', no date.

PUNJAB

24. The Economic Adviser to the Government of Punjab, Chandigarh, 'An Economic Classification of the Punjab Government Budget for 1970/71', 1971.

RAJASTHAN

25. Directorate of Economics and Statistics, Rajasthan, Jaipur, 'Economic Classification of Budget of Government of Rajasthan 1960/61 to 1965/66'.

TAMIL NADU

26. The Director of Statistics, Madras, 'Economic Classification of the Madras Government Budget for 1965/66', 1968.
27. The Director of Statistics, Tamil Nadu, 'Economic Classification of the Tamil Nadu Government Budget 1966/67 and 1967/68', 1969.

UTTAR PRADESH

28. Director of Statistics, Uttar Pradesh, Lucknow, 'Economic Classification of State Budget of Uttar Pradesh for 1970/71' (in Hindi), no date.

APPENDIX B

The calculation of expenditure centralization ratios from data on a national accounts basis

In Table 6.2 the degree of centralization of government expenditure was calculated from data reclassified by the Indian C.S.O. on a national accounts basis. Appendix B considers whether there are valid objections to this.

The national accounts approach has been described as one designed 'to show the outlay actually made by each [level of] government for goods and services and transfer payments regardless of the source of funds'.[1] Thus all transfers between levels of government, e.g. central grants to states, or state grants to municipalities, are shown once only. They are shown as part of the expenditure of the receiving government. This implies that the states' measured share in total expenditure will be higher on a national accounts basis than on any other. If these inter-level transfers are counted twice, once as the expenditure of the receiving government and once as the expenditure of the donor government (which is what Reddy seems to have done) the states' measured share will obviously be reduced. This is indicated by a comparison of the figure for 1968 in Table 6.1 (using Reddy's statistics) which is 50.3 per cent with the figure for 1968/69 in Table 6.2, which is 56 per cent. Counting inter-level transfers once, but as the expenditure of the donor government would reduce the states' share even further, assuming that states always receive more in such transfers than they pass down to local authorities.

It may be asked whether, if such transfers are an exercise of power by the higher-level government to determine the spending patterns of the lower-level government, counting them once, and towards the donor's expenditure, would not give a more realistic picture of the degree of expenditure centralization. This can be answered with two arguments, one general in nature, the other connected with specific developments in India.

The general objection to abandoning the national accounts approach is that it makes the measure of expenditure centralization

1 Bird (1970), p. 33; cf. Pryor (1968), p. 70, note 1.

more arbitrary. In order to achieve the added realism which is wanted, it would be necessary to distinguish between types of inter-level transfer, according to the closeness of their link with specific patterns of spending. After all, some of these inter-level transfers are given for the purpose of general budgetary assistance, which, if anything, expands the scope for local autonomy. Yet such distinctions are very hard to draw. It is not even true that matching grants, which presumably embody the greatest degree of central direction, always infringe local autonomy. They can substitute for the local finance of the programme; they do not always stimulate spending on a programme that would otherwise not have been undertaken. To decide their effect in particular cases would require knowledge of, or guesses about, what the receiving government would have been prepared to spend themselves on the particular programme which is being supported. Further, there is every incentive for a receiving government to conceal its true intentions, and deny that matching grants have any substitution effects. These difficulties indicate why it may be more reliable, as well as more convenient, to retain the national accounts approach.

Nevertheless, it must be asked whether, in India, there is evidence of changes in the indirect centralization of expenditure which Table 6.2 implicitly ignores. This is the question, often aired in the literature, whether the states were becoming increasingly dependent on the centre for the finance of their expenditure.[2] This problem can be formulated in a number of different ways. But a crude approximation of the degree of states' financial self-reliance can be obtained by asking how much of their total expenditure had to be financed by means other than direct and indirect taxation and the surpluses of departmental public enterprises. The amount of state spending financed by none of these methods may be termed the 'expenditure gap', which will be largely bridged by various forms of assistance from the centre. (It is not an exact measure, because to a small extent it is bridged by fees, income from property and interest receipts from non-government sources.) Table B.1 gives figures for this gap in absolute terms, and as a percentage of total states expenditure.

As the table shows, although the absolute gap was rising, there is no indication of an increasing gap relative to total expenditure. The share of spending which had to be financed from sources other than taxation and enterprise surpluses was declining slightly. It is true that the figures of tax yield used in the calculation include the amounts of centrally-levied taxes assigned to the states on the recommendation of the Finance Commission. But these tax transfers are, of all the forms of

2 See Chelliah (1969), p. 159; Sastri (1966), pp. 1–9; Venkataraman (1968), p. 19; Watson (1965), pp. 123–4.

TABLE B.1 *States' spending 'gap' as a percentage of their total spending, 1960/61 to 1969/70*

(1) Year	(2) States spending 'gap' (Rs. lakhs)	(3) 'Gap' as a percentage of total spending (%)	(4) Col. (3) taking 5-year averages (%)
1960/61	44372	37	
1961/62	54624	41	
1962/63	57505	38	37
1963/64	52375	33	
1964/65	61614	35	
1965/66	84696	40	
1966/67	70950	32	
1967/68	90775	35	34
1968/69	96875	34	
1969/70	105658	32	

Source: C.S.O. unpublished data.

central assistance to the states, those most distinctly in the nature of general budgetary support. Although they should be excluded from any measure of the revenue-raising performance of the states, this does not seem to be necessary when the aim is to measure the degree of state autonomy in deciding its own expenditure patterns. The channels of central influence over state spending are (a) central grants which are conditional on certain state expenditures and (b) central loans intended to finance specific projects agreed in the process of planning. There is the other evidence, based on R.B.I. data, that these two channels diminished in relative quantitative importance in the 1960s.[3] Moreover, the centre's Article 282 grants, which were a particularly strong channel of central influence were modified in 1969 to permit greater state autonomy.[4]

Thus, while it is perfectly true that expenditure centralization ratios based on national accounts data ignore 'indirect' centralization by means of inter-level transfers that affect state expenditure patterns, it does not appear that the degree of this indirect centralization changed very much in India in the 1960s. (Constancy of indirect centralization may not be true as between the early 1950s and early 1960s,

3 Toye (1973), p. 265, Table 2.
4 A.R.C. (1969), p. 10; Planning Commission (1970), pp. 54–7.

or between the late 1960s and early 1970s – but that is irrelevant here.) Therefore the changes noted in the text in the centralization ratio do not seem to have been in any way offset by changes in the degree of indirect centralization.

APPENDIX C

Problems arising in the preparation of statewise constant price expenditure series

As argued in the text, in the presence of general inflation expenditure series at current prices exaggerate the changes in the volume of resources being absorbed by the government as its inputs – and in the volume of government outputs also, if these are assumed to be directly correlated with inputs.

Theoretically, inflation can involve a further complication, when it is accompanied by a change in the relative price of a key input, such as labour. Government activities, in India as elsewhere, have an above average labour content.[1] Faster rising labour productivity in the private sector may lead to an increase in the relative price of labour. In such circumstances, even a constant price expenditure series will understate spending growth in terms of actual cost.[2] This complication has been ignored for three main reasons. First, reliable estimates of governmental labour productivity do not exist.[3] Second, in the small Indian modern manufacturing sector, the real earnings of workers seem to have been static in the 1960s.[4] Finally, in developed economies, such as the U.K., the required adjustment for the relative price effect is small, only 0.6 per cent per annum.[5] For India, therefore, it would be a work of supererogation to attempt any refinement on a normal constant price series.

Obviously, for inter-state comparisons the current price data must be deflated by indices which reflect geographical differences in the rate of general inflation. A priori, such differences could be expected to be significant. Economic activity takes place in sets of regional markets which are poorly integrated. The ready movement of goods and factors between markets which would minimize such differences cannot be assumed; rather, where we have evidence, as with foodgrain prices, it is for the 'unreasonable' persistence of inter-state differentials.[6]

1 Ovens (1968), p. 152.
2 Rees and Thompson (1972).
3 Cf. Pryor (1968), pp. 403–4.
4 Ministry of Labour and Rehabilitation (1972), p. 61, Table 4.8.
5 H.M. Treasury (1972), p. 25.
6 Raj (1966), pp. 49–52.

Only one Indian price index relevant to government spending is geographically differentiated – the urban non-manual consumers' index, for the major population centres including the state capitals. Assuming, as seems to be the case, that state governments have increased dearness allowances (i.e. cost-of-living bonuses on top of normal pay) in line with the cost of living, this index can be used to deflate expenditure arising from payment of employees.

For other expenditure, a cruder method of deflation had perforce to be resorted to. Estimates of national income at current and constant prices, taken in conjunction with each other, imply an index of price change. The same argument applies to estimates of state domestic product at current and constant prices. Despite the serious doubts that must exist about the state income estimates made by the different state statistical bureaux, the price indices implicit therein have been applied to expenditure other than payment of employees. The difficulty with this method is that the S.S.B.s do not all use the same methodology in preparing their income estimates. The states most obviously out of line are Assam, Madhya Pradesh, Mysore and Rajasthan. Their price indices, for example, can only be given a 1960/61 base by illegitimate arithmetic manipulation.

It is a characteristic of the price indices implicit in the income estimates of these four states that they show slower price inflation than is general in the other states. It would be useful to have some independent check on whether this feature is a mere accident or whether it is the result of their constant prices income series having base years earlier than 1960/61. Such a check is available in the form of wholesale price indices for these states, which are set out in Table C.1. As the table shows, in general the wholesale price indices do suggest a somewhat faster rate of inflation than the indices derived from state income estimates. But the discrepancy only appears to be a serious one in the case of Rajasthan. The very high calculated expenditure growth rate for Rajasthan (using the implicit price index as deflator) accordingly is probably spurious. If it is assumed that the wholesale price index is the true deflator for the non-labour element of expenditure, the expenditure growth rate falls from 8.8 to 4.7 per cent per annum. We have accepted this assumption, and used the lower growth rate in all inter-state comparisons. For Assam, Madhya Pradesh and Mysore, however, the growth rates calculated with the implicit price index as a deflator have been allowed to stand, on the supposition that they are not seriously misleading.

TABLE C.1   *Comparison of price indices in four states, 1960/61 and 1969/70*

	1960/61	*1969/70*
1 *Assam*		
a Implicit from state income estimates; base 1948/49	123	191
b Index of wholesale prices; base 1953	135	243
2 *Madhya Pradesh*		
a Implicit from state income estimates; base 1952/53	111	223
b Index of agricultural wholesale prices; base 1959/60 to 1961/62	100	222
3 *Mysore*		
a Implicit from state income estimates; base 1956/57	120	173
b Index of agricultural wholesale prices; base 1952/53	141	237
4 *Rajasthan*		
a Implicit from state income estimates; base 1954/55	134	178
b Index of wholesale prices; base 1952/53	123	242

Sources: Lines 1–4a calculated from C.S.O. unpublished data on state income.
Line 1b Government of Assam, *Economic Survey of Assam, 1970* pp. 71–2.
Line 2b Directorate of Economics and Statistics, Madhya Pradesh, *Economic Survey of Madhya Pradesh 1970/71*, p. 111.
Line 3b Government of Mysore, *Economic Development of Mysore 1956–69*, p. 184. Figure for 1968/69.
Line 4b Government of Rajasthan, *15 Years of Rajasthan's Economy*, p. 28; *Statistical Abstract of Rajasthan, 1969*, p. 99.

LIST OF WORKS CITED

(This list excludes works that appear only as sources of statistical information. Such works are cited in full at the end of the relevant table).

Addy, P. and I. Azad 1975 'Politics and Society in Bengal' in R. Blackburn (ed.) 1975, *Explosion in a Sub-Continent*, London: Penguin.

Alavi, H. 1972 'The State in Post Colonial Societies: Pakistan and Bangladesh' in K. Gough and H. P. Sharma (eds.) 1973, *Imperialism and Revolution in South Asia*, New York and London: Monthly Review Press.

Anon 1967 'Not Useful Enough', *Economic and Political Weekly*, 8 July.

1968 'Kashmir: Merry Living on Grants', *Economic and Political Weekly*, 1 June.

1969 'New Bearings for Rail Bhavan', *Economic and Political Weekly*, 15 June.

1973 'Losing Struggle', *Economic and Political Weekly*, 19 May.

A.R.C. (Administrative Reforms Commission) 1968a *Report on Finance, Accounts and Audit*, Delhi.

1968b *Report of the Study Team on Financial Administration*, Delhi.

1969 *Report on Centre – State Relations*, New Delhi.

Austin, G. 1966 *The Indian Constitution: Cornerstone of a Nation*, Oxford: Clarendon Press.

Bagchi, A. K. 1971 'The Theory of Efficient Neocolonialism', *Economic and Political Weekly*, Special Number, July.

Baran, P. A. 1973 *The Political Economy of Growth*, London: Pelican.

Bator, F. M. 1962 *The Question of Government Spending*, New York: Collier Books Edition.

Bauer, P. T. 1974 'Debt Cancellation for Development?', *National Westminster Bank Quarterly Review*, November.

Berki, R. N. 1971 'On Marxian Thought and the Problem of International Relations', *World Politics*, October.

Bhagwati, J. N. 1966 *The Economics of Underdeveloped Countries*, London: Weidenfeld and Nicolson.

Bhagwati, J. N. and S. Chakravarthy 1971 *Contributions to Indian Economic Analysis: A Survey*, Bombay: Lalvani.

Bhagwati, J. N. and P. Desai 1970 *India: Planning for Industrialisation. Industrialisation and Trade Policies since 1951*, Oxford University Press, for O.E.C.D. Development Centre.

Bhagwati, J. N. and T. N. Srinivasan 1975 *Foreign Trade Regimes and Economic Development: India*, New York: Columbia University Press for N.B.E.R. (U.S. National Bureau for Economic Research).

Bird, R. M. 1969 'The Determinants of State and Local Expenditures: A Review of U.S. Studies', University of Toronto *IQASEP Working Paper No. 6907*.

1970 *The Growth of Government Spending in Canada*, Toronto: Canadian Tax Foundation.

1971 '"Wagner's Law" of Expanding State Activity', *Public Finance/Finances Publiques*, No. 1.

Burkehead, J. and J. Miner 1971 *Public Expenditure*, London: Macmillan.

Byres, T. J. 1969 'Thor, Adam Smith, Marx – and Myrdal', *Asian Review* Vol. 2 No. 3, April.

1972 'Industrialisation, the Peasantry and Economic Debate in Post-Independence India' in A. B. Bhuleshkar (ed.) 1972, *Towards Socialist Transformation of the Indian Economy*, Bombay: Popular Prakashan.

Caiden, N. and A. Wildavsky 1974 *Planning and Budgeting in Poor Countries*, New York: Wiley Interscience.

Census of India 1971 *Provisional Population Totals*, New Delhi.

Chanda, A. 1965 *Federalism in India*, London: Allen and Unwin.

Chatterji, A. 1971 *The Central Financing of State Plans in the Indian Federation*, Calcutta: K. Mukhopadhyay.

Chattopadhyay, P. 1970 'State Capitalism in India', *Monthly Review*, March.

Chaudhuri, P. 1978 *India: Poverty and Development*, London: Crosby, Lockwood, Staples.

Chaudhuri, P. (ed.) 1971 *Aspects of Indian Economic Development*, London: Allen and Unwin.

Chelliah, R. J. 1966 'Tax Potential and Economic Growth in Countries of the ECAFE Region', *UN Economic Bulletin for Asia and the Far East*, Vol. XVII No. 2, September.

1967 'Fiscal Policy Must be Reoriented', *Economic and Political Weekly*, 20 May.

1968 'Public Sector Investment and the Financial Plan – A General Framework and Some Policy Issues', *UN Economic Bulletin for Asia and the Far East*, Vol. XX No. 3, December.

1969 *Fiscal Policy in Underdeveloped Countries*, London: Allen and Unwin Second Edition.

Clark, T. W. (ed.) 1970 *The Novel in India*, London: Allen and Unwin.

Clarkson, S. 1972 'In Search of a Communist Development Model: The Soviets' Political Economy of India', *Economic and Political Weekly*, 18 March.

1973 'Non-Impact of Soviet Writing on Indian Thinking and Policy', *Economic and Political Weekly*, 14 April.

Clow, A. G. 1928 *The State and Industry*, Calcutta: Government of India, Central Publications Branch.

C.S.O. (Central Statistical Organisation) 1966 *Statistical System in India*, New Delhi.

1971 *Estimates of National Product, 1960/61–1969/70*, Delhi.

1973 *Estimates of National Product, Saving and Capital Formation, 1960/61–1971/72*, New Delhi.

1974 *First Report of the Committee on Regional Accounts*, New Delhi.

1975 *National Accounts Statistics 1960/61–1972/73*, Delhi.

1976a *National Accounts Statistics 1960/61–1973/74*, Delhi.

1976b *National Accounts Statistics 1960/61 – 1974/75*, Delhi.

Cutt, J. 1969 *Taxation and Economic Development in India*, New York: Praeger.

Dandekar, V. M. and N. M. Rath 1971 'Poverty in India', *Economic and Political Weekly* I and II, 2 and 9 January.

Davey, B. 1975 *The Economic Development of India: A Marxist Analysis*, Nottingham: Spokesman Books.

Desai, A. V. 1967 'Small Thoughts on the Elections', *Economic and Political Weekly*, 4 March.

Desai, M. 1975 'India: Emerging Contradictions of Slow Capitalist Development' in R. Blackburn (ed.) 1975, *Explosion in a Sub-Continent*, London: Penguin.

Desai, P. and J. N. Bhagwati 1975 'Socialism and Indian Economic Policy', *World Development*, Vol. 3 No. 4.

Deshmukh C. D. 1957 *Economic Development in India: A Personal Retrospect*, Bombay: Asia.

1972 *Reflections on Finance, Education and Society*, Delhi: Motilal Banaridass.

Dobb, M. 1937 'The Trend of Modern Economics' in E. K. Hunt and J. G. Schwartz 1972, *A Critique of Economic Theory*, London: Penguin.

Durbin, E. F. M. 1949 *Problems of Economic Planning*, London: Routledge.

Eapen, A. T. 1970 'A Critique of Indian Fiscal Federalism', *Public Finance/Finances Publiques*.

Edwards, C. T. 1969 'Financing Government Spending in Ceylon,

India and Pakistan', *UN Economic Bulletin for Asia and the Far East*, Vol. XX No. 3, December.

Ezekial, H. 1971 'Capacity Utilization, Investment Pattern and Income Growth', *Economic and Political Weekly*, 12 June.

Fabricant, S. 1952 *The Trend of Government Activity in the United States since 1900*, New York: N.B.E.R. (U.S. National Bureau for Economic Research).

Finance Commission 1969 *Report*, New Delhi.

Finance, Ministry of (Department of Economic Affairs) 1955 *Report of the Taxation Enquiry Committee, 1953–4*, Vol. 1, New Delhi.

1972 *Economic Survey, 1971/72*, Delhi.

Forrester, D. B. 1968 'Electoral Politics and Social Change', *Economic and Political Weekly*, Special Number, July.

Franda, M. F. 1968 *The Federalizing Process in West Bengal*, Princeton: Princeton University Press.

1970 'Federalizing India: Attitudes, Capacities and Constraints', *South Asian Review*, Vol. 3 No. 3, April.

Frankel, F. R. 1978 *India's Political Economy 1947–1977*, Princeton: Princeton University Press.

Gadgil, D. R. 1972 *Planning and Economic Policy in India*, Poona: Gokhale Institute of Economics and Politics, revised edition.

Gandhi, V. P. 1970 'Are There Economies of Size in Government Current Expenditures in Developing Countries?' *The Nigerian Journal of Economic and Social Studies*, Vol. 12 No. 2, July.

1971 'Wagner's Law of Public Expenditure: Do Recent Cross-Section Studies Confirm It?', *Public Finance/Finances Publiques*, No. 1.

Goffman, I. and D. J. Mahar 1971 'The Growth of Public Expenditures in Selected Developing Nations', *Public Finance/Finances Publiques*, No. 1.

Gopal, S. 1975 *Jawaharlal Nehru: A Biography, Volume One 1889–1947*, London: Jonathan Cape.

Government of Andhra Pradesh (1970? n.d.) *An Economic and Functional Classification of Budgetary Transactions*, Hyderabad.

Government of Assam 1970 *An Economic Classification of Assam Government Budget 1969–70*, Shillong.

Government of Rajasthan 1970 *Statistical System in the States of India*, Jaipur.

Greenwood, M. J. 1971 'An Analysis of the Determinants of Internal Labour Mobility in India', *Annals of Regional Science*, June.

Griffiths Sir P. 1969 'Deficit Financing in the States of India', mimeograph.

Grubel, H. 1969 *The International Monetary System*, London: Penguin.

Gupta, B. N. 1970 *Indian Federal Finance and Budgetary Policy*, Allahabad: Chaitanya.

Gupta, S. P. 1973 'The Role of the Public Sector in Reducing Regional

Income Disparity in Indian Plans', *Journal of Development Studies*, January.

Habib, S. I. 1975 'The State Sector in the Indian Economy' in M. Kurien (ed.) 1975, *India: State and Society*, Bombay: Orient Longmans.

Hanson, A. H., 1968 'Power Shifts and Regional Balances' in P. Streeten and M. Lipton (ed.), 1968, *The Crisis of Indian Planning*, London: Oxford University Press for Royal Institute for International Affairs.

Harrison, S. S. 1960 *India: The Most Dangerous Decades*, Princeton: Princeton University Press.

Head, J. G. 1973 'Public Goods and Multi-Level Government' in W. L. David (ed.) 1973, *Public Finance, Planning and Economic Development*, London: Macmillan.

Hicks, U. K. 1968 'Federal Finance Problems in India and Australia', *Public Finance/Finances Publiques*, Vol. 23.

Hinrichs, H. 1966 *A General Theory of Tax Structure Change during Economic Development*, Cambridge, Mass.: Harvard Law School International Tax Program.

Hirsch, W. Z. 1970 *The Economics of State and Local Government*, London: McGraw-Hill.

Hirschman, A. O. 1958 *The Strategy of Economic Development*, New Haven: Yale University Press.

H. M. Treasury 1972 *Public Expenditure White Papers: Handbook on Methodology*, London: H.M.S.O.

Holland, S. 1972 *The State as Entrepreneur*, London: Weidenfeld and Nicolson.

Hone, A. 1968a 'Retrieving Ten Years of Industrial Effort', *Asian Review*, Vol. 1 No. 3, April.

  1968b 'Tangled Wires of State Electricity Boards', *Economic and Political Weekly*, 2 July.

Hutchison, T. W. 1964 *'Positive' Economics and Policy Objectives*, London: Allen and Unwin.

Jha, P. S. 1973 'What Happens When Exploding Expenditure Leaves Income Behind', *The Guardian*, 23 May.

Johnson, H. G. 1967 *Economic Policies Towards Less Developed Countries*, London: Allen and Unwin.

Kalecki, M. 1972 *Selected Essays in the Economic Growth of the Socialist and the Mixed Economy*, Cambridge: Cambridge University Press.

Kapoor, A. 1974 *Planning for International Business Negotiations*, Cambridge, Mass: Ballinger.

Kidron, M. 1965 *Foreign Investments in India*, London: Oxford University Press.

Kothari, R. 1970 *Politics in India*, New Delhi: Orient Longmans.

Labour and Rehabilitation, Ministry of 1972 *Indian Labour Statistics*, New Delhi.

Lakdawala, D. T., Y. K. Alagh and A. Sarma 1974 *Regional Variations in Industrial Development*, Bombay: Popular Prakashan.

Lakdawala, D. T. and K. V. Nambiar 1972 *Commodity Taxation in India*, Bombay: Popular Prakashan.

Leuthold, A. and J. F. Due 1970 'A Fiscal Policy Model for Economic Development', *Public Finance/Finances Publiques*, No. 4.

Lewis, W. A. 1954 'Economic Development with Unlimited Supplies of Labour', *The Manchester School*, May. Reprinted in A. N. Agarwala and S. P. Singh (ed.) 1963, *The Economics of Underdevelopment*, Oxford: Galaxy Books.

1966 *Development Planning*, London: Allen and Unwin.

1978 *The Evolution of the International Economic Order*, Princeton: Princeton University Press.

Lipton, M. 1977 *Why Poor People Stay Poor*, London: Temple Smith.

Little, I. M. D. and J. A. Mirrlees 1968 *Manual of Industrial Project Analysis in Developing Countries*, Vol. II, Paris O.E.C.D. Development Centre.

1974 *Project Appraisal and Planning for Developing Countries*, London: Heinemann Educational Books.

McGee, T. G. 1971 *The Urbanisation Process in the Third World: Explorations in Search of a Theory*, London: Bell.

Maddison, A. 1971 *Class Structure and Economic Growth*, London: Allen and Unwin.

Malaviya, N. M. 1918 *Note* in Indian Industrial Commission, 1916–18 *Report*, Calcutta.

Malenbaum, W. 1971 *Modern India's Economy*, Columbus, Ohio: Merrill.

Margolis, J. 1954 'A Comment on the Pure Theory of Public Expenditure' in R. W. Houghton (ed.) 1970, *Public Finance: Selected Readings*, London: Penguin.

Martin, A. and W. A. Lewis 1956 'Patterns of Government Revenue and Expenditure', *The Manchester School*, Vol. XXIV No. 3, September.

Martinussen, J. 1976 'The Public Sector in Indian Industry', *Papers for Fifth European Conference on Modern South Asian Studies*, Leiden.

Matthews, R. 1973 'Budget Structure and Organisation in Developed and Developing Countries', in W. L. David (ed.) 1973, *Public Finance, Planning and Economic Development*, London: Macmillan.

Maurice, R. (ed.) 1968 *National Accounts Statistics: Sources and Methods*, London: H.M.S.O.

Maxwell, J. A. 1969 *Financing State and Local Governments*, revised edition, Washington D.C.

Maxwell, N. 1972 *India's China War*, London: Pelican.

Medhora, P. B. 1968a 'Income Shifts as a Factor in the Recession', *Economic and Political Weekly*, 27 July.

1968b 'Income Shifts and the Recession: A Rejoinder', *Economic and Political Weekly*, 7 December.

1972 'Approach to the Fifth Plan: Issues and Pseudo-Issues', *Economic and Political Weekly*, 8 July.

1973 'Managerial Reforms in India's Public Sector', *South Asian Review*, Vol. 7 No. 1, October.

Melzer, A. 1974 *The Social Use of India's Television Satellite*, Zurich. Swiss Federal Institute of Technology, Research Monograph, New Series Vol. II.

Mirrlees, J. 1968 'Targets and Investment in Industry' P. Streeten and M. Lipton (ed.) 1968, *The Crisis of Indian Planning*, Oxford University Press for Royal Institute for International Affairs.

Mitra, A. 1970 'Population and Foodgrain Output in India: A Note on Disparate Growth Rates', E. A. G. Robinson and M. Kidron (ed.) 1970, *Economic Development in South Asia*, London: Macmillan for International Econ Assoc.

1977 *Terms of Trade and Class Relations*, London: Frank Cass.

Morris-Jones, W. H. 1967 'The Indian Congress Party: A Dilemma of Dominance', *Modern Asian Studies*, Vol. I No. 2.

Morss, E. 1966 'Some Thoughts on the Determinants of State and Local Expenditure', *National Tax Journal*, March.

Mukherjee, M. and G. S. Chatterjee 1967 'Trends in the Distribution of National Income, 1950–51 to 1965–66', *Economic and Political Weekly*, 15 July.

Musgrave, R. A. 1961 *The Theory of Public Finance*, Tokyo: Asian Student Edition.

1969 *Fiscal Systems*, London and New Haven: Yale University Press.

Myrdal, G. K. 1968 *Asian Drama: An Enquiry into the Poverty of Nations*, London: Pelican.

Nairn, T. 1975 'The Modern Janus', *New Left Review*, No. 94, November–December.

Nambiar, K. V. and M. Govinda Rao 1972 'Tax Performance of States', *Economic and Political Weekly*, 20 May.

Nath, V. 1970 'Regional Development in Indian Planning', *Economic and Political Weekly*, Annual Number, January.

Nayar, B. R. 1972 *The Modernisation Imperative and Indian Planning*, Delhi: Vikas.

Nayyar, D. 1976 *India's Exports and Export Policies in the 1960s*, Cambridge: Cambridge University Press.

N.C.A.E.R. (National Council of Applied Economic Research) 1960

Economic–Functional Classification of Central and State Government Budgets 1957–58, Delhi.

1961 *Economic–Functional Classification of Government Accounts 1951–52 and 1957–58,* New Delhi.

Nehru, J. 1961 *The Discovery of India,* Bombay: Asia.

O'Connor, J. 1969 'Scientific and Ideological Elements in the Economic Theory of Government Policy', E. K. Hunt and J. G. Schwartz (eds.), 1972, *A Critique of Economic Theory,* London: Penguin.

O.E.C.D. (Organisation for Economic Cooperation and Development) 1972 *National Accounts in Developing Countries of Asia,* Paris.

Ohlsson, I. 1953 'Treatment of Government Economic Activity in the National Accounts' in M. Gilbert (ed.), 1953, *Income and Wealth,* Series III, Cambridge: Bowes and Bowes.

Oshima, H. T. 1965 'National Accounts for the Analysis of Asian Growth' in *Asian Studies in Income and Wealth,* London: Asia Publishing House.

Ovens, D. 1968 'Investment in Human Capital', P. Streeten and M. Lipton (eds.), 1968, *The Crisis of Indian Planning,* London: Oxford University Press for Royal Institute of International Affairs.

Owen, W. 1968 *Distance and Development: Transport and Communication in India,* Washington: Brookings Institution.

Patnaik, P. 1972 'Imperialism and the Growth of Indian Capitalism' in E. R. J. Owen and R. B. Sutcliffe (eds.), 1972, *Studies in the Theory of Imperialism,* London: Longmans.

Pattanaik, P. 1971 *Voting and Collective Choice,* Cambridge: Cambridge University Press.

Paul, S. 1968 'Income Shifts and Recession: A Comment', *Economic and Political Weekly,* 31 August.

Peacock, A. T. and G. K. Shaw 1971 *The Economic Theory of Fiscal Policy,* London: Allen and Unwin, first edition.

Peacock, A. T. and J. Wiseman 1967 *The Growth of Public Expenditure in the United Kingdom,* London: Allen and Unwin, revised edition.

Petras, J. 1977 'State Capitalism and the Third World', *Development and Change,* Vol. 8 No. 1.

Plamenatz, J. 1963 *Man and Society,* Vol. 2, London: Longmans.

Planning Commission 1952 *The First Five Year Plan: A Summary,* New Delhi.

1956 *Second Five Year Plan,* New Delhi.

1962 *Third Five Year Plan,* New Delhi.

1964 *Resource Development Regions and Divisions of India,* New Delhi.

1970 *Fourth Five Year Plan, 1969–74,* New Delhi.

1973 *Approach to the Fifth Plan, 1974–79*, New Delhi.

1974 *Draft Fifth Five Year Plan, 1974–79*, Vol. I, New Delhi.

1976 *Fifth Five Year Plan 1974–79*, New Delhi.

Planning Commission (Committee on Plan Projects) 1957 *Report of the Team for Study of Community Projects and National Extension Service*, New Delhi.

Post, K. and P. Wright 1978 'Some Comments on *The "Intermediate Regime" and Industrialisation Prospects'*, *Development and Change*, Vol. 9 No. 4.

Premchand, A. 1966 *Control of Public Expenditure in India*, second revised edition, Bombay: Allied.

1967 'Towards a Functional Budget', *Economic and Political Weekly*, 11 March.

1969 *Performance Budgeting*, New Delhi and Bombay: Academic Books.

Prest, A. R. 1969 *Transport Economics in Developing Countries*, London: Weidenfeld and Nicolson.

Pryor, F. L. 1968 *Public Expenditure in Communist and Capitalist Nations*, London: Allen and Unwin.

Raj, K. N. 1966 'Regional Variations in Foodgrain Prices', *Economic and Political Weekly*, 20 August.

1967 'The Fourth Plan and Future Economic Policy' *Economic and Political Weekly*, March.

1970 'Some Issues Concerning Investment and Saving in the Indian Economy', in E. A. G. Robinson and M. Kidron (eds.), 1970, *Economic Development in South Asia*, London: Macmillan for the International Economic Association.

1971 'Planning from Below with Reference to District Development and State Planning: A Note', *Economic and Political Weekly*, Special Number, July.

Rangnekar, S. B. and associates 1958 *Central and State Governments in India: An Economic Classification 1958–59*, Punjab University (Department of Economics).

R.B.I. (Reserve Bank of India) 1970 *Bulletin*, September.

Reddy, K. N. 1970 'The Growth of Government Expenditure and National Income in India 1872–1966', *Public Finance/Finances Publiques*, No. 1.

1972 *The Growth of Public Expenditure in India*, New Delhi: Sterling.

Rees, P. M. and F. P. Thompson 1972 'The Relative Price Effect in Public Expenditure: Its Nature and Method of Calculation', *Statistical News*, No. 18, August.

Reynolds, L. G. 1971 'Public Sector Saving and Capital Formation', in G. Ranis (ed.) 1971, *Government and Economic Development*, New Haven and London, Yale.

Rider T. D. 1971 *The Tariff Policy of the Government of India and its Development Strategy 1864–1924*, unpublished Ph.D. thesis, University of Minnesota.

Roy, A. 1965 *Planning in India: Achievements and Problems*, Calcutta: National Publishers.

Roy, R. 1966–67 'Selection of Congress Candidates' Parts I and IV, *Economic and Political Weekly*, 31 December 1966, 11 February 1967.

Rudolph, L. I. and S. H. 1969 'Regional Patterns of Education: Rimland and Heartland in Indian Education', *Economic and Political Weekly*, 28 June.

Rudra, A. 1975 *Indian Plan Models*, Delhi: Sterling.

Ruggles, R. and N. 1970 *The Design of Economic Accounts*, New York: National Bureau of Economic Research.

Sachs, I. 1964 *Patterns of Public Sector in Underdeveloped Economies*, Bombay: Asia.

Samuelson, P. A. 1954 'The Pure Theory of Public Expenditure', *Review of Economics and Statistics*, Vol. XXXVI, November.

Sastri, K. V. S. 1966 *Federal–State Fiscal Relations in India*, Oxford: Oxford University Press.

Seers, D. and R. Jolly 1966 'The Treatment of Education in National Accounting', *Review of Income and Wealth*, Series 12 No. 3, September.

Sen, S. K. 1966 *Studies in Economic Policy and Development of India 1848–1926*, Calcutta: Progressive Publishers.

Shah, K. T. (ed.) 1949 *Report: National Planning Committee*, Bombay: Vora.

Sheth, D. L. 1971 'Profiles of Party Support in 1967', *Economic and Political Weekly*, Annual, January.

Shils, E. A. 1965 *Political Development in the New States*, The Hague: Mouton.

Shirokov, G. K. 1973 *Industrialisation of India*, Moscow: Progress Publishers.

Siddhartan, N. S. 1967 'Voting Pattern in the Fourth General Election, I: D.M.K. Success in Madras', *Economic and Political Weekly*, 17 June.

Simha, S.L.N. (ed.) 1974 *Inflation in India*, Bombay: Vora.

Sinha, N.C. and P.N. Khera 1962 *Indian War Economy (Supply, Industry and Finance)*, New Delhi: Orient Longmans.

Sitaramaswami, K. 1968 'Role of the Private Sector in Promoting India's Industrial Growth', *Capital*, 4 July.

Spencer, D. L. 1959 *India: Mixed Enterprise and Western Business*, The Hague: Martinus Nijhoff.

Stanfield, R. J. 1973 *The Economic Surplus and Neo-Marxism*, Massachusetts: Lexington Books.

States Reorganisation Commission 1955 *Report*, New Delhi.

Subrahmanyam, K. 1973 'Indian Defence Expenditure in Global Perspective', *Economic and Political Weekly*, 30 June.

Sundrum, R. M. 1972 'Studies in Planning Techniques III – Decentralisation of Planning', *Economic and Political Weekly* 20 May.

Swamy, S. 1967 'Structural Changes and the Distribution of Income by Size: The Case of India', *Review of Income and Wealth*, June.

1971 *Indian Economic Planning: An Alternative Approach*, Delhi Vikas.

Thakurdas, Sir P. et al. 1945 *Memorandum Outlining a Plan of Economic Development for India (Parts One and Two)*, London: Penguin.

Thirlwall, A. P. 1972 *Growth and Development with special reference to Developing Economies*, London: Macmillan.

Thorn, R. S. 1967 'The Evolution of Public Finances during Economic Development', *The Manchester School*, Vol. XXXV No. 1, January.

Tinbergen, J. 1967 *Development Planning*, London: Weidenfeld and Nicolson.

Toye, J. F. J. 1973 'Structural Changes in the Government Sector of the Indian States 1955–1970', *Journal of Development Studies*, January.

1976 'Economic Theories of Politics and Public Finance', *British Journal of Political Science*, October.

1977 'Economic Trends and Policies in India During the Emergency', *World Development*, April.

1981 'Public Expenditure Reform in India and Malaysia', *Development and Change*, forthcoming.

Toye, J. F. J. (ed.) 1978 *Taxation and Economic Development*, London: Frank Cass.

Tullock, G. 1967 'The General Irrelevance of the General Impossibility Theorem', *Quarterly Journal of Economics*, Vol. LXXXI.

Tyson, G. 1966 *Nehru: The Years of Power*, London: Pall Mall.

Ulyanovsky, R. and V. Pavlov 1973 *Asian Dilemma: A Soviet View and Myrdal's Concept*, Moscow: Progress Publishers.

U.N. (United Nations) 1958 *Manual for Economic and Functional Classification of Government Transactions*, New York.

1970 *A Manual for Government Accounting*, New York.

1975 *Public Administration and Finance for Development*, New York: ST/ESA/SER.E/1.

United Nations (Industrial Development Organisation) 1979 *Industrial Priorities in Developing Countries*, New York.

United Nations (Statistical Office) 1968 *A System of National Accounts*, Series F No. 2 Rev. 3, New York.

Van Arkadie, B. 1973 'National Accounting and Development Planning: A Review of Some Issues', *Development and Change*, Vol. IV.

Van Arkadie, B. and C. R. Frank Jr 1969 *Economic Accounting and Deve-*

lopment Planning, revised edition (American), New York: Oxford University Press.

Venkataraman, K. 1965 *Local Finance in Perspective*, New Delhi.

1968 *States' Finances in India*, London: Allen and Unwin.

Visvesvaraya, Sir M. 1934 *Planned Economy for India*, Bangalore: Bangalore Press.

1951 *Memoirs of My Working Life*, private.

Ward, M. 1974 'Problems of Determining and Measuring the Reliability of National Accounts in Developing Countries: Comment', *Review of Income and Wealth*, series 20 No. 2, March.

Warren, W. M. 1973 'Imperialism and Capitalist Industrialisation', *New Left Review*, No. 81, September–October.

Watson, M. M. 1965 'Federalism and Finance in the Modern Commonwealth', *Journal of Commonwealth Political Studies*, Vol. III.

Winch, D. 1969 *Analytical Welfare Economics*, London: Penguin.

Zahir, M. 1972 *Public Expenditure and Income Distribution in India*, New Delhi: Associated.

INDEX

Printed in the United States
By Bookmasters